Modeling and Simulation in Python

Modeling and Simulation
in Python

Jason M. Kinser

CRC Press
Taylor & Francis Group
Boca Raton London New York

CRC Press is an imprint of the
Taylor & Francis Group, an **informa** business

A CHAPMAN & HALL BOOK

First edition published 2022
by CRC Press
6000 Broken Sound Parkway NW, Suite 300, Boca Raton, FL 33487-2742

and by CRC Press
4 Park Square, Milton Park, Abingdon, Oxon, OX14 4RN

CRC Press is an imprint of Taylor & Francis Group, LLC

Library of Congress Cataloging-in-Publication Data

Names: Kinser, Jason M., 1962- author.
Title: Modeling and simulation in Python / Jason M. Kinser.
Description: First edition. | Boca Raton, FL : CRC Press, 2022. | Includes bibliographical references and index.
Identifiers: LCCN 2021059491 | ISBN 9781032116488 (hbk) | ISBN 9781032128702 (pbk) | ISBN 9781003226581 (ebk)
Subjects: LCSH: Computer simulation. | Python (Computer program language)
Classification: LCC QA76.9.C65 K56 2022 | DDC 003/.3--dc23/eng/20220124
LC record available at https://lccn.loc.gov/2021059491

ISBN: 978-1-032-11648-8 (hbk)
ISBN: 978-1-032-12870-2 (pbk)
ISBN: 978-1-003-22658-1 (ebk)

DOI: 10.1201/9781003226581

Typeset in Latin Moderrn font
by KnowledgeWorks Global Ltd.

Publisher's note: This book has been prepared from camera-ready copy provided by the authors.

Access the companion website: https://github.com/jmkinser/ModSim411

This book is dedicated to Betty and Budd.

Contents

Preface

The use of Python as a powerful computational tool is expanding with great strides. Python is a language which is easy to use, and the libraries of tools provide it with efficient versatility. As the tools continue to expand, users can create insightful models and simulations.

While the tools offer an easy method to create a pipeline, such constructions are not guaranteed to provide correct results. A lot of things can go wrong when building a simulation – deviously so.

Users need to understand more than just how to build a process pipeline. For example, why are certain steps selected to be used? What are the steps accomplishing? What are the limits of each step? How can the simulation fail to provide a correct answer?

Without these answers, a simulation may be merely a computer exercise and have no connection to reality.

This textbook presents foundations of modeling and simulation through theory, code, and applications. It begins with simple constructs and then reaches into some real-world applications. However, reality is more complicated than the scope of this text allows, so the models and simulations present only foundations applications.

Topics in this book are selected to delve into different facets of modeling. For example, some chapters deal with connectivity, some deal with kinematic motion, and some deal with rule-based applications. Unfortunately, the book cannot cover the breadth of topics in modeling and simulation.

I do hope that you find this book to be educational, foundational, and in some aspects a bit of fun.

Jason M. Kinser George Mason University Fairfax, VA, USA

Software

Several Python functions have been written for this book. Many of these are provided in the text. Some functions though are only partially presented, as repetitive code is not printed on the pages. One example is the Chess chapter in which a function has several lines dedicated to one player, and then it has nearly identical lines for the other player. The latter are omitted with comments about what has been omitted. A few functions in this book are quite simple to write and are not shown on the pages.

All Python functions written for this book are archived on GitHub. This directory contains both the Python scripts and data files created for the projects therein. Data retrieved from other sources are not included in the archive, but URLs are provided in the text as to the location of the data.

```
https://github.com/jmkinser/ModSim411
```

## CHAPTER 1

Introduction

E MERGING COMPUTATIONAL prowess is creating new levels of knowledge and analysis. To be effective, these new models and simulations must have ties to realities, thus providing value to commercial, medical, and defensive applications. For example, massive programs are used to simulate vehicle collisions with enough detail to determine the action of each bolt. However, if those bolts are not realistic (perhaps modeled as plastic instead of metal), then the simulation is merely an academic exercise with little value to the automotive industry.

Such programs need years to build and test. In this example, collecting the data, which requires the disassembling of an entire vehicle, can consume months of work. While such simulations would be fun to employ, they are well beyond the scope of this text. Rather, these chapters will focus on simpler, self-contained models and simulations. It does include a variety of applications which have significant differences, in order to span some of the width of this field. Examples in this text must necessarily be simple, in order to complete the demonstrations within a reasonable volume of pages.

The simplest concept prevalent in many simulations is that of a stochastic process. Such simulations rely on randomness within predefined boundaries. Thus, the first few chapters review random number concepts and provide some applications.

The Monte Carlo process (Chapter 4) builds on this theory, providing demonstrations of smaller systems. Following it is a review of Schelling's model which, in fact, organizes data through a random process.

Chapter 6 advances the use of stochastic processes to build Hidden Markov Models (HMMs). Several following chapters use the HMM for a variety of applications, ending in a light-hearted finale with the ability to create new Shakespearean text.

Chapter 10 shifts into a different aspect of modeling. Often events, or data collected from an event, are connected, and these models of analyzing such connections are considered.

Models often are based on mathematical descriptions. Chapter 11 reviews a normalization process applied to gene expression arrays, and it converts this theory into an application.

The tone of the text changes in Chapter 12 as it ventures into modeling mathematical and physical phenomena. This chapter begins the journey with effective

DOI: 10.1201/9781003226581-1

methods of solving simultaneous linear equations. Chapter 13 models linear and accelerated motion. This leads into Chapter 14 which models oscillatory motion. This chapter will also present issues in the model which creates errors. While this chapter explains the cause and provides a couple of fixes, the real solution comes in the next chapter.

Building on previous chapters, Chapter 15 considers coupled equations, modeling systems with multiple variables dependent on each other. Perhaps this chapter is the most important to converting theory into realistic applications.

With most of the theory in place, the final chapters consider several applications. These include solving puzzles, modeling the spread of a virus, and creating a program that can play chess.

The goal of this text is to introduce foundations of simulation and modeling. Several theories and applications are provided, each with working Python scripts. In all cases, much more complicated applications do exist, but as the goal of the book is to introduce concepts and applications, these complicated applications are not pursued.

All applications are presented with Python scripts. The Python language is chosen because it is freely available, powerful, and quite popular. The text assumes that the reader has a good foundation in Python and the *numpy* module. Explanations of *numpy* functions will be provided when they are employed, but the foundation concepts of *numpy* are assumed. Readers do not have to be Python experts, but a working knowledge of the language is required.

Finally, a few typesetting conventions are employed to maintain clarity:

- Python module names are in italics.

- Python function names are in boldface.

- Python variables are in equally-spaced, teletype font.

- Mathematical variables are in italics.

- Mathematical matrices are in boldface.

The journey begins with a review of random numbers.

## CHAPTER 2

Random Values

$\mathcal{C}$OMPUTERS are calculating machines, and no matter how fancy an algorithm becomes, the real work is performed in manipulating bytes which represent numbers or are associated with text in a specifically prescribed manner.

From this is born the paradox of *random numbers*. The concept of a random number is easy in that it is a number arbitrary value within a given range. Yet, the computer, which is purely a calculating machine, must be able to generate an arbitrary random number.

Random numbers are important to simulations as they allow for injudicious decisions to be made during the process. This could be as simple as creating a simulation to play a card game requiring the deck of cards to be shuffled before play begins. Or this simulation could be enormously complicated in which random values can be used to drive a host of interacting phenomena.

This chapter reviews some aspects of random numbers and Python commands to generate these numbers. Work from this chapter will be used in several subsequent chapters.

2.1 DEFINING RANDOM

A computer script to generate a random number requires some parameters to be defined. First is the range, defining the lowest and highest allowed values. Second is the distribution, defining the probabilities within that range of generating a number. Of these, the easiest is a range from 0 to 1 with an equal probability distribution. The latter means that the probability of generating a number in the middle of the range is the same as generating a number at the ends of the range. The system has the same chance of returning a 0.5 as it does a 0.9.

One popular formula for generating a random number is

$$x_{n+1} = (P_1 x_n + P_2) \mod N, \tag{2.1}$$

where P_1 and P_2 are parameters, N defines the range, and mod is the modulo operator. The value of x_n is a number which is usually the previous random number or obtained from other source. Park and Miller [1] suggested $P_1 = 16807$, $P_2 = 0$, and $N = 2^{31} - 1$.

DOI: 10.1201/9781003226581-2

This equation is realized in Code 2.1. Each value of x1 generates a new value of x2. The output values are divided by N to confine to a range of 0 to 1. If the sequence of numbers is random, then there would not be any relationships between consecutive values. None seems apparent upon first glance.

Code 2.1 Employing a random number generator function.

```
1   P1 = 16807
2   P2 = 0
3   N=2**31 - 1
4   x1 = 10000
5   for i in range(10):
6       x2 = (P1 * x1 + P2) % N
7       print(x2/N)
8       x1 = x2
9
10  0.07826369259425611
11  0.37788143166242233
12  0.053221950332271846
13  0.5013192344928715
14  0.6723741216922058
15  0.5918632809034844
16  0.44616214486125955
17  0.6471686831895116
18  0.9640583661217514
19  0.9289594082762298
```

The initial value of x1 is the seed, and each seed generates the same sequence of values. However, two seeds quite close to each other in value generate vastly different sequences. Without user input, the seed is obtained from an internal source such as the computer's clock.

Coding this equation is not necessary, as Python offers multiple functions to generate random values. Two functions such functions generate random values with an equal probability distribution between 0 and 1.

The first function to consider is the **random** function from the *random* module. Line 1 in Code 2.2 imports the *random* module, and line 2 calls the **random** function and it returns a number between 0 and 1. Repeated use of this function returns different values.

Code 2.2 Using the **random** function from the *random* module.

```
1   import random
2   random.random()
3   Out[]: 0.8665363574885081
```

The second function is the **rand** function from the *numpy.random* module. This also returns a random number between 0 and 1 as seen in lines 1 through 3 in Code 2.3. This function, though, has the option of generating several random values in a single command. The integer argument shown in line 4 indicates how many random numbers are returned. Used in this manner, the function returns a Python array, which will be a convenience in subsequent tasks. Thus, subsequent applications will use this function.

Code 2.3 Using the **rand** function from the *numpy.random* module.

```
1  import numpy as np
2  np.random.rand( )
3  Out[]: 0.9196282186557251
4  np.random.rand( 4 )
5  Out[]: array([0.78928349, 0.64147685, 0.83711364,
       0.26165368])
```

The random values in a Python array provide the opportunity to use the math tools available in *numpy*. One example is the computation of the average of many random values, which can be conveniently be determined by the **mean** function. The example shown in line 1 of Code 2.4 creates an array of 1000 random values. Line 2 computes the average, and the result is shown in line 3. The random values are equally distributed between 0 and 1, and therefore half of the random values in the array should be greater than 0.5. The average of a large number of random values should be close to 0.5.

This computation is sensitive to the number of values in the array. Consider the extreme case, in which the array contains a single value. The average of the array is that value, and that value can be anywhere between 0 and 1. If this test is run several times, then it is expected half of the trials would have an average above 0.5. Consider a second round of tests, in which two random numbers are generated in each trial. Half of the trials should have one value above 0.5 and one value below 0.5; thus, the average should be closer to 0.5 than in the first set of trials. The average of random values gets closer to 0.5 if there are more values in the array.

Code 2.4 Computing the average of random values.

```
1  v = np.random.rand( 1000 )
2  v.mean()
3  Out[]: 0.48591086027452335
4  v = np.random.rand( 100000 )
5  v.mean()
6  Out[]: 0.4995598835683946
```

In Code 2.4, 1000 values are created and the average is close to 0.5 but not exactly 0.5. Line 4 creates an array of 100,000 random values, and the average (line 6) is much closer to 0.5. The important lesson is that results are more predictable if the quantity of random values is large. Code 2.5 shows a trial that considers the average value of different sized arrays. Larger array sizes produce averages which are closer to 0.5. The converse idea is that if a certain precision is required, then a certain number of random values should be used.

Code 2.5 The average of arrays of different sizes.

```
for n in N:
    v = np.random.rand( n )
    print(n,v.mean())
10  0.5012245989677024
1000  0.5030188283033385
10000  0.4980787898491217
100000  0.49967970851291466
1000000  0.4993184663852726
```

Predictably, the average of many random values is 0.5, but the prediction of the standard deviation of many random values is less obvious. However, there is a simple way of predicting this value. A sequence of equally distribute random values should have the same average and standard deviation as equally spaced values over the same range.

Line 1 in Code 2.6 creates 10,000 equally spaced values between 0 and 1 via the **linspace** function. The standard deviation is computed by the **std** function in line 2, and the result is shown to be 0.2887 in line 3. Line 4 computes the standard deviation of the 1000 random values created in line 1 of Code 2.4. The standard deviation of these values is 0.2882. The equally spaced values predicted the standard deviation of a large sequence of random values.

Code 2.6 The standard deviation of many random values.

```
espace = np.linspace(0,1,10000)
espace.std()
Out[]:  0.2887040035517924
v.std()
Out[]:  0.28825847963168166
```

2.2 REPLICATING RANDOM SEQUENCES

A *random sequence* is a series of random values, which can be obtained using **random()** from the *numpy* module. Be able to generate the same sequence is important for testing, so that unexpected results can be explored.

The random number generating function such as Equation (2.1) requires an input value, x_n. Consider a case in which the user defines the first value of x_n. The equation computes x_{n+1}, and that value is used to be x_n for the next computed value, and so on. A sequence is computed as thus. If the user starts over with the same initial value of x_n, the computation will generate the same sequence of values. Even though the values are considered to be random, the sequence can be exactly replicated.

This initial value is a *seed*. Random number generators can obtain a seed value from an internal mechanism such as the computer's clock, or it can receive the seed value from the user. In this latter case, the user has the ability to replicate a sequence. Code 2.7 shows a case in which two sequences are generated, but they are given the same seed using the **seed** function. As seen, they produce the same random sequence.

Code 2.7 Using the **seed** function.

```
1  np.random.seed( 2354 )
2  np.random.rand(3)
3  Out[]: array([0.34939732, 0.15531535, 0.4103861 ])
4
5  np.random.seed( 2354 )
6  np.random.rand(3)
7  Out[]: array([0.34939732, 0.15531535, 0.4103861 ])
```

One of the beauties of this process is that the series will be replicated on any format. The user can use a Mac, PC, or UNIX computer, and the results will be the same. They will not necessarily be the same for different random generators. For example, **math.random.random()** and **numpy.random.rand()** will not return the same value even if given the same seed.

2.3 BIAS AND OFFSET

The functions thus explained generate values between 0 and 1, but some applications need a different range. Management of the range of values is performed through adjustments to the scale and bias. Consider the first line in Figure 2.1 which shows the number line between 0 and 1. This is the range of the random number generator. To make the range from 0 to 2 (the second line), a scaling is required. In this example, the random values are multiplied by the value of 2. A bias is the lateral shift in the number line. The third line shows the effect of subtracting 1 from the values. Through the scale and bias, the range of the random numbers is now from -1 to $+1$. The random number generator creates values between 0 and 1, but the scale and bias are applied to obtain the desired range.

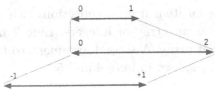

Figure 2.1: Adjusting the range of random values with a bias and a scale.

The example shown in Code 2.8 generates a large number of random values so that the smallest and largest values are close to the limits. Line 1 creates 10,000 random values, and line 2 prints the smallest and largest, and as expected these are values quite close to 0 and quite close to 1. Line 4 multiplies these values by a scale of 2 thus making the range from 0 to 2. This is confirmed in lines 5 and 6. The final step is to shift the values by a bias of -1. Line 9 confirms that the new range of values is from -1 to +1.

Code 2.8 Adjusting the range of the random values.

```
1  v = np.random.rand( 10000 )
2  print(v.min(), v.max())
3  4.756980881870376e-05  0.9999672331785702
4  v = v*2 # adjust scale
5  print(v.min(), v.max())
6  9.513961763740753e-05  1.9999344663571403
7  v = v-1 # adjust bias
8  print(v.min(), v.max())
9  -0.9999048603823626  0.9999344663571403
```

2.4   OTHER TYPES OF RANDOM VALUES

Generating random values is just one possible use of randomization. Three others are shown here,

- random integers,
- random choices, and
- random arrangements.

Random integers are generated by the **randint** function, but since these cannot be in a range of 0 to 1, a new range must be defined. Three examples are shown in Code 2.9. Line 1 shows the function with a single argument, which defines the high value for the choices. This function will return 0, 1, or 2. Line 3 uses two arguments which are the low and high values. Like most Python functions, the low value is included and the high value is excluded. Thus, this function can return a 1 but not a 9. The use of a third argument (line 5) indicates how many integers are to be returned.

Random choice selects an item from a collection such as a list, tuple, or array. Line 1 of Code 2.10 creates an array of integers. Line 2 uses the **choice** function to select one item from that array. A second argument to the function will return a specific number of values as shown in lines 4 and 5.

The input to this function can be a list or a tuple. However, the function returns an array, and as such, the data type returned must be uniform. Line 7 creates a small list with an integer and a float. The request for random selections is in line 8. The

---

Code 2.9 Creating random integers.

```
1  np.random.randint(3)
2  Out[]: 1
3  np.random.randint(1,9)
4  Out[]: 2
5  np.random.randint(0,9,4)
6  Out[]: array([6, 2, 0, 0])
```

Code 2.10 Selecting choices.

```
1   a = np.array((4,5,6,7,8,9))
2   np.random.choice(a)
3   Out[]: 7
4   np.random.choice(a,3)
5   Out[]: array([7, 6, 5])
6   b = [5,7.6]
7   np.random.choice(b,5)
8   Out[]: array([5. , 7.6, 5. , 5. , 7.6])
9   c = (6,7,3,4,5,1,2,3,3,3,3)
10  np.random.choice(c,5,replace=False)
11  Out[]: array([3, 3, 6, 7, 2])
```

---

output shows that all returned values are floats, even though one of them was an integer in the original list.

Line 7 also requests more returned values than exist in the original data. The function must return more than one instance of at least one data item. In some cases, this may be undesirable, and instead the purpose is to extract only one instance of data from an input. In this current implementation, an item is selected but not removed from further consideration. This is a "random selection with replacement." Line 10 turns this default option to **False**, which means that items can be chosen only once. Such an option cannot be applied to line 7 as the requested number of items exceeds the length of the input. Line 10 shows an example "random selection without replacement," which will return only one instance of any item. The output in line 11 shows two 3's, but this is allowed since there are two 3's in the input.

The final topic of randomization is to rearrange a given sequence. Consider a case in which a sequence has one 1, two 2's, three 3's, and four 4's. The goal is to have a random array with these values. The values are established in line 1 of Code 2.11. Line 2 uses the **shuffle** command to rearrange these values. The output is shown in line 4.

Code 2.11 Rearranging values.

```
1  a = np.array((1,2,2,3,3,3,4,4,4,4))
2  np.random.shuffle(a)
3  a
4  Out[]: array([3, 3, 4, 4, 2, 3, 2, 4, 4, 1])
```

2.5 ALTERNATE DISTRIBUTIONS

The **random** and **rand** functions provide random values that have an equal probability distribution between 0 and 1. The *numpy.random* module has functions generating other types of distributions. This module has dozens of different types of distribution functions, but only one of these will be reviewed here, and that is perhaps the most popular among them.

Consider the bell curve shown in Figure 2.2. It is constructed from

$$y = \exp(-(x - \mu)^2/(2\sigma^2), \tag{2.2}$$

where μ is the average, σ is the standard deviation, and the equation computes the output value for a given input x. This curve estimates a distribution of values measured in x, but instead of being equally distributed, these values are in a Gaussian distribution. The horizontal center of the curve is the average value μ. The half-width at the half-maximum is the standard deviation σ. Thus the full-width at half-maximum is 2σ as shown in Figure 2.2.

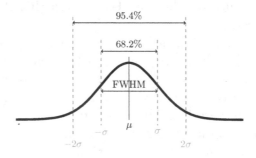

Figure 2.2: The Gaussian distribution for a given μ and σ.

The σ is important in this type of distribution. Between $\mu - \sigma$ and $\mu + \sigma$ lies more than 68% of the random values, and between $\mu - 2\sigma$ to $\mu + 2\sigma$ lies 95% of the values. The distribution of data represented by a bell curves goes by other names including a *Gaussian distribution* and a *normal distribution*.

The **normal** function performs the calculation of Equation (2.2) with the inputs being μ and σ as shown in the example in Code 2.12. Line 1 calls the function, and it returns a random value based on a normal distribution with $\mu = 0.4$ and $\sigma = 0.3$. Like many of the functions in the *numpy.random* module, an additional argument will indicate how many values are to be returned. Line 3 returns an array of 100,000 values within this distribution.

Code 2.12 The **normal** function.

```
1  np.random.normal(0.4,0.3)
2  Out[]:  0.7472685525759929
3  v = np.random.normal(0.4,0.3,100000)
4  v.mean()
5  Out[]:  0.3999020649321314
6  v.std()
7  Out[]:  0.29961843486581985
```

The arguments to the **normal** function define the mean and standard deviation of the collection of random values. This is easy to confirm. Line 4 computes the average of the random values, and indeed it is quite close to 0.4. Likewise, line 6 computes the standard deviation of these values, and it is close to 0.3.

2.6 CONFIRMING RANDOMNESS

Many of these functions return an array of random values. At least, that is the claim of the function, but are the values really random? This question evokes complicated answers, but for here, simple tests confirm the quality of randomness of a sequence.

Consider a sequence of random integers with values between 1 and 10. There are 10 different values which are available, so within a large array of random values, it is expected that each integer is 10% of the array. In other words, the number 3 should be 10% of the values in the array. This concept is shown in Code 2.13. Line 1 creates 1,000,000 random integers between 1 and 10. Line 2 counts the number of 3's in the array. For this case, there are 100,173 of such instances which is 10.0173% of the numbers in the array.

Code 2.13 Computing the number of occurrences of a value.

```
1  vals = np.random.randint(1,11,1000000)
2  (vals==3).sum()
3  Out[]:  100173
```

While a random sequence would have this quality, this quality does not mean that a sequence is random. It is possible to have a sequence in which the first 100,173 values are the number 3, and the number 3 does not appear in the rest of the sequence. So, another test is needed. If a sequence is random then it is expected that on average every tenth value is 3. This can also be easily tested.

A similar test is to compute the average distance between two instances of the same integer. For example: what is the average distance between any two 1's? This answer is expected to be around 10. Using the same random sequence from Code 2.13, line 1 in Code 2.14 finds all locations of the integer 1. The first few of these are shown in line 3. Line 4 computes the distances between consecutive 1 values by measuring the distances in the array `temp`. The first four of these are printed in line

6. The distance between the first two 1's in the sequence is 1. This is correct, because the first two instances are at locations 4 and 5. The next distance is 18 because consecutive values of 1 are at locations 5 and 23. The final step is to compute the average of these distances which is quite close to the theoretical value of 10 (line 8). Again, a random sequence would have this quality, but it does not prove that the sequence is random.

Code 2.14 Computing the average distance between similar integers.

```
1  temp = (vals==1).nonzero()[0]
2  temp[:10]
3  Out[]: array([ 4,  5, 23, 32, 41, 45, 50, 51, 52, 61],
       dtype=int64)
4  diff = temp[1:] - temp[:-1]
5  diff[:4]
6  Out[]: array([ 1, 18,  9,  9], dtype=int64)
7  diff.mean()
8  Out[]: 9.991976258518356
```

The final test shown here is to determine which values follow a given integer. Line 2 in Code 2.15 displays the first 7 integers of the sequence. The integer 1 is located at positions 4 and 5, but this was already known from line 3 in Code 2.14. The integer that follows the first instance of a 1 is also a 1. The integer that follows the second instance of a 1 is 5. This collection of data is performed for the whole sequence. In an equal probability distribution, each integer should be 10% of the values that follow a number 1.

Code 2.15 Computing the percentage of following integers.

```
1  vals[:7]
2  Out[]: array([9, 2, 7, 7, 1, 1, 5])
3  ndx = (vals==1).nonzero()[0]
4  ndx = np.array( ndx ) + 1
5  print((nvals==2).sum())
6  10136
7  10126/len(ndx)
8  Out[]: 0.10118006774648028
```

The variable **ndx** from line 3 is the locations of the number 1 in the sequence. The location of the next values is at locations **ndx + 1** which is computed in line 4. Line 5 finds the number of times that the number 2 is at the locations in **ndx**. This value, 10,136 is divided by the length of **ndx**, and the result shows that the number 2 is 10.1% of the numbers which follow the number 1.

Of course, this test can use any values, for example, to search for the number of times a 4 follows a 9. Furthermore, the test could change distance between the numbers. For example, the modified test would search for the number of times that a 4 follows a 9 by three spaces in the original sequence. For any two integers and any distance, the percentage of occurrences should be about 10%.

A more complicated scenario would be to look for sequences which follow a number. For example, how many times does the sequence 47 follow a 2? In this case, the expected value is 1%. Again, this can be performed for any integer values and any distance. The purpose of these tests is to determine if there is a repeating pattern in the array of integers. The code as written demonstrates the idea, but would be a wholly inefficient way to perform the tests for a large array since there are so many possibilities. Other math tools exist which would be far more efficient in confirming a sequence's randomness, but the foundations of these tools are beyond the scope of this chapter.

2.7 SUMMARY

Random numbers and sequences are the foundations for several simulations. Python can easily generate random numbers for given distributions and ranges. Python also offers functions to generate random integers as well as random selections and shuffling of data.

PROBLEMS

1. Create an array of 100,000 random values equally distributed between -2 and +3.3. Print the lowest and highest values of this array.

2. Create an array of 100,000 values which are each the sum of two different random values. Print the average of the values in this array.

3. Create an array of 100,000 values which are each the multiplication of two different random values. Print the average of the values in this array.

4. Create an array of 100,000 values using a normal distribution with an average of 0.3 and a standard deviation of 1.2. Print the average and standard deviation of the values in this array.

5. Create two arrays, a and b, where each are 100,000 random integers with values between 0 and 20. Create a new array, c, from $c[i] = a[i] - b[i-1]$. Of course, the c array will have a length of 99,999. Create a histogram of these values with a range of -20 to +21.

6. Create an array of 100,000 values from a normal distribution with an average of 3 and a standard deviation of 1.2. Plot the histogram of these values with a range of -0.6 to +0.6 and a bin width of 0.05.

7. Create an array of 100,000 random values between 0 and 1. Collect the distances between the occurrences of the 1's. Plot a histogram of these distances.

## CHAPTER 3

Application of Random Values

A COMPUTER SIMULATION creates the opportunity to explore thousands of possible outcomes, which is particularly useful if the number of total outcomes far exceeds the capabilities of the computer. Consider a playing card game in which the outcome is completely reliant on the initial distribution of the playing cards. There are 52 cards in a deck, and thus there are $52! = 8 \times 10^{67}$ variations on the arrangement of cards. It is not possible to compute the outcome of a game for all of these possibilities.

One approach is to assume that the statistics of a large number of games would be similar to the statistics from all possible games. Thus, only a few thousand games would be played instead of 8×10^{67}. Thus, if player 1 wins 60% of a thousand games, then it will be assumed that player 1 would win 60% of the games if all possible games could be played.

To demonstrate this point, this chapter will simulate a simple card game which is wholly reliant on the initial distribution of cards. Players do not make any decisions during the game. Thousands of games will be ran to gather statistics. Alterations to the game will be administered, and alterations to the results will be examined.

3.1 THE CARD GAME NAMED WAR

There are hundreds of card games from which a simulation can be written. For this chapter the requirements were to find a game with simple rules and one in which the players do not have to make logical decisions. Once the cards are distributed, the simulation can accurately compute the output of the game. The game of War is such a game.

The rules are simple. Each player, and for now there are just two players, starts with a stack of cards which are face down. They each turn over the top card and compare the values (Figure 3.1). The player with the largest values keeps both cards. Play continues until one person has all cards.

A deck has 52 cards, with 13 cards in each of 4 suits (spades, diamonds, clubs, and hearts). The cards have face values (1, 2, 3, 4, 5, 6, 7, 8, 9, 10, jack, queen, king,

DOI: 10.1201/9781003226581-3

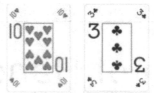

Figure 3.1: The comparison of two cards.

and ace). In this game, the suit does not matter, thus there are 4 cards for each value. As such is the case, occasionally, two cards of the same face value will be played. The resolution of this tie is to play three cards face down so the values are unknown, and then play a fourth card with the value showing (Figure 3.2). The winner is the one with the highest value in these fourth cards, and this player keeps the 10 played cards. If these fourth cards are a tie, then the three-down process repeats.

Figure 3.2: The resolution of a tie.

The play continues until either one player runs out of cards or until the players gets bored with the game. The latter occurs because, in reality, the game takes too long to play.

3.2   PYTHON IMPLEMENTATION

The creation of a Python simulation uses the following steps:

1. Create a deck of cards and shuffle them (randomize the order),

2. Distribute the cards,

3. Play a single round, including the possibility of a tie, and

4. Iterate to simulate an entire game.

The suit of the cards are not used, so the deck of cards need only their value. There are four instances of each value in the deck. The values include (2, 3, 4, 5, 6, 7, 8, 9, and 10), but there are also other cards. To make the Python implement easy, these cards are assigned numerical values (jack=11, queen=12, king=13, and ace=14). Thus, the only task of determining the winner of a round is to compare numerical values of the played cards.

The first step to create the deck of cards. Line 2 in Code 3.1 creates a list of the 13 values and then multiplies the list by 4. This makes a new list which has the given list repeated four times. Line 3 shuffles the deck. When playing a card game, the cards are dealt to the players one at a time. The dealer gives a card to each player, and then repeats this action. For the simulation, this style of dealing cards is not necessary. The cards are in random order, so the program can simply deliver the first 26 cards to player 1 and the last 26 cards to player 2, as seen in lines 4 and 5.

Code 3.1 Creating the deck of cards.

```
1  import random
2  deck = list(range(2,15)) * 4
3  random.shuffle(deck)
4  p1 = deck[:26]
5  p2 = deck[26:]
```

Each player has a list which contains their cards. A second list is needed to contain the cards currently being played. So player 1 has the list `p1` which contains their cards and the list `pile1` which will contain their cards currently in play. Initially, this list is empty. These commands are encapsulated in the **Start** function shown in Code 3.2. The deck is created and distributed. The `p1count` variable will collect the number of cards that player 1 has at the end of each round. This will be used to track progress of the game. Since player 1 is starting with 26 cards, this value is placed in the list.

Code 3.2 The initialization function.

```
1  # war.py
2  def Start():
3      deck = list(range(2,15)) * 4
4      random.shuffle( deck )
5      p1 = deck[:26]
6      p2 = deck[26:]
7      p1count = [26]
8      pile1=[]; pile2=[]
9      return p1, p2, p1count, pile1, pile2
```

At the beginning of a round, each player removes the first card in their list. These are moved to the player's pile list, as shown in the first two lines in Code 3.3. The **pop** function removes the first item from a list, and the **append** function places it at the end of another list.

The next step is to compare the last two cards in the player's piles. There will be cases in which this comparison will create a tie and more cards are appended to the pile. Then the last cards are compared to determine the round's winner. So, the last card in the piles are the ones used in comparison, not the first. For most rounds, each pile has only one card, so the first and last are the same card.

Three results are possible, the players play cards of the same value, player 1 wins the round, or player 2 wins the round. The outline of the logic is shown in Code 3.3. Line 4 tests for a tie, line 6 tests for player 1 being the winner, and line 8 tests for player 2 being the winner. The comment on line 5 is a placeholder which will be filled in soon.

Code 3.3 The skeleton of a round of play.

```
pile1.append( p1.pop(0) )
pile2.append( p2.pop(0) )

if pile1[-1]==pile2[-1]:
    # It's a tie
elif pile1[-1]>pile2[-1]:
    WinRound(p1,pile1,pile2)
elif pile1[-1]<pile2[-1]:
    WinRound(p2,pile2,pile1)
```

The last two choices are easier to implement. Code 3.4 shows the **WinRound** function which is called if one player wins the round. The input `pwin` is either p1 or p2 depending on who is the winner. The `pilewin` is the pile list for the winner, and the `pilelose` is the pile list for the loser. If a player wins, then the cards from both piles are added to their deck. This is done in lines 3 and 4. The two pile lists are then emptied by using the **clear** function as seen in lines 5 and 6.

Code 3.4 The **WinRound** function.

```
# war.py
def WinRound(pwin,pilewin,pilelose):
    pwin.extend(pilewin)
    pwin.extend(pilelose)
    pilewin.clear()
    pilelose.clear()
```

A tie presents a couple of issues which must be managed. One is the appending of more cards to the player's piles. The other is the situation in which one player has only a single card which is involved in the tie. Thus, this player does not have any more cards to attempt to break the tie. In this case, the game was finished.

Lines 4 and 5 in Code 3.3 become that shown in Code 3.5. Lines 2 through 5 manage the situation if one player only has one card. The appropriate arguments are sent to the **WinRound** function. Line 6 calls the **Tie** function which will take the first steps necessary to resolve a tie.

Code 3.5 The steps following a tie.

```
1  if pile1[-1]==pile2[-1]:
2      if len(p1)==0:
3          WinRound(p2,pile2,pile1)
4      if len(p2)==0:
5          WinRound(p1,pile1,pile2)
6      Tie(p1, p2, p1count, pile1, pile2)
```

The purpose of the **Tie** function is to put the three face-down cards into the players' piles. If both players have more than three cards, then this is an easy step, but eventually, one player will have fewer than three cards. The rule for this player is to put all cards into the pile except for one, which will soon be used to resolve the tie. Code 3.6 shows part of the function. This part considers player 2. The value of N calculated in line 4 is the number of cards that player 2 can put into the pile, which is 3 or less. These cards are moved from the player's deck to the player's pile in lines 5 and 6. This function has similar code for player 1, but it is not shown here.

Code 3.6 Adding cards to the piles in a tie.

```
1  # war.py
2  def Tie(p1,p2,p1count, pile1, pile2):
3      if len(p2)>1:
4          N = min((3,len(p2)-1))
5          for i in range(N):
6              pile2.append(p2.pop(0))
7      . . .
8      # similar code for p1
```

The parts are constructed and collected into the **Play1** function shown in Code 3.7. Lines 3 through 14 have been discussed. Line 15 archives the number of cards player 1 has for subsequent analysis. Lines 16 and 17 return **False** if the game has ended as one player has run out of cards. Line 19 returns **True** which indicates the game can continue for another round.

The function **Play1** plays one round of the game. To complete a game, this function is repeatedly called until one player runs out of cards. This process is shown in Code 3.8. The **Play1** function returns a Boolean value which is True as long as

Code 3.7 The function to play one round.

```
# war.py
def Play1(p1, p2, p1count, pile1, pile2):
    pile1.append( p1.pop(0) )
    pile2.append( p2.pop(0) )
    if pile1[-1]==pile2[-1]:
        if len(p1)==0:
            WinRound(p2,pile2,pile1)
        if len(p2)==0:
            WinRound(p1,pile1,pile2)
        Tie(p1, p2, p1count, pile1, pile2)
    elif pile1[-1]>pile2[-1]:
        WinRound(p1,pile1,pile2)
    elif pile1[-1]<pile2[-1]:
        WinRound(p2,pile2,pile1)
    p1count.append( len(p1))
    if len(p1)<1 or len(p2)<1:
        return False
    else:
        return True
```

both players have cards remaining in their deck. Thus, play continues until one player has all the cards.

Code 3.8 Code to play one game to completion.

```
p1, p2, p1count, pile1, pile2 = Start()
ok = True
while ok:
    ok = Play1(p1, p2, p1count, pile1, pile2)
```

The list `p1count` appends the number of cards player 1 has at the end of each round. At the end of the game, the last value in this list will either be 0 or 52, thus indicating which player won the game. The values of this list for one example are plotted in Figure 3.3. Player 1 had about half of the cards for thirty rounds, and then luck turned against this player. The game ended in favor of player 2 after 120 rounds.

A single game is managed by the function **RunGame** (Code 3.9), which receives initialized lists and plays enough rounds to come to a winner. This function returns two variables. The first is at 1 or 2 depending on which player wins the game, and the second is the integer `rounds` which is the number of iterations required for this game. The last three lines are sufficient to run a single game and print the results.

Now it is possible to collect statistics over a large number of games, using the function **Go** shown in Code 3.10. The input N is the number of games to play. Line 5

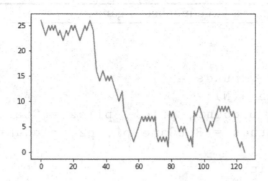

Figure 3.3: The number of cards for player 1 for each round.

```
1  # war.py
2  def RunGame(p1, p2, p1count, pile1, pile2):
3      ok = True
4      rounds= 0
5      while ok:
6          ok = Play1(p1, p2, p1count, pile1, pile2)
7          rounds += 1
8      if len(p1)>1:
9          return 1, rounds
10     else:
11         return 2, rounds
12
13 p1, p2, p1count, pile1, pile2 = Start()
14 RunGame( p1, p2, p1count, pile1, pile2 )
15 Out[]: (1, 120)
```

starts a single game and line 6 plays the game. The variable `ct` collects the number of games that player 1 wins. The variable `wrounds` is a list that collects the number of iterations required in the games player 1 wins.

Code 3.10 Code to play a large number of game.

```python
# war.py
def Go(N=1000):
    ct = 0;        wrounds = []
    for i in range(N):
        p1, p2, p1count, pile1, pile2 = Start()
        win, rounds = RunGame(p1, p2, p1count, pile1,
            pile2)
        ct += win
        if win:
            wrounds.append( rounds )
    wrounds = np.array( wrounds )
    return ct, wrounds
```

Figure 3.4a shows a bar chart indicating the number of iterations for player 1 to be victorious. One game required about 1000 iterations. This chart is difficult to view, so Figure 3.4b reorders the data from low to high. Thus, it is easy to see that about 3/4 of the games required 200 iterations or less, and a small number needed more than 800.

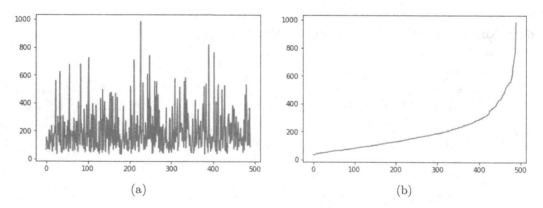

(a)   (b)

Figure 3.4: (a) The number of iterations for each win of player 1. (b) The same data sorted.

3.3 ALTERATIONS

With the ease of running thousands of simulations, the next step is to consider what happens if the game is altered. Two such cases are pursued here. Both of these alter the starting configuration of the game and then run many trials to gather statistics about the outcomes.

3.3.1 One Ace

The first simulation is an extreme. Player 1 starts with just one card, an ace. This player has a very high probability of winning the first round. Most of the **Start2** function is shown in Code 3.11. The deck is created and shuffled in lines 3 and 4 as before. Line 5 assigns just one ace to player 1, and this is removed from the shuffled deck in line 6. The rest of the cards are given to player 2 in line 7. The remainder of the **Start2** program is the same as in **Start1**, therefore it is not shown here.

Code 3.11 Player 1 starts with just one ace.

```
1   # war.py
2   def Start2():
3       deck = list(range(2,15)) * 4
4       np.random.shuffle( deck )
5       p1 = [14]
6       deck.remove(14)
7       p2 = deck
8           . . .
```

A small alteration is needed for the **Go** function, in that it needs to call **Start2** instead of **Start**. A simulation ran 1000 games, and player 1 actually won 125 of those contests. So, under this scenario, player 1 wins 12.5% of the contests.

3.3.2 Four Aces

The second alteration is for player 1 to start with all four aces. In this scenario, player 1 has the four highest cards and is therefore guaranteed to win the first four rounds. In doing so, player 1 collects four new cards. Now it is possible to have ties and the opportunity to lose those aces. Even though the player starts with the four highest cards, victory is not assured.

The alteration to the start of the game is shown in Code 3.12. The logic is similar to the previous case. Line 5 assigns the four aces, and lines 6 and 7 removes these from the shuffled deck. The rest of the cards are given to player 2 in line 8.

Again, the **Go** function is altered so it calls **Start3**. Out of 1000 trials, player 1 won 656 games. Thus, a player starting with just the four aces has about a 2 in 3 chance of winning the game.

3.4 SUMMARY

This chapter considered a case in which the rules of a system were easy to simulate, but the variations in the starting parameters were too numerous to calculate the outcome of all possibilities. Therefore, a simulation was created which calculated the

---

Code 3.12 Player 1 starts with four aces.

```
1  # war.py
2  def Start3():
3      deck = list(range(2,15)) * 4
4      np.random.shuffle( deck )
5      p1 = [14,14,14,14]
6      for i in range( 4 ):
7          deck.remove(14)
8      p2 = deck
9      . . .
```

---

outcomes for a thousands of random initialization. From this, behavior of the system were obtained. Finally, a few alterations were considered, to demonstrate the behavior of the system beginning with unusual circumstances.

PROBLEMS

1. Define V as the average of the initial cards for player 1. Collect the value of V for 1000 games, and calculate the average of these values.

2. Define V as the average of the initial cards for player 1. Collect the value of V for 1000 games for only the games that player 1 wins. Calculate the average of these values.

3. Create a bar chart which plots the percentage of wins for player 1 for cases of playing 3 games, 10 games, 20 games, 40 games, 80 games, 160 games, 320 games, 640 games, and 1280 games.

4. For a single game, count the number of times that cards of value 2, 9, and aces change from one player to the other. Divide these values by the number of rounds in the game. This is called the transfer rate. Repeat this for 1000 games. What is the average transfer rate for these three types of cards?

5. Start the game with each player having two instances of each type of card. Thus, they have exactly the same starting deck, and player 1 should have a 50% chance of winning the game. Play 10,000 iterations to see if this prediction is supported.

6. In the original game, three cards were placed face-down during a tie. For 10,000 games compute the average number of rounds needed for player 1 to win and the standard deviation. Print these two values. Change the max number of cards in a Tie from 3 to 5. Compute the average and standard deviation for the number of rounds needed for player 1 to win a game. Print these two values. Change that value to 5. Run 1000 games and calculate the number of rounds for each game. Plot these values from low to high. Are there significant differences to the original version of this game.

7. Count the number of cards player 1 has in the initial deck that are valued higher than 10 before each game. Call this value H. Collect separately the value of H for a player 1 win and for a player 1 loss. Run 1000 games. Print the average and standard deviation of the H values for player 1 wins, and the average and standard deviation of player 1 losses.

8. Count the number of cards player 1 has in the initial deck that are valued higher than 10 before each game. Call this value H. Run 1000 iterations. Create a scatter plot where the horizontal value is the number of high-valued cards and the vertical value is the number of rounds required for player 1 to win.

9. Change the behavior of a tie. Instead of adding 4 cards to the `plists`, simply remove from play the two cards that caused the tie. Run 1000 games and collect the number of cards player 1 has after their wins. Sort these values from low to high and plot.

## CHAPTER 4

The Monte Carlo Method

RANDOM VALUES were used in the previous chapter to initialize a simulation. The next step is to understand the effect of the distribution of random values. A card game example is inappropriate to use here because it had 64 dimensions to the input space, which is hard to visualize. This chapter will consider a much simpler case so that the effects can be clearly displayed. The chapter reviews the Monte Carlo method in which several examples of random input values are considered, and information about the distributions are collected. The examples use two-dimensional points which can be visualized, but the techniques are easily translated to higher dimensions. Before this method is considered, a review of random-valued vectors is presented.

4.1 RANDOM VECTORS

Consider the case of generating a random point in a three-dimensional space. The x, y, and z components of the vector would need to be random numbers. The **rand** function from the *numpy.random* module can return multiple random values in an array (Code 4.1). The argument to the **rand** function is the number of random values to be generated. The returned data is a numpy array, and thus it can be considered as a vector.

Code 4.1 Creating a vector of random values.

```
1  import numpy as np
2  vec = np.random.rand(3)
3  print(vec)
4  [0.15482926 0.738941   0.00314528]
```

Creating a large number of random vectors is accomplished in a single command by creating a matrix of random values as shown in line 1 of Code 4.2. This function receives a single argument which is a tuple of two integers representing the size of the matrix. In this case, the matrix will have 100 rows and 3 columns. This can be interpreted as 100 vectors, each of length 3.

DOI: 10.1201/9781003226581-4

Code 4.2 The average of 100 random vectors.

```
1  mat = np.random.ranf((100,3))
2  np.set_printoptions(precision=3)
3  print(mat[:4])
4  [[0.818 0.527 0.219]
5   [0.313 0.389 0.734]
6   [0.957 0.706 0.7  ]
7   [0.164 0.877 0.479]]
8  mat.mean(0)
9  Out[]: array([0.540, 0.500 , 0.554])
```

The **set_printoptions** function limits the number of decimals which are printed to the console. This command does not change the accuracy of the computation, it merely limits what is shown. In line 2, this option is set to 3, thus making a cleaner presentation of the first four rows of the matrix.

The average vector should be a vector in which all elements are close to 0.5. This is confirmed in lines 8 and 9, by computing the average of all columns.

4.2 ROLLING DICE

Rolling a six-sided die is a common example for random number generators. The desire is to have a random integer from the value of 1 to 6. The **randint** function generates random integers, which are equally distributed. Line 1 in Code 4.3 generates a random number between 1 (inclusive) and 7 (exclusive). This is the function which simulates the rolling of a single die. Line 4 adds another argument which is the number of random values to make. This line is equivalent to rolling one die ten times or ten dice one time each.

Code 4.3 Generating random integers.

```
1  np.random.randint(1,7)
2  Out[]: 4
3
4  np.random.randint(1,7,10)
5  Out[]: array([5, 3, 5, 6, 3, 5, 2, 2, 1, 6])
```

Some games require more than one die to be rolled in a turn. The third argument to **randint** controls the number of values returned. By sending a tuple to this argument, the returned values will be in the shape of the values within that tuple. Consider Code 4.4 which sends (5,2) as the third argument. The returned values are in a matrix which is 5×2.

Now, consider a game in which the player wins big if he rolls five of a kind. This means that all five dice have the same value, but it doesn't matter what that value

---

Code 4.4 Generating five sets of rolling two dice.

```
1  np.random.randint(1,7,(5,2))
2  Out[*]:
3  array([[2, 2],
4         [6, 2],
5         [2, 1],
6         [5, 2],
7         [1, 1]])
```

---

is. The player wins if they roll all 1's or all 6's. The question is, how often is this expected to occur?

Code 4.5 provides a simulation of rolling 5 dice 10,000,000 times. Line 2 creates these rolls. The next task is to find all of the cases in which the dice have the same value. Equivalently, the task is to find the rows in `mat` which have the same value in all columns.

Code 4.5 Playing the five of a kind game.

```
1  N = 10000000
2  mat = np.random.randint(1,7,(N,5))
3  minus = np.zeros((N,4))
4  for i in range(4):
5      minus[:,i] = abs(mat[:,0]-mat[:,i+1])
6
7  adds = minus.sum(1)
8  ct = (adds==0).sum()
9  7712
```

Line 3 creates a new matrix which has only four columns. The `for` loop started in line 4 populates this new matrix. The value in `minus[m,n]` is the absolute value of the difference of `mat[m,0]` and `mat[m,n+1]`. Basically, it is the difference of one of the values in the row to the first value in the row. If all of the values in a row are the same, then all of the values in the row in `minus` will be 0.

Line 7 sums horizontally. This produces a vector of 10,000,000 elements. If a row n in `mat` has the same values, then `adds[n]` will be 0. The converse is true as well. If `adds[n]` is 0, then all of the values in row n are the same. So, the problem is now reduced to counting the number of times that 0 appears in `adds`. This is done in line 8.

The answer is 7712, which means of the 10,000,000 rolls, only 7712 were rolls in which all dice had the same value. That is about 1 time in 1300 tries.

4.3   THE MONTE CARLO METHOD

The Monte Carlo method generates random data and receives results from the interaction of that data. A very simple example is to generate points in a defined space and determine which side of a decision surface the points reside. A few examples are shown here which start with an easy problem. The complexity increases, but the protocol remains the same. Random points are generated and compared to decision surfaces.

4.3.1   Horizontal Barrier

The first task is to determine the area below a line within a given environment. The simplest form of this is a horizontal line, and for this example, the line is $y = 0.5$. The desired output is shown in Figure 4.1 in which random points are generated and determined if they are above or below a decision line. Since the points are evenly distributed the space is sampled uniformly. Thus the ratio of the number of points below the line to the total number of points should be similar to the ratio of the area below the line to the total area of the environment.

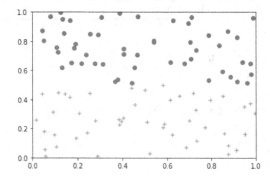

Figure 4.1: Random points above and below a horizontal line.

Line 1 in Code 4.6 creates the 100 vectors which are (x, y) points in two-dimensional space. Line 2 compares the y values of these vectors to the threshold 0.5. This returns the array named **above** which has True values for points which are above the line. Line 3 returns an array with those locations. Thus, any value in **ndx** is the index of a vector that is above $y > 0.5$. Line 4 creates a scatter plot for these points. Those points which are not above the line are below the line. Line 5 switches the Boolean values, thus making **ndx** the indexes of the points below the line. A second scatter plot is created for these points, and the result is shown in Figure 4.1.

As seen, the random points are separated by the decision surface. The area of each sector can be estimated by the ratios of An/m, where n is the number of points in a sector, m is the total number of points, and A is the area of the encompassing environment. In this case, half of the points are in the first class, so $1 \times 50/100 = 0.5$. The total area of the **True** sector is 0.5.

Code 4.6 Color-coded random vectors divided by a horizontal line.

```
1  vecs = np.random.ranf((100,2))
2  above = vecs[:,1]>0.5
3  ndx = above.nonzero()[0]
4  plt.scatter( vecs[ndx,0], vecs[ndx,1])
5  ndx = (1-above).nonzero()[0]
6  plt.scatter( vecs[ndx,0], vecs[ndx,1], marker='+')
7  plt.xlim(0, 1); plt.ylim(0, 1)
```

4.3.2 Slanted Barrier

The second task is to divide the random points by a slanted line as shown in Figure 4.2. The dividing line is defined by,

$$y = mx + b, \tag{4.1}$$

and in this example $m = -1.3$ and $b = 0.8$. The m and b are the slope and intercept, and these are defined in lines 1 and 2 in Code 4.7. Line 3 creates 100 random vectors.

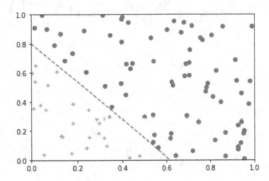

Figure 4.2: Random points above and below a slanted line.

In the previous task, the y value was known for all locations to be 0.5. In this task, the y value depends on the x value. Thus, the y value is computed for the x values in the random vectors. These y values are computed in line 4 and stored in yline. To determine if an (x, y) point is above the line, the y value of the point is compared to the corresponding value in yline. This is done in line 5. The output ndx is the indexes of the vectors which are above the line. Line 7 finds the indexes of the points below the line.

Lines 9 through 11 create the dashed line in Figure 4.2. To make this line, a series of equally spaced x values were created by **linspace**, and their corresponding y values were created in line 10. Line 11 defines this to be a dashed, green line. As seen, the points are color-coded based on their relative location to the dashed line. Once again, the area of the sector can be estimated by An/m.

Code 4.7 Color-coded random vectors divided by a slanted line.

```
1  slope = -1.3
2  intercept = 0.8
3  vecs = np.random.ranf((100,2))
4  yline = vecs[:,0]*slope + intercept
5  ndx = (vecs[:,1] > yline).nonzero()[0]
6  plt.scatter( vecs[ndx,0], vecs[ndx,1])
7  ndx = (vecs[:,1] < yline).nonzero()[0]
8  plt.scatter( vecs[ndx,0], vecs[ndx,1], marker='+')
9  x = np.linspace(0,0.7,20)
10 yline2 = x*slope + intercept
11 plt.plot( x, yline2,'--',color='green')
12 plt.xlim(0, 1); plt.ylim(0, 1)
```

4.3.3 Integration

Consider the function in Figure 4.3, which was generated by

$$y = \sin\left(8\cos 7(x+10))^4\right)^2 + \exp\left(\frac{x+0.5}{0.9}\right). \tag{4.2}$$

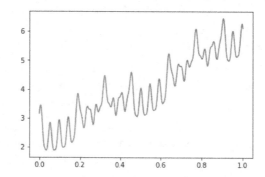

Figure 4.3: A difficult function to integrate.

Once again, the goal is to count the number of values below a line. However, this case has an actual application. The math operation of integration measures the area under a curve. Mathematical operations can convert the function that defines the curve into a direct solution. However, such as this case, the function can be difficult to manipulate. The Monte Carlo method offers an estimate of the area of the curve and thus an estimate of the integration value.

Consider Code 4.8. Line 1 generates 100 pairs of points. Both the x and y values range between 0 and 1. The figure shows that the x values do lie within a range of 0 to 1, but the y values are in a range of 0 to 6. So, line 2 multiples all of the y values by 6 to bring the random data to the correct scale. Line 3 just makes a copy of the x values for clarity. Otherwise the next lines gets even more difficult to read.

Code 4.8 Monte Carlo method applied to integration.

```
1  xpts = np.random.ranf((100,2))
2  xpts[:,1] *= 6
3  x = xpts[:,0]+0
4  yline = (np.sin((np.cos((x+10)*7))**4*8))**2 + (np.cos((x
       +10)*70))**4 + np.exp((x+0.5)/0.9)
5  a = xpts[:,1] < yline
6  a.sum()
7  Out[*]: 67
```

The addition of a 0 is a Python trick. This will ensure that the values of one array are duplicated. Consider a case in which b is a Python array, and the Python command is a = b. This will give two names to the same data. If the user changes a value in b then a will show this change. Both of these variables are pointing to the same location in memory. The command a = b + 0 will create a duplicate copy of the data. In this case, a and b now point to different locations in the memory. Changes in b are not seen in a.

Line 4 in Code 4.8 computes the y value for the 100 x values. All of these points lie on the curve in the plot. The values xpts[:,1] are the random y values. Consider just one random point xpts[k], which has a random x location denoted by xpts[k,0]. At this particular locations, the height of the function is yline[k] as defined by line 4. If the y-part of the random point is below the line, then xpts[k,1] < yline[k]. This is measured in line 5. A **True** value means that the random point is below the function. This Python script performs these comparisons for all points.

The answer indicates that 67 of the 100 points are below the line. Since random numbers are involved, each trial can generate a slightly different answer.

Is this answer correct? The average of the function would be a straight line that cuts the figure about in half. Thus, there is the same amount of area above and below the graph. But that is not actually true. The minimum value on the y axis is not 0. It is 2. So, about of third of the area used in the simulation is not shown in the graph. In that case, the answer is expected to be about 2/3 of the area is below the curve. 67 points out of 100 is about 2/3, so the evidence suggests that the calculation is accurate.

4.3.4 Square

The next example increases the complexity by increasing the number of dimensions. In this example, the target area is in the lower left quadrant of a 1×1 square (Figure 4.4). This target consumes one-fourth of the total environment, and the expectation is that one-fourth of the total random values land inside of the target. This, for 10,000 random points, the expectation is that 2,500 will be in the target (Figure 4.4).

The first step is to generate 10,000 random points. The environment space ranges from 0 to 1 in both the horizontal and vertical dimensions, and so it is not necessary

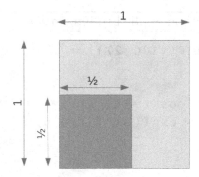

Figure 4.4: Monte Carlo example.

to bias or offset the random values. Code 4.9 creates 10,000 random points in line 1. Line 2 prints the first 5 rows and all of the columns (of which there are only 2). Each row is considered to be a random point in two-dimensional space.

Code 4.9 10,000 random points.

```
vecs = np.random.ranf((10000,2))
print(vecs[:5])
[[0.16806095 0.28518224]
 [0.80259647 0.28171387]
 [0.39965307 0.82203232]
 [0.13059667 0.49126246]
 [0.03156632 0.97971138]]
```

The second step is to determine if a point is inside of the target area or not. In this case the target area has four boundaries:

- $x > 0$

- $x < 0.5$

- $y > 0$

- $y < 0.5$

If all four conditions are met, the point is inside the target. Consider the first data point (line 3 from Code 4.9). The x value is 0.16 which is both greater than 0 and less than 0.5. The y value is 0.28 which is both greater than 0 and less than 0.5. So, this point is inside of the target area.

In this case, two of the conditions are automatically met. All random values are above 0, so the first and third test do not require code. Had the region of interest not been in the lower left corner, then these conditions would also require lines of Python script.

The situation becomes that of finding those (x, y) points in which both $x < 0.5$ and $y < 0.5$ are **True**. Lines 1 and 2 in Code 4.10 performs these comparisons. Each test produces an array of True or False values. These can be treated as 1 and 0. To find the cases in which both conditions are True, the intermediate results xless and yless are multiplied together (line 3). Those elements which are True have met both conditions. Counting the number of points in the defined region is achieved by a summation (line 7). The output is 2538, which is quite close to the expected 25% of the total number of points.

Code 4.10 Finding points in the region of interest.

```
1  xless = vecs[:,0] < 0.5
2  yless = vecs[:,1] < 0.5
3  both = xless * yless
4  print( both[:5] )
5  [ True False False  True False]
6
7  print( both.sum() )
8  2538
```

4.3.5 Estimation of π

Consider the task of estimating the value of π. Figure 4.5 shows a circle inscribed inside of a square. The radius of the circle is $r = 1$, and thus the length of the sides of the square is 2. In this simulation, the computer will generate random locations inside of the square. The ratio of the points inside of the circle to the total number of points is directly related to π,

$$\frac{N_c}{N} = \frac{A_c}{A_s}. \tag{4.3}$$

where N_c is the number of points inside of the circle, N is the total number of points, A_c is the area the circle, and A_s is the area of the square. The area of the circle is $A_c = \pi r^2$, but $r = 1$, thus in this case $A_c = \pi$. The area of the square with side lengths of 2 is 4. So, the equation reduces to,

$$\frac{N_c}{N} = \frac{\pi}{4}. \tag{4.4}$$

This equation is easily rearranged to solve for π,

$$\pi = 4\frac{N_c}{N}. \tag{4.5}$$

Thus, π can be estimated by the ratio of the number of points inside the circle to the total number of points.

The simulation defines the (0,0) point to be at the center of the circle, which defines the distance of a random point to the center of the environment as,

$$d = \sqrt{x^2 + y^2}. \tag{4.6}$$

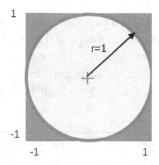

Figure 4.5: The environment to estimate π.

The radius of the circle is 1, and therefore, if $d < r$ then the point is inside of the circle.

The function **PIbyDarts** in Code 4.11 generates the random points, computes their distances to the center, and then computes Equation (4.5). The inputs are the number of random vectors to generate and the length of those vectors, which has a default of 2. This function is adaptable to vectors of any length. The slew of random vectors is created in line 3, with all values being between -1 and +1. This places the random vectors inside of the square. Line 4 computes the distance of each vector to the center of the environment. Line 5 counts the number of those in which the distance is less than 1. The comparison `dists < 1` produces an array of `True` and `False` values which can be treated as 1 and 0. Thus, the sum is also the count. Finally, line 6 uses Equation 4.5 to compute the answer. Line 9 runs the function, generating 1,000,000 random points. As seen, the output is close to the value of π.

Code 4.11 The **PIbyDarts** function.

```
# montecarlo.py
def PIbyDarts( NumDarts, DM=2 ):
    vecs = 2 * np.random.ranf((NumDarts,DM)) - 1
    dists = np.sqrt((vecs**2).sum(1))
    NdartsIn = (dists < 1 ).sum()
    answer = 4.0 * NdartsIn / NumDarts
    return answer

estPi = PIbyDarts(1000000)
print(estPi)
3.143628
```

4.4 HYPER-DIMENSIONAL BALL

Now the problem is increased in dimension. In the previous example, the area of the circle was π, and the area of the square was 4. Their ratio is 0.7834. This means that 78% of the environment is inside of the circle. Now, increase the dimensions from 2 to 3. The volume of a sphere is, $V = \frac{4}{3}\pi r^3$ which is 4.189 for $r = 1$, and it is inscribed in a cube such that all faces of the cube touch the sphere. Since the sphere radius is 1, the length of each side of the cube is 2, thus the volume of the cube is $2^3 = 8$. The ratio is then 0.523. The value of the volume went up, but the ratio went down. In the 2D case, 78% of the environment was inside the circle, but in the 3D case, only about half of the points are inside of the sphere.

The volume of a higher dimensional spheres (hypersphere) are considered. The equation for volume is,

$$V_n(r) = \frac{\pi^{n/2}}{\Gamma\left(\frac{n}{2} + 1\right)} r^n, \tag{4.7}$$

where r is the radius, n is the dimension, and Γ represents the *gamma function*, which is,

$$\Gamma(n) = (n - 1)! \tag{4.8}$$

when n is an integer, but for this application,

$$\Gamma\left(n + \frac{1}{2}\right) = \left(n - \frac{1}{2}\right) \times \left(n - \frac{3}{2}\right) \times \ldots \times \frac{1}{2} \times \sqrt{\pi}. \tag{4.9}$$

Fortunately, Python offers the gamma function through two functions **math.gamma** or **scipy.special.gamma**. Either of these will work here. Code 4.12 shows the dimension number, the sphere volume, and the ratio of the volume of the sphere to the square. Interestingly, the volume of the unit hypersphere increases, but after $n = 5$ it decreases. Furthermore, the ratio decreases, and values become quite close to 0 for larger values of n. For $n = 9$, 99% of the space is outside of the sphere, yet each side of the hypercube touches the hypersphere.

Code 4.12 Volume of a hypersphere and the ratio to the enclosing hypercube.

```
for n in range(2,10):
    v = math.pi**(n/2)/math.gamma(n/2 + 1)
    print(n,"{:.2f}".format(v),  "{:.2f}".format(v/(2**n)))

2 3.14 0.79
3 4.19 0.52
4 4.93 0.31
5 5.26 0.16
6 5.17 0.08
7 4.72 0.04
8 4.06 0.02
9 3.30 0.01
```

Code 4.13 shows the Monte Carlo implementation in which 1000 n-dimensional vectors are created. For each, the distance to the center is computed in line 6. If this distance is less than 1, then the integer **count** is increased by 1. The ratio of the count to the number of total points is the same as the ratio of the volume of the sphere to the volume of the cube. The example uses $n = 6$ and the output is the same as in Code 4.12.

Code 4.13 Estimating the volume of a hypersphere.

```
1  n = 6
2  count = 0
3  Npts = 1000
4  for i in range(Npts):
5      v = np.random.rand(n)*2-1
6      rad = np.sqrt((v*v).sum())
7      if rad < 1:
8          count += 1
9  print(count/Npts)
10
11 0.081
```

4.5 PROPER SAMPLING

Sometimes we learn by through errant investigations. In this section, the reader is challenged to find the error in the approach, and the answer will be revealed at the end of the section.

Figure 4.6 shows a problem in which a square is inscribed in a circle. The task is different than the previous. The environment is a circle, and the goal is to find all points inside of the square.

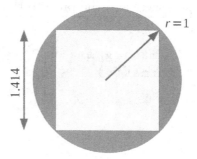

Figure 4.6: A right triangle.

All data points must lie within the unit circle. An easy method of generating these points is to create random points using polar coordinates. Each random point will have a radius of less than 1.0 and an angle between 0 and 2π. Line 1 in Code 4.14 sets the scales for the two types of random numbers, the first is for the radius with the maximum value being 1, and the second is for the angle where the maximum value is 2π. Line 2 generates the random points and multiplies these by this scale. The points in the first column range between 0 and 1, and the points in the second column range between 0 and 2π.

Code 4.14 Generating 1000 points in radial polar space.

```
1  scale = np.array((1,2*np.pi))
2  vecs = np.random.ranf((1000,2)) * scale
```

The radius of the circle is 1, and thus the diagonal of the inscribed square is length 2. The length of any side is $\sqrt{2}$, and the x and y values of the points inside the square must both be between $-\frac{\sqrt{2}}{2}$ and $+\frac{\sqrt{2}}{2}$. These points are counted in Code 4.15.

Code 4.15 Counting the points inside of the square for one example.

```
1  a1 = (vecs[:,0] > -0.707)*(vecs[:,0] < 0.707)
2  a2 = (vecs[:,1] > -0.707)*(vecs[:,1] < 0.707)
3  ndx = (a1 * a2).nonzero()[0]
4  print(len(ndx),len(vecs))
5  788 1000
```

The ratio of points inside of the square to the total number of points is 0.788. This can be easily checked. The area of the square is $\sqrt{2} \times \sqrt{2} = 2$, and the area of a circle with $r = 1$ is π. This ratio of the areas is 0.6366.

Theory states that the ratio should be 0.6366, but the simulation produced a value of 0.788. As stated at the beginning of this section, something is amiss with this process, and the reader's task was to identify the problem before going on to the next paragraph.

The issue is shown in Figure 4.7. The selection of points in the radial-polar space caused a problem. The script created the same number of points for each radius. There are the same number of points for a small radius as there are for a large radius, However, the larger radius has a larger circumference, so its points are spread farther apart. Thus, the space is not sampled uniformly, violating the main condition of the simple Monte Carlo method.

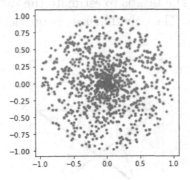

Figure 4.7: The density of the random points.

The proper method would have been to generate the points inside the larger square that contains the circle. Points outside the circle are discarded. From the remaining points, those inside the inscribed square are counted as before. Code 4.16 shows the proper simulation. Line 1 creates the points in the environment which is a square with length 2 on both sides, just as in previous problems. Line 2 computes the distance for each point to the center. Line 3 finds those points which have a radius of less than 1, thus being inside of the circle. Line 5 finds the points that are within the x range of $-\sqrt{2}/2$ and $-\sqrt{2}/2$. Line 6 repeats the same for the y variable. Line 7 combines these, finding those in which the condition is **True** for both dimensions, thus isolating those points which are inside of the inscribed square. Line 8 prints the total number of points inside of the square, the total number of points inside of the circle, and their ratio, which matches the theory. 10,000 points were generated but only 7,825 were valid for this computation. The rest were ignored as they were outside of the circular environment.

Code 4.16 The proper method of finding the ratio of points inside the square.

```
1  pts = np.random.ranf((10000,2))*2-1
2  dist = np.sqrt((pts**2).sum(1))
3  incirc = dist < 1
4  lm = np.sqrt(2)/2
5  a = (pts[:,0] > -lm) * (pts[:,0] < lm )
6  b = (pts[:,1] > -lm) * (pts[:,1] < lm )
7  insquare = a*b
8  print(insquare.sum(), incirc.sum(), insquare.sum()/incirc.
       sum())
9  4981 7825 0.6365495207667732
```

4.6 ESTIMATING THE AREA OF A STAR

The tools created in the previous section can be expanded to estimate the area of complicated geometric structures. Figure 4.8 shows a star pattern inscribed in a rectangle of unknown size. The task is to estimate the ratio of the area of the star to the area of the environment. The only dimensions provided is that the length of each line in the star is 1.

Figure 4.8: The star in an inscribed box.

Once again, the Monte Carlo process is to generate a large number of random points inside of an environment and then determine if those points are inside of an object. This problem is more complicated than the previous for two reasons. First, the dimensions of the environment are not known, and second, the perimeter of the object (the star) is defined by line-segment boundaries. These steps define the process used to find a solution:

1. Define the geometric properties of the problem,

2. Determine the theoretical percentage of space consumed by the star,

3. Create a method to determine if a point is inside the star, and

4. Run the simulation and compare experimental values to the theoretical values.

4.6.1 Geometric Properties

The star is created from five lines which are equal in length. The five-pointed star is symmetric, as a rotation of 72° creates a replica of the original image. Thus, the angle inside of each star point is 36°. This creates five triangles and a pentagon.

Figure 4.9 labels lines and regions of the star. Each line is identified by a capital letter, and each region is defined by a number. The length of the lines are equal, but that length is not technically defined. Since the goal is to determine a percentage of the space consumed by the star, the numerical value of the length is not important, so it is set to 1.0.

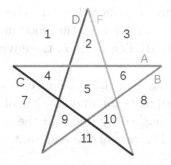

Figure 4.9: The star with labels.

In the previous problems, the origin of the space was defined as the center of the environment, but since the environment is not known, a center needs to be defined. For now, the center of line A is defined as (0,0). This will be changed after more information becomes available. The length of line A is 1, and thus, the endpoints of line A are $(-0.5, 0)$ and $(0.5, 0)$.

One end of line B is at $(0.5, 0)$, it has a length of 1, and it makes an angle of 36° to line A. Figure 4.10 shows the geometry of this configuration. The vertical location of the other endpoint is $-\sin(36°)$, and the horizontal location is $0.5 - \cos(36°)$. The computation is in Code 4.17. Python trigonometric functions use radians, thus the angle is converted use the **radians** function. The second end point is at $(-0.309,$ $-0.588)$, and similarly the other endpoint for line C is $(0.309, -0.588)$. Using similar logic, the endpoint at the top of the star is $(0, 0.363)$.

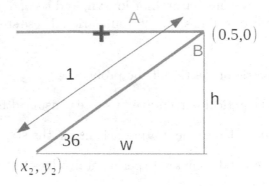

Figure 4.10: Values for line B.

Code 4.17 One endpoint for line B.

```
1  -np.sin(np.radians(36))
2  Out[*]:  -0.5877852522924731
3
4  0.5-np.cos(np.radians(36))
5  Out[]:  -0.30901699437494745
```

The extent of the environment is now known. The vertical location of the top point is 0.363, and the vertical location of the bottom point is -0.588. Thus, the height of the environment is 0.951. The width of the environment is the length of line A which is 1.

Code 4.18 begins the calculations. Line 1 converts the two angles into radians, and line 2 sets the known endpoints for line A. One of the line B endpoints is the same as one in Line A as established by line 3 in the script. The other endpoint in line B is computed in line 4. The rest of the endpoints are similarly calculated and printed.

A programming convenience can be gained by re-defining the location of the origin (0,0). Instead of being at the center of line A, it is moved to the center of the environment. This is merely a vertical shift of 0.112 as shown in Figure 4.11, and the calculations are performed in Code 4.20. The vector **shift** is moves all points 0.112 in the y direction.

The y values of all known points are:

- Line A: $(-0.5, 0.112)$ $(0.5, 0.112)$

- Line B: $(0.5, 0.112)$ $(-0.309, -0.476)$

- Line C: $(-0.5, 0.112)$ $(0.309, -0.476)$

Code 4.18 The end points of the lines in the star.

```
1  t1 = np.radians(36); t2 = np.radians(72)
2  la1 = np.array((-0.5,0)); la2 = np.array((0.5,0))
3  lb1 = la2+0
4  lb2 = np.array((0.5-np.cos(t1),-np.sin(t1)))
5  print('endpoint line B',lb2)
6  endpoint line B [-0.30901699 -0.58778525]
7
8  lc1 = la1+0
9  lc2 = np.array((-0.5+np.cos(t1),-np.sin(t1)))
10 print('endpoint line C', lc2)
11 endpoint line C [ 0.30901699 -0.58778525]
12
13 ld2 = lb2+0
14 ld1 = np.array((ld2[0]+np.cos(t2),ld2[1]+np.sin(t2)))
15 print('endpoint line D', ld1)
16 endpoint line D [0.         0.36327126]
17
18 le2 = lc2+0
19 le1 = np.array((le2[0]-np.cos(t2),le2[1]+np.sin(t2)))
20 print('endpoint line E', le1)
21 endpoint line E [0.         0.36327126]
```

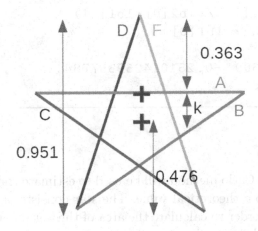

Figure 4.11: Determining the new origin.

Code 4.19 Adjusting the center of the environment.

```
1  yshift = -(le1[1] + lb2[1])/2
2  shift = np.array( (0,yshift))
3  la1 += shift; la2 += shift
4  lb1 += shift; lb2 += shift
5  lc1 += shift; lc2 += shift
6  ld1 += shift; ld2 += shift
7  le1 += shift; le2 += shift
```

- Line D: $(-0.309, -0.476)$ $(0, 0.476)$

- Line E: $(0.309, -0.476)$ $(0, 0.476)$

With the endpoints known, the next step is to compute the slope and intercept for the five lines. Code 4.20 computes these for line B. A computation is not needed for line A since it is horizontal and at $y = 0.112$. The other slopes and intercepts are similarly computed and the results are:

- Line A: $(0, 0.112)$

- Line B: $(0.727, -0.251)$

- Line C: $(-0.727, -0.251)$

- Line D: $(3.077, 0.476)$

- Line E: $(-3.077, 0.476)$

Code 4.20 Computing the slopes and intercepts.

```
1  mB = (lb2[1]-lb1[1])/(lb2[0]-lb1[0])
2  bB = lb1[1] - mB * lb1[0]
3  print(mB,bB)
4  0.7265425280053609  -0.2510142698577841
5  # similar code for the other lines
```

4.6.2 Theoretic Ratio

Eventually, the Monte Carlo method will be used to estimate the area of the star, and it can be compared to a theoretical value. The star consists of five similar triangles and one pentagon. In order to calculate the area of these geometric shapes, two more measurements are needed. The distances f and g shown in Figure 4.12 provide enough information to calculate the area of the triangles and pentagon in the star.

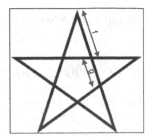

Figure 4.12: Needed measurements for the area computations.

The length of a line is 1, and thus $2f + g = 1$. The location of the intersection of lines A and E is needed to find f and g. Each line is defined by the equations $y = m_A x + b_A$ and $y = m_E x + b_E$. The intersection is when both equations have the same values of x and y. If both equations have the same y value, then,

$$m_A x + b_A = m_E x + b_E. \tag{4.10}$$

This equation is rearranged to give,

$$x = \frac{b_E - b_A}{m_A - m_E}. \tag{4.11}$$

This is the horizontal location of the intersection, and the vertical location is obtained from either of the equations for line A or E. In this case, the first is chosen,

$$y = m_A x + b_A. \tag{4.12}$$

The computation is performed in Code 4.21, where line 1 computes Equation (4.11), and line 2 computes Equation (4.12). The values are placed into a vector and printed in line 5.

Code 4.21 The intersection of lines A and E.

```
1  x = (bE-bA)/(mA-mE)
2  y = mA * x + bA
3  corner = np.array((x,y))
4  print(corner)
5  [0.11811749 0.112      ]
```

The distance f is the distance from the top endpoint of line E to this newly calculated corner. This is calculated in line 1 of Code 4.22. Since the total length of line E is 1, the distance g is $g = 1 - 2f$, and it is calculated in line 2.

Code 4.22 The distances of f and g.

```
1  distf = np.linalg.norm(corner-le1)
2  distg = 1-2*distf
```

Heron's formula is used to compute the area of a triangle for the cases in which all three sides are known. It is,

$$A_\triangle = \sqrt{p(p - s_1)(p - s_2)(p - s_3)} \tag{4.13}$$

where s_1, s_2, s_3 are the side lengths, and $p = (s_1 + s_2 + s_3)/2$. This formula is realized in Code 4.23.

Code 4.23 The area of a single triangle.

```
p = (distf+distf+distg)/2
atriang = np.sqrt( p*(p-distf)*(p-distf)*(p-distg))
print('Area of a single triangle', atriang)
Area of a single triangle 0.0428
```

The formula for computing the area of a regular pentagon (all sides have the same length) is,

$$A_\varhexagon = \frac{d^2}{4}\sqrt{5(5 + 2\sqrt{5})}, \tag{4.14}$$

where d is the length of one side of the pentagon. The computation is performed in Code 4.24, and the result is that the area is 0.0954.

Code 4.24 The area of a pentagon.

```
apent = 0.25 * np.sqrt(5*(5+2*np.sqrt(5)))*distg**2
print('Area of the pentagon', apent)
Area of the pentagon 0.0954
```

The total area of the star, the environment, and the ratio of these values is now well within reach. The area of the star is the is the $5A_\triangle + A_\varhexagon$, and the area of the environment is the height times the width. These values and their ratio is computed in Code 4.25. Line 3 prints the area of the star, and line 7 prints the area of the environment. Their ratio is 0.325 which means about one-third of the environment is filled by the star. This is the target value for the Monte Carlo method employed in the next section.

4.6.3 Monte Carlo Estimate of the Star Area Ratio

The star (Figure 4.9) has 11 eleven regions, and several of these (2,4,5,6,9,10) are inside the star. The Monte Carlo method will generate random points, and the task is to determine which region the points are in. These regions are not rectangular or circular which makes this determination slightly more complicated.

The regions are defined by a combination of straight lines, and the origin is inside of region 5. The points in each region will be defined by which sides of the lines they are on. A point is considered to be on the near side if it is on the same side as the

Code 4.25 The areas of the star, the environment, and their ratio.

```
1  astar = 5*atriang + apent
2  print('Area of the star', astar)
3  Area of the star 0.3095
4
5  aenv = (le1[1]-lb2[1])*1
6  print('Area environment: ',aenv)
7  Area environment:   0.9510
8
9  print('Ratio: ', astar/aenv)
10 Ratio:   0.32549
```

origin, and it is considered to be on the far side otherwise. For example, consider a random point which lands in region 1. It is on the far side on line A, the near side of line B, the near side of line C, the far side of line D, and the near side of line E.

4.6.3.1 Determining Side of Line

Dot products are useful in determining which side of a line a point is on. Figure 4.13 shows two example points, one line, and the origin. The slope and the intercept of the line are known. This image also shows the perpendicular line from the origin to the given line, which is denoted as $\vec{v}_\perp = (x_\perp, y_\perp)$. The slope of the perpendicular is related to the slope of the original line by,

$$\frac{1}{m_\perp} = -m. \tag{4.15}$$

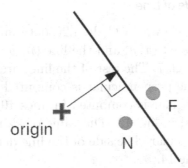

Figure 4.13: Consider points on both sides of the line.

The inner product of the perpendicular line with itself is,

$$\vec{v}_\perp \cdot \vec{v}_\perp = x_\perp^2 + y_\perp^2. \tag{4.16}$$

The value of the dot product, k, is constant for all points on the line. The inner product is a projection, and thus, the inner product of any point on the line $\vec{v}_l =$

(x_l, y_l) produces the same k value,

$$\vec{v}_\perp \cdot \vec{v}_l = x_\perp x_l + y_\perp y_l = k. \tag{4.17}$$

The inner product of a random point $\vec{v} = (x, y)$ with $\vec{v}_\perp$ will be less than k if the point $\vec{v}$ is on the near side of the line,

$$\vec{v}_\perp \cdot \vec{v} < k. \tag{4.18}$$

Likewise, a point on the far side of the line will create an inner product greater than k,

$$\vec{v}_\perp \cdot \vec{v} > k. \tag{4.19}$$

A region in the star image is denoted by which side of the five lines it is on with respect to the origin which is inside of region 5. Region 5 is denoted by NNNNN since all points are on the near side. A point in region 2 is on the far side of line A. It is on the near side of all of the other lines. So, the designation of region 2 is FNNNN. The designation of all of the regions inside of the star are:

- Region 2: FNNNN

- Region 4: NNNFN

- Region 5: NNNNN

- Region 6: NFNNN

- Region 9: NNFNN

- Region 10: NFNNN

4.6.3.2 Python Script for Side of Line

The function **SideOfLine** shown in Code 4.26 determines which side of a line a point is on. It receives the point (x, y) and the line (m, b). The special case of $m = 0$ is considered in lines 4 through 7. The rest of the lines are considered starting in line 9. For these, the slope of the perpendicular is computed in line 9. The intersection of the line and the perpendicular is computed in lines 10 and 11. The value of k of Equation (4.16) is computed in line 12. The value of k2 is the inner product of the given point and the perpendicular. The side of the line determination is inside of the if statement starting on line 14.

The **GetCode** function shown in Code 4.27 returns the near-far code for a given point. Line 3 creates an empty list named answ. It gathers the five letters (either N or F). Line 9 uses the **join** function to convert a list of individual letters to a string. The output of this function is a five letter code indicating which region the point is in. The example in Code 4.28 uses the point (0, 0.12) as an example. The returned code is FNNNN which indicates this point is in region 2.

Code 4.26 The **SideOfLine** function.

```
1   # star2.py
2   def SideOfLine( x,y, m, b):
3       if m==0:
4           if y > b:
5               return 'F'
6           else:
7               return 'N'
8       else:
9           mp = -1/m
10          xp = -b/(m-mp)
11          yp = mp * xp
12          k = xp*xp + yp*yp
13          k2 = xp*x + yp*y
14          if k2>k:
15              return 'F'
16          else:
17              return 'N'
```

Code 4.27 The **GetCode** function.

```
1   # star2.py
2   def GetCode(x,y):
3       answ = []
4       answ.append( SideOfLine(x,y, 0,.112) ) # line 1
5       answ.append( SideOfLine(x,y,.727,-.251)) # line 2
6       answ.append( SideOfLine(x,y,-.72,-.251)) # line 3
7       answ.append( SideOfLine(x,y,3.077,.476)) # line 4
8       answ.append( SideOfLine(x,y,-3.077,.476)) # line 5
9       answ = ''.join(answ)
10      return answ
```

The function **IsInsideStar** shown in Code 4.29 checks for a match for the codes of the six regions inside of the star. The function simply checks the computed string against a list of strings, and then returns either True or False.

The **RandomPoint** function shown in Code 4.30 creates a random point inside of the enclosing rectangle. Each random point is between -0.5 and $+0.5$ in the horizontal and -0.475 and $+0.475$ in the vertical.

The final function is **ManyRandomPoints** as shown in Code 4.31. This function calls **RandomPoint** in line 5, and if it is inside of the star (line 6) then the counter is incremented (line 7). The output is the number of points landing inside of the star to the number of random points. The final two lines run the program and print the result.

Code 4.28 Testing with a point in Region 2.

```
1  print( star2.GetCode( 0,0.12) )
2  'FNNNN'
```

Code 4.29 The **IsInsideStar** function.

```
1  # star2.py
2  def IsInsideStar(x,y):
3      incodes = ['FNNNN','NFNNN','NNFNN','NNNFN', 'NNNNF', '
            NNNNN']
4      c = GetCode( x,y )
5      if c in incodes:
6          return True
7      else:
8          return False
```

Code 4.30 The **RandomPoint** function.

```
1  # star2.py
2  def RandomPoint( ):
3      x = 1*random.random() - 0.5
4      y = .951*random.random() - .475
5      return (x,y)
```

Code 4.31 The **ManyRandomPoints** function.

```
1  # star2.py
2  def ManyRandomPoints( Nvectors ):
3      ct = 0
4      for i in range( Nvectors ):
5          x,y = RandomPoint()
6          if IsInsideStar( x,y ):
7              ct += 1
8      return ct/Nvectors
9
10 ManyRandomPoints(1000000)
11 Out[]: 0.326683
```

In this trial, 32.7% of the points landed inside of the star which matches well to the theoretical value, confirming that the star consumes about 1/3 of the space in the environment.

4.7 UNEQUAL DISTRIBUTIONS

So far, the examples have used equal distribution random points. There are cases in which other types of distributions are warranted. Consider the case of a laser beam shining onto a surface with a rectangular hole. The quest is to estimate the percentage of photons which go through the whole. The profile of a laser beam is not uniform, as there are more photons in the center the of the beam than near the edges. Thus, the equal distribution of points is inappropriate.

As a simple estimate, the profile of the laser beam is assumed to be Gaussian, and for the first part of the simulation, only one dimension is considered. The Gaussian profile creates a bell curve which is wider than the square aperture. Thus, the tails of the Gaussian beam do not go through the opening. Of course, the simulation is given the known values for the mean and standard deviation of the Gaussian function and the dimension of the aperture.

The *numpy* module provides functions to generate random points in a Gaussian distribution. The first function is **numpy.random.normal** which has three optional arguments. The first is the mean, the second is the standard the deviation, and the third is the number of points to generate. Code 4.32 runs this simulation. Line 1 declares the number of random points, and line 2 calls the **normal** function. In this case, the mean is 3.0 and the standard deviation is 1.0. This generates, 10,000 points which abide by this distribution. The opening of the surface that the laser beam shines on is from location 2.0 to 4.0. Line 3 finds which of the random points are in this region, and the ratio of 0.687 is printed to the console.

Code 4.32 A Monte Carlo simulation with a Gaussian distribution.

```
1  N = 10000
2  pts = np.random.normal(3.0,1.0,N)
3  ct = ((pts>2)*(pts<4)).sum()
4  print(ct/N)
5  0.6874
```

This result can easily be checked. It is well-known that for a Gaussian distribution, 68.2% of the points lie between $\mu - \sigma$ and $\mu + \sigma$ (where μ is the average and σ is the standard deviation). The example does have a standard deviation of 1 and the width of the opening is twice that, thus, making the opening equal to $\mu \pm \sigma$. The answer of 0.687 then matches the theoretical value.

Python also offers functions of normal distributions in more than one dimension. These are called multivariate distributions and the *numpy* function reflects this name. The **numpy.random.multivariate_normal** function (Code 4.33) receives the same three types of input. However, the mean is now a vector. For a problem in two dimensions, this vector is of length 2. The second argument is now the covariance matrix, which for this simulation is 2×2. The aperture is also in two dimensions which are defined on line 5 and 6. The test in these lines is to determine which random points are inside of the opening, and the final tally is computed in line 7. In this example, almost 50% of the photons went through the opening.

Code 4.33 A simulation with a multivariate distribution.

```
1  N = 10000
2  mu = np.array((2.0,3.5))
3  sigma = np.array(((1.0,0.5),(0.5,1.0)))
4  pts = np.random.multivariate_normal(mu,sigma,N)
5  vtrue = (pts[:,0]>1.0) * (pts[:,0]<3.0)
6  htrue = (pts[:,1]>2.5) * (pts[:,1]<4.5)
7  truth = vtrue * htrue
8  print(truth.sum()/N)
9  0.4984
```

4.8 SUMMARY

The Monte Carlo method creates random data points which are so numerous that it thoroughly samples the environment. Simple examples shown here place random points inside of an environment and then determines which points are inside of a geometric shape. These simple samples help visualize and confirm the Monte Carlo process. Of course, the Monte Carlo method is not restricted to geometry. It can certainly be expanded to complicated processes which are too involved to be presented here.

PROBLEMS

1. Generate 1,000,000 random vectors of length 10. The range of the first elements of the vectors is from 0 to 1, which is written as $v_i[0] \in [0:1]\ \forall i$. The $v_i[0]$ is the first element of all vectors, v, and [0:1] is the value of the range. The range of the rest of the elements in the vectors follows, $v_i[k] \in [0:k+1]\ \forall i$. For these vectors, compute the average vector and the standard deviation vector.

2. Employ the Monte Carlo method for a 2D environment which is a 1×1 square. The target area is a rectangular region in the upper right corner, from $0.8 < x < 1$ and $0.9 < y < 1$. Create 1,000,000 random points uniformly distributed in this environment. How many points land in the target region?

3. Employ the Monte Carlo method for a 2D environment which is a 1×1 square. The target area is a circular region centered at (0,1) with a radius of 0.5. Create 1,000,000 random points uniformly distributed in this environment. How many points land in the target region?

4. Employ the Monte Carlo method for a 2D environment which is a 1×1 square. The target area is an ellipse, centered in the environment, with a major axis of length 0.8 and a minor axis of length 0.4. Create 1,000,000 random points uniformly distributed in this environment. How many points land in the target region?

5. Consider a pyramid with a square bottom surface. The sides of the square are length 1, and the height of the pyramid is 1. The volume of a pyramid is $v = lwh/3$ were l and w are sides of the base and h is the height. Employ the Monte Carlo method on a 3D environment of size $1 \times 1 \times 1$ which completely contains this pyramid. Create 1,000,000 random points uniformly distributed in this environment. How many points land in the pyramid?

6. Start with a square 1×1 environment which contains a 0.5×0.5 square target region centered in the environment. For 1,000,000 uniformly distributed random points, count how many points are inside of the target. Compute the ratio of number of points inside the target to the number of points. Increase this problem to 3D in which the length of each side of the environment is 1 and the length of each side of the target region is 0.5. Compute the ratio of the number of points inside of the target to the total number of points. Repeat this problem for increasing dimensions up to a ten-dimensional space. Print the computed ratios for each dimension.

7. In the star problem there were 5 triangles and 1 pentagon. Repeat the star problem. For 1,000,000 random points count the number that are in each triangle and the pentagon separately. Print those 6 values.

8. Generate 1,000,000 values for a Gaussian distribution with $\mu = 3.5$ and $\sigma = 1.28$. For these points, compute the average and standard deviation.

9. Modify the laser beam example of Section 4.7. The laser beam is centered at (0,0) and its Gaussian profile has a standard deviation of 0.5 in both directions. This beams strikes a surface with a circular opening of radius 0.25 located at (0,0). Assume the beam has 1,000,000 photons. How many go through the opening?

10. Modify the laser beam example of Section 4.7. The laser beam is centered at (0,0) and its Gaussian profile has a standard deviation of 0.1 in both directions. The beam strikes a surface with an opening in the shape of the star with the same dimensions as given in Section 4.6.1. The beam has 1,000,000 photons. How many go through the star?

## CHAPTER 5

Modeling Self-Organization

THE 1967 FILM *Planet of the Apes* had elaborate costumes that were difficult to put on and take off. The cast had to eat their lunches while still in costume. The star of the movie, Charlton Heston, noted "an instinctive segregation on the set. Not only would the apes eat together, but the chimpanzees ate with the chimpanzees, the gorillas ate with the gorillas, the orangutans ate with the orangutans, and the humans would eat off by themselves. It was quite spooky." [2]

Two years later, James Franciscus starred in *Beneath the Planet of the Apes*, and he noted a similar phenomenon. "During lunch I looked up and realized, 'My God, here is the universe,' because at one table were all the orangutans eating, at another table were the apes, and at another table were the humans. The orangutan characters would not eat or mix with the ape characters, and the humans wouldn't sit down and eat with any one of them." [2]

The actors self-organized. No one told the actors where to have lunch, they each made their own decision, and in the end, they were organized solely by their costume. While psychologists and sociologists would have a grand time exploring the reasons for this, the interest in this chapter lies in algorithms that can produce a similar phenomenon. There are several, but one of the earliest algorithms will be sufficient for demonstration.

5.1 SCHELLING'S MODEL

Just a few years after those movies were released, Thomas Schelling published a simple model, which considered the nature of self-organizing in terms of housing. The model supported the idea that humans, at that time, selected to live in neighborhoods among people of similar ethnicity. Schelling's model, however, relaxed the decision-making property of the humans. Instead of moving to a house in a specific neighborhood, the entities in his model moved to a randomly selected empty house. Segregation still occurred.

In lieu of teetering on the edge of social discrimination, this model will be presented here in terms of cats and dogs. The environment is two-dimensional grid, and a cell in this grid can contain only one animal. An animal will desire to move if it is surrounded by the other type of animal. Figure 5.1a shows just nine cells from the larger grid, and this image, the dog in the center is surrounded by other dogs

DOI: 10.1201/9781003226581-5

or empty cells. This dog is happy and has no desire to move. Figure 5.1b shows a different part of the grid, and this dog is surrounded by cats, and therefore the dog wants to move.

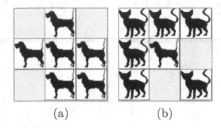

Figure 5.1: (a) The dog is surrounded by other dogs and thus will not move. (b) The dog is surrounded by cats and thus wants to move.

The measure of unhappiness is the number of neighboring cells which contain the opposing animal. Usually, that value is between 4 and 6, but for the following example, the value is set to 3 in order to keep the images simple. The variable γ is used to represent this value, and thus, it is named the gamma value.

Figure 5.2a shows twelve cells, and three animals are considered as unhappy because they have three neighboring cells occupied by the other animal. One of these unhappy animals is selected and is moved to a randomly selected cell, and the result is shown in Figure 5.2b. Still, two animals are unhappy, and one of these is selected to move as shown in Figure 5.2c. The final result, coincidentally, resolves the social issues of both unhappy animals. All animals are happy in Figure 5.2d. Furthermore, segregation has been achieved. The cats are on the left, and the dogs are on the right.

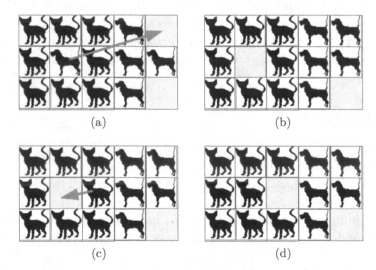

Figure 5.2: (a) The unhappy dog moves to a randomly selected open cell. (b) Still there are unhappy animals. (c) Of these, random selection picks the unhappy cat to move. (d) Now all animals are happy, and the segregation is complete.

5.2 MODELING IN PYTHON

The first decision to make in creating a model is how to represent the environment and the three occupants of the cells (dog, cat, empty). The occupants need no other information than their identities, thus the simple encoding of empty=0, cat=1, dog=2 can be used. The environment becomes a two-dimensional Python array which contains integers.

The simulation starts with a random distribution of the occupants. However, the user must make a few decisions: the size of the environment, the percentage of cells which are empty, and the threshold to determine if an occupant wants to move. The first two are needed for the initialization.

The **Init** (Code 5.1) creates the environment and the initial population. The first two inputs are the vertical and horizontal size of the environment, and the last argument is the percentage of empty cells. Line 3 creates the environment. Line 4 generates a random number for each cell. These will be used to determine which occupant is in each cell. Since there are three entities (dog, cat, empty), two thresholds are required. The first threshold, `t1`, separates the empty cells from the animals. If the random number is below `t1` then the cell will be declared as initially empty. Thus, `t1` is set to `pctempty` in line 5. The second threshold separates the two animals. This is set at halfway between `t1` and 1.0 in line 6. Lines 7 and 8 creates new binary matrices which contain **True** or **False** values depending on the animal selection. These matrices act as gateways and are called *masks*. The `mask1` will contain **True** values in the cells just determined to have cats. Likewise, `mask2` will contain **True** values at the location for dogs. Line 9 combines these masks with the integers that represent the animals, thus completing the initialization.

Code 5.1 Initializing Schelling's model.

```
1   # schelling.py
2   def Init(V,H,pctempty):
3       grid=np.zeros((V,H),int)
4       r = np.random.rand(V,H)
5       t1 = pctempty # first threshold
6       t2 = (1-t1)/2 + t1 # second threshold
7       mask1 = (r>t1)*(r<=t2)
8       mask2 = (r>t2)
9       grid = grid + mask1 + mask2*2
10      return grid
```

An iteration consists of finding the animals which are unhappy and moving one of them. Unhappiness is defined as having too many of the other animal in the neighboring cells. This requires the user to define this threshold. For the following examples, the threshold is set to 5, and thus, if animal has 5 neighbors of the opposite kind, then it will want to move. This calculation must exclude empty cells.

This operation requires that each cell be considered, which is a double nested loop. Each consideration is to retrieve the value of the surrounding cells, which is another double nested loop. In Python, a four-nested loops will be inefficient, so a different approach is used. The **Unhappy** function in Code 5.2 counts the number of opposing neighbors for all cells. Line 2 imports the **shift** function which will shift a matrix in a specified direction without a wrap-around. If the matrix is shifted upward, then the bottom row is filled with 0's. The top row does not wrap-around to become the bottom row.

Line 4 creates an empty matrix which will accumulate the count of opposing neighbors. Line 5 defines all possible shifts. For the 2D array, eight shifts exist. Each of these are considered in the loop starting one line 6. Line 7 shifts the grid by one of the eight possible shifts. Line 8 compares the shifted grid to the original. As an example, consider the shift of (1,0) which moves the grid down one row and places 0's in the top row. Line 8 overlays this shifted grid over the original thus comparing a cell in the original grid with one above it. If they differ, then the count for that cell is increased by 1. However, this process also captures the cases which compare an animal to an empty space, which is not to be included in the count. Thus, line 9 is used to remove these cases which are when the shifted cell is 0. Line 10 removes the cases in which the original grid cell is 0.

Code 5.2 Finding candidates to be moved.

```
1  # schelling.py
2  import scipy.ndimage.interpolation as ndi
3  def Unhappy( grid ):
4      unhappy = np.zeros( grid.shape, int )
5      shifts = ((-1,-1),(-1,0),(-1,1),(0,-1),(0,1),(1,-1)
            ,(1,0),(1,1))
6      for sh in shifts:
7          alt = ndi.shift(grid, sh )
8          temp = grid != alt
9          unhappy +=  temp * (alt!=0)
10     unhappy *= (grid!=0)
11     return unhappy
```

Originally, the problem was described as four nested loops. This code is more efficient because the two largest loops are now performed in *numpy* functions. Are handled by the list **shifts**, which has combined the two loops into one.

The **CollectGrumps** function(Code 5.3) identifies which of the cells have a unhappiness value that exceeds γ. The inputs are the output from **Unhappy** and the threshold which defines the minimum number of opposing animals which are needed to make an occupant want to move. Since the information is stored in an array, this operation is a simple threshold as shown in line 3. Line 4 collects the locations of the occupants which are unhappy.

Code 5.3 The **CollectGrumps** function.

```
# schelling.py
def CollectGrumps(uhap, gamma=5):
    mask = uhap>=gamma
    v,h = mask.nonzero()
    return v,h
```

This function finds the occupants which are eligible to move to a new location. The next step is to find the empty cells. This is performed in the function **FindEmpty** shown in Code 5.4. Line 3 finds the location of the cells which have a value of 0. It is a simple task to find these cells.

Code 5.4 The **FindEmpty** function.

```
# schelling.py
def FindEmpty(grid):
    ev,eh = (grid==0).nonzero()
    return ev,eh
```

The lists returned by **CollectGrumps** are the occupants who qualify to move, and the lists returned from the **FindEmpty** function are the locations to where they can move. The next step is to randomly select one occupant to move, randomly select one empty location, and to perform the move. Code 5.5 shows the **Move1Unhappy** function. This must check to make sure there is as least one unhappy occupant to prevent errors. Lines 5 and 6 pick the occupant to move, and lines 8 and 9 pick the empty cell. Line 10 moves the occupant, and line 11 makes the occupant's old location empty.

Code 5.5 Moving one occupant.

```
# schelling.py
def Move1Unhappy(v,h,ev,eh,grid):
    N = len(v)
    if N>0:
        me = np.random.randint(0,N)
        mover = v[me],h[me]
        M = len(ev)
        me = np.random.randint(0,M)
        newloc = ev[me],eh[me]
        grid[newloc] = grid[mover]
        grid[mover] = 0
```

The components are built. The next step is to combine them into a single iteration. Code 5.6 shows the **Iterate** function which performs the four steps in a single iteration. To run the full simulation, the **Iterate** function is called until a user-defined condition is met, such as the number of iterations, or the number of changes between iterations, etc. This could be a limit on the number of iterations or the number of unhappy occupants falling below a threshold. The *schelling* module contains a **Go** which performs this loop.

Code 5.6 A single iteration.

```
1  # schelling.py
2  def Iterate(grid):
3      u = Unhappy(grid)
4      v,h = CollectGrumps(u,4)
5      ev,eh = FindEmpty(grid)
6      Move1Unhappy(v,h,ev,eh,grid)
```

5.3 TRIALS

Consider a case in which the size of the grid is 100×100 and the initial configuration has 10% empty cells. Figure 5.3 shows a single trial after 10,000, 20,000, and 30,000 iterations. The brightest pixels represent the cats, the medium pixels represent the dogs, and the few black pixels are the empty cells. Initially, the occupants are randomly distributed, but after 10,000 iterations, organization is apparent. This improves to 20,000 iterations, but that improvement does not carry on to 30,000 iterations. Yet, the occupants are not fully organized.

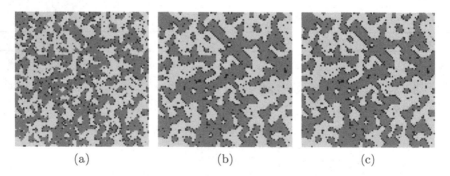

      (a)   (b)   (c)

Figure 5.3: (a) The distribution after 10,000 iterations. (b) The distribution after 20,000 iterations. (c) The distribution after 30,000 iterations.

Two competing concepts are involved. The first is that system is not fully segregated, and thus there should be unhappy occupants. The second is that the system has stopped evolving, and thus all occupants must be happy. The latter option is the actual case. Those occupants at the boundaries are actually surrounded by many empty cells. Technically, they are satisfied with their current position, as there are only a small number of animals in an unhappy position. Yet, the segregation has occurred.

The solution is to reduce the number of empty cells. Figure 5.4 shows the case in which only 1% of the cells are empty. The images are for 10,000 iterations, 30,000 iterations, and 70,000 iterations. The segregation is more extreme in this case, thus confirming that too many empty cells will inhibit segregation.

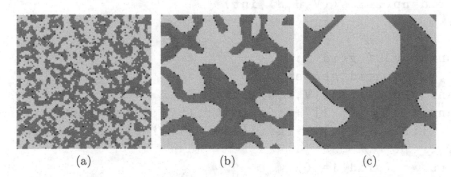

(a)   (b)   (c)

Figure 5.4: (a) The distribution after 10,000 iterations. (b) The distribution after 30,000 iterations. (c) The distribution after 70,000 iterations.

This raises the question as to what is the correct number of empty cells? Consider a case in which the desire is to have all cats on one side of a straight line and all dogs on the other. For a 100×100 grid, there needs to be 100 empty cells out of 10,000. Thus, 1% of the cells need to be empty, which is the case shown in Figure 5.4. The desired straight line could be achieved if the initial boundaries were located in the middle of the environment. In other words, if an initial boundary were at $x = 50$ then the desired single line segregation could emerge. Segregation boundaries, though, emerge from a chaotic distribution, and thus the desired single line boundary is unlikely to emerge.

5.4 ALTERATIONS TO THE ALGORITHM

Once the algorithm is complete, then alterations to the theory can be considered. One such alteration would be to get rid of the edge effects with a wrap-around. Cells in the left-most column would consider cells in the right-most column as neighbors, and vice-versa. The same would apply to the top and bottom rows. Thus, all cells would have 8 neighbors.

Another alteration would be to expand the environment from two dimensions to three dimensions. Instead of eight neighbors, each cell would have twenty-six neighbors. The γ threshold, used to determine if an entity is eligible to move, also increases. Several alterations are needed to convert to a 3D environment. The **Iterated3D** function (not shown here) calls four functions similar to Code 5.6, but each function name is modified with the letters 3D.

These four functions need modifications. The initialization performed by **Init3D** needs to create a 3D environment instead of a 2D environment. The script modified from **Init** is shown in lines 2 and 3 of Code 5.7. The rest of the function (represented by the ellipses in line 4 is the same as in the original function.

Code 5.7 Modifications to the script to create a 3D simulation.

```python
# schelling.py
def Init3D(V,H,N,pctempty):
    grid=np.zeros((V,H,N),int)
    . . . .    # lines of code not shown

def Unhappy3D( grid ):
    V,H,W = grid.shape
    ans = np.zeros((V,H,W),int)
    ans[:-1,:-1,:-1] += (grid[1:,1:,1:] != grid
        [:-1,:-1,:-1])*(grid[1:,1:,1:]!=0).astype(int)
    . . . .     # many lines not shown
    ans *= (grid != 0)
    return ans

def CollectGrumps3D(uhap, gamma=13):
    mask = uhap>=gamma
    v,h,w = mask.nonzero()
    return v,h,w

def FindEmpty3D(grid):
    ev,eh,ew = (grid==0).nonzero()
    return ev,eh,ew

def Move1Unhappy3D(v,h,w,ev,eh,ew,grid):
    N = len(v)
    M = len(ev)
    if N>1 and M>1:
        me = np.random.randint(0,N)
        mover = v[me],h[me],w[me]
        me = np.random.randint(0,M)
        newloc = ev[me],eh[me], ew[me]
    . . . . # code not shown
```

The **Unhappy3D** needs two types of alterations. The first is to convert all computations to 3D arrays as shown in lines 7, 8, and 9. In this new model, each cell has 26 neighbors instead of 8. The second modification is to create 25 more lines similar to line 9. These are not shown here, but they are in the *schelling.py* module. The **CollectGrumps3D** and **FindEmpty3D** functions are modified to accommodate 3D arrays. The **Move1Unhappy3D** function needs more input arguments, and lines 28 and 30 are also modified to be in 3D.

Of course, more dimensions increases the computational load. In the original 2D model, a 100 grid contained 10,000 cells. In the 3D case, a grid that is $50 \times 50 \times 50$ has $125,000$ cells, which is more than a ten-fold increase. Furthermore, each cell has 26 neighbors instead of 8 which increases the number of shifts required to count the neighbors of each cell. Finally, more iterations are needed in order to get segregation. On a standard laptop, the $50\times50\times50$ grid with 10% empty cells and 100,000 iterations required 30 minutes to compute. Even then, the segregation was not complete.

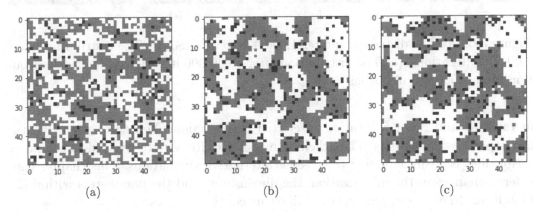

Figure 5.5: (a) The first (x, y) plane, (b) the middle (x, y) plane, and (c) the neighboring plane of the previous.

Partial results after 100,000 iterations are shown in Figure 5.5. As it is not possible display a 3D image on a 2D page, a few planes are shown. Figure 5.5a shows the first (x, y) plane $(w = 0)$. Figures 5.5b and 5.5c show two neighboring planes from the middle of the 3D cube $(w = 25$ and $w = 26)$. As seen, segregation is evolving with better results in the middle of the cube. The neighboring planes are shown to show that segregation is contiguous across the planes. Several hundred thousand iterations would be needed to vastly improve the segregation.

Two alterations thus discussed are removing the effects of the edges and to increase the dimensions. A third alteration is to use four types of occupants instead of two. This requires the alteration of the **Init** function, which now needs to divide the cells into five categories. Figure 5.6a shows the distribution after 1,000,000 iterations. Pockets of organization are appearing, but most of the space still appears to be random. The chances of a moving occupant to find a neighborhood where they can be happy is much more difficult to find, and thus more iterations are need.

Figure 5.6b shows the state after 2,000,000 iterations, and the pockets of organization are growing. The result of 3,000,000 iterations is shown in Figure 5.6c. Most of the randomness is gone. More iterations will create large sections of like entities. However, 4,000,000 iterations does require some time to run.

5.5 SUMMARY

The Schelling model demonstrates the self-organization ability for a system based on random numbers. Entities which are candidates to move to new locations are selected

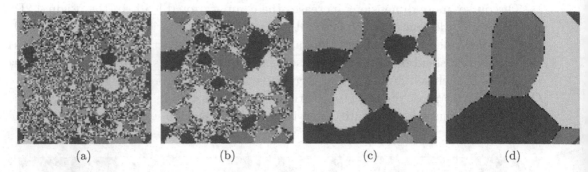

Figure 5.6: (a) The distribution after 1,000,000 iterations. (b) The distribution after 2,000,000 iterations. (c) The distribution after 3,000,000 iterations. (d) The distribution after 4,000,000 iterations

at random, and the new location is selected from random. Yet, this system eventually separates the entities. The Schelling model is quite easy to realized in computer script, and is easily modified to consider alternative simulations. This chapter considered changes in the initialization, the dimensions, and the parameters within the algorithm. In all cases, segregation still occurred.

PROBLEMS

1. Run the standard Schelling model with a grid size of 100×100, 1% empty spaces, using $\gamma = 6$. Display the grid after 10,000 iterations.

2. Run the standard Schelling model with a grid size of 100×100, 1% empty spaces, using $\gamma = 2$. Display the grid after 10,000 iterations.

3. Run the standard Schelling model with a grid size of 100×100, and 1% empty spaces. Start with $\gamma = 7$. Run the simulation for 24,000 iterations, but after every 4000 iterations reduce γ by 1. At the end of the simulation, the γ value should be 2. Show the grid from the final iteration.

4. Run the standard Schelling model with a grid size of 100×100, 1% empty spaces, using $\gamma = 4$. Initialize the grid such that there is about ten times more of one entity than the other (e.g., ten times more cats than dogs). Since the initialization does use random numbers, it is not necessary to have *exactly* ten times more of one entity than the other. Show the grid after 10,000 iterations.

5. Run the standard Schelling model with a grid size of 100×100, 1% empty spaces, using $\gamma = 4$. Modify the program such that the second entity (cats) prefer to drift to the right. Modify the **Move1Unhappy** function such that the second entity considers two choices for the me value used to compute the newloc. The cat always chooses the me value which is farther to the right. Show the grid after 10,000 iterations.

6. Modify the Schelling model of size 100×100 such that there are 0 empty cells. Instead of selecting one entity and moving it to an empty cell, find two entities (one from each class) that are qualified to move, and then swap their locations. In other words, within a single iteration, find one unhappy dog and one unhappy cat, and switch their locations. Show the grid after 10,000 iterations. Use $\gamma = 4$.

7. The Schelling model is designed to segregate by finding unhappy animals and moving them. The opposite would be to build a model that integrates. This can be done by making a single modification in the **CollectGrumps** functions. Run a simulation for a 100×100 grid, 1% empty cells, $\gamma = 4$, for 10,000 iterations. Show the final grid.

8. The output from **Unhappy** contains information about how many opposing entities surround each cell. If an entity is completely surrounded by its own kind then the cell's unhappy value is 0. It is also 0 for empty cells. Run a simulation with a 100×100 grid, 1% empty cells, and $\gamma = 4$. Run the simulation for a large number of iterations, 100,000. After every 100 iterations, count the number of the first entity (cats) which are completely surround by its own kind (other cats). Create a line plot of these values versus the number of iterations.

9. Modify the Schelling simulation by creating two grids (each 100×100 with 1% empty cells and $\gamma = 4$). In this simulation, a single iteration has four steps: 1) Find an unhappy dog in grid 1 and move it to an empty square in grid 2, 2) find an unhappy cat in grid 2 and move it to an empty square in grid 1, 3) find an unhappy animal in grid 1 and move it to an empty square in grid 1, and 4) find an unhappy animal in grid 2 and move it to an empty square in grid 2. The last two steps are the standard Schelling actions. Show both grids after 10,000 iterations.

## CHAPTER 6

Hidden Markov Models

T HE MONTE CARLO METHOD in Chapter 4 reviewed the concept of sampling a space with random points. The order of the sampling didn't matter. In other words, changing the order in which the sampling points were generated would not change the results. Schelling's model from Chapter 5 allowed data points to consider the state of their local neighbors, but not beyond.

This chapter will consider the nature of the sequence of data. Consider a written paragraph, for which it is possible to count the number of letters, but in that there is no sense to the meaning of the paragraph. Rather, the meaning is born from the sequence of letters. The arrangement of the letters is highly important, which opposes the philosophy used in the Monte Carlo method.

The Hidden Markov Model (HMM) is a common tool used in analyzing or even predicting the nature of a sequence. This chapter will review two types of models and construct the models in Python. The following chapters will create involved applications of the HMM, presenting some of its versatility. This chapter will review the basics of some of the popular instantiations of the HMM.

A typical HMM is a set of connected nodes as shown in Figure 6.1. The information flow through the network from left to right. Probabilities are contained in either the nodes or the connections between the nodes. In this system, information enters from the left and exits to the right. The path that it took the probabilities used in the calculation.

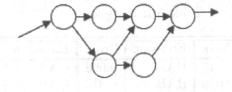

Figure 6.1: A simple HMM.

DOI: 10.1201/9781003226581-6

6.1 AN EMISSION HMM

An emission HMM contains nodes which can have several states and a probability of emission. The example in Figure 6.2 has three possible states with the respective probabilities. The probabilities add to exactly 1.0 since there is a 100% chance that the node will emit a state. In the example, the "C" state would be selected 50% of the time.

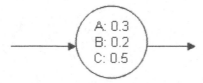

Figure 6.2: An emission node.

The HMM network is built from a collection of these nodes as seen in Figure 6.3. This simple model has three nodes and is capable of returning the probability of a particular sequence. For example, BAB would activate the B emission in the first node, the A emission in the second node, and the B emission in the third node: $0.2 \times 0.1 \times 0.6 = 0.012$. This node has a probability of 1.2%. Table 6.1 shows the probabilities for all possible sequences, and these also add up to 1.0. This means that there is a 100% chance of the network emitting one of these sequences.

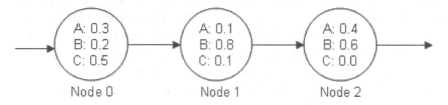

Figure 6.3: An emission HMM built from three nodes.

Table 6.1: Emissions.

Emission	Prob.	Emission	Prob.	Emission	Prob.
AAA	0.012	BAA	0.008	CAA	0.020
AAB	0.018	BAB	0.012	CAB	0.030
AAC	0	BAC	0	CAC	0
ABA	0.096	BBA	0.064	CBA	0.160
ABB	0.144	BBB	0.096	CBB	0.240
ABC	0	BBC	0	CBC	0
ACA	0.012	BCA	0.008	CCA	0.020
ACB	0.18	BCB	0.012	CCB	0.030
ACC	0	BCC	0	CCC	0

Each node contains a data label, a probability, and a connection to a subsequent node (or nodes). An approach is to employ a Python dictionary to contain the HMM. Code 6.1 shows the **TrialSystem** function which creates the network of Figure 6.3. Line 3 creates an empty dictionary, and the next three lines populate this dictionary. The key to each entry is the node identifier, and the value is a tuple. Each tuple contains two items. The first is another dictionary which contains the possible states at as the keys and the emission probabilities as the values. The second item in the tuple is the identification of the next node in the sequence.

Code 6.1 The **TrialSystem** function.

```
# hmm.py
def TrialSystem():
    hmm = {}
    hmm[0] = ({'A':0.3, 'B':0.2, 'C':0.5 } , 1 )
    hmm[1] = ({ 'A':0.1, 'B':0.8, 'C':0.1} , 2)
    hmm[2] = ({ 'A':0.4, 'B':0.6} , -1 )
    return hmm
```

Returning the probability of a sequence is performed by **ERecall** shown in Code 6.2. It receives the HMM and the sequence. Line 7 gathers the probabilities. The index i is the node identifier, and thus `hmm[i][0]` is the first item in the tuple for node i, and it is the dictionary which contains the information for a single node. A single letter in the sequence is denoted by `strng[i]`. Thus, `hmm[i][0][ strng[i] ]` is the probability for a single emission from a single node. The probabilities of each node are multiplied to form the final answer. Lines 8 through 10 handle the case in which a letter in the input sequence does not exist in the node.

Code 6.2 The **ERecall** function.

```
# hmm.py
def ERecall( hmm, strng ):
    prb = 1
    N = len( strng )
    for i in range( N ):
        if strng[i] in hmm[i][0]:
            prb *= hmm[i][0][ strng[i] ]
        else:
            prb = 0
            break
    return prb
```

The functions are called in Code 6.3. Line creates this specific HMM, and line 2 returns the probability for the sequence BAB, which matches the theoretical value. The emission HMM is quite easy to build using tuples, lists, and dictionaries.

However, this is not the most common type of HMM. Instead, many employ a transition HMM which is depicted in the next section.

Code 6.3 Creating and using an emission HMM.

```
1  net = hmm.TrialSystem()
2  prob = hmm.ERecall(net, 'BAB')
3  print(prob)
4  0.012
```

6.2 A TRANSITION HMM

An example transition HMM is shown in Figure 6.4. In this system, the probabilities are associated with the connecting lines instead of the emission of a node. The numbers in the square boxes are the node identifiers. An example case is to calculate the probability for a sequence ABAB. The first A is associated with node 0, and the first B is associated with node 1 as it is the only node with that state of B connected to node 0. The probability of this transition is 0.6. The next two letters are associated with nodes 3 and 7. The transition probabilities are $0.6 \times 1.0 \times 0.7 = 0.42$. The sequence ABAB represents 42% of the data set.

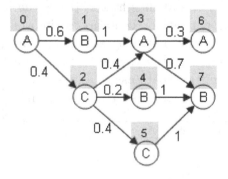

Figure 6.4: A transition HMM.

Since each node (except the exit nodes) has a 100% chance of going to another node, the transitions that exit the node sum up to 1. Table 6.2 shows the probabilities for the possible sequences. This is the complete set of possible sequences, these probabilities add to 1.

6.2.1 Data Structures for the Transition HMM

Python dictionaries are useful in representing this HMM. Each node is contained in a tuple (Code 6.4) which has two components. The first is the state of the node. The second is a dictionary in which the keys are the identifier of a possible next node in the sequence, and the data is the transition probability. This example represents

Table 6.2: Transition probabilities.

Emission	Prob.
ABAA	0.180
ABAB	0.420
ACAA	0.048
ACAB	0.112
ACBB	0.080
ACCB	0.160

node 0. It's state is 'A', and it can connect to node 1 with a probability of 0.6 or node 2 with a probability of 0.4.

Code 6.4 Encoding in Python.

```
1  ('A', {1:0.6,2:0.4} ))
```

To simplify the explanation of the programs, Figure 6.5 shows a simpler HMM with just four active nodes. A *begin* node and an *end* node are added to the network for programming convenience providing a single entry and exist to the network.

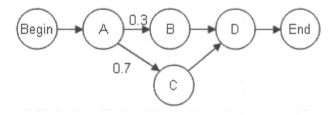

Figure 6.5: The HMM for Figure 6.4.

Code 6.5 shows the **SimpleTHMM** function which creates the HMM shown in Figure 6.5. The collection of nodes are contained in a dictionary with the node identifier as the key and the tuple of node information as the data. The function is called in the last line.

Computing the probability for a transition HMM requires the knowledge of which node follows the current node. The networks starts with node 0, but it needs to know if the next node is node 1 or 2 before collecting information about the transition probability. Thus, the function **NextNode** is warranted. Line 2 in Code 6.6 receives the HMM, the node being considered, and the data for the ensuing node. For the given node, it searches through the nodes which are connected in the `for` loop starting on line 5. When it finds the node with the matching value (line 6) then it gathers the node identifier and probability. An example is shown in line 11. The input is node 0 and the desire is to find the probability to the node with the next letter in the sequence ('B'). The output shows the next node is `net[1]` with a transition probability of 0.3.

Code 6.5 The **SimpleTHMM** function.

```python
# hmm.py
def SimpleTHMM( ):
    net = {}
    net['begin'] = ('',{0:1.0} )
    net[0] = ('A', {1:0.3,2:0.7} )
    net[1] = ('B', {3:1.0} )
    net[2] = ('C', {3:1.0} )
    net[3] = ('D', {'end':1.0} )
    net['end'] = ('',{} )
    return net

net = hmm.SimpleTHMM()
```

Code 6.6 The **NextNode** function.

```python
# hmm.py
def NextNode( net, k, ask ):
    t = net[k][1].keys()
    hit = []
    for i in t:
        if net[i][0]==ask:
            hit = i, net[k][1][i]
            break
    return hit

print( hmm.NextNode( net, 0, 'B' ))
(1, 0.3)
```

The entire sequence is considered by the **TProb** function shown in Code 6.7. It receives the HMM and the test string, and the search begins with that *begin* node as established in line 5. The procedure considers each letter in the input sequence via a `for` loop. Using **NextNode** the program retrieves the transition probabilities and multiplies them together (line 9). An example is called in line 12.

Code 6.7 The **TProb** function.

```
1  # hmm.py
2  def TProb( net, instr ):
3      L = len( instr )
4      pbs = 1.0
5      k = 'begin'
6      for i in range( L ):
7          tran = NextNode( net,k,instr[i])
8          k = tran[0]
9          pbs *= tran[1]
10     return pbs
11
12 print( hmm.TProb(net,'ABD'))
13 0.3
```

6.2.2 Constructing a Transition HMM

Creating a transition HMM from a set of data is a two-step process. The reason is that all nodes need to be created and assigned an identifier before the transitions can be calculated. The first step is to create the nodes, and the second step is to create the connections between them. The example data to be used in this process are three DNA strings (GTATC, GTTTC, and GT-AC) where the last string has a gap. Furthermore, the strings do not have the same number of occurrences. In this case, the second string is seen twice in the data, and the other strings have only a 25% each.

Function **NodeTable** in Code 6.8 creates a table which is used to identify the nodes in the network. It receives two arguments. The first is the list of data strings, and the second is the alphabet which is all letters used in the data: ACGT-. The matrix NT is the node table initially with all values set to −1. The number of rows is the length of the alphabet, and the number of columns is the length of the strings. The `for` loops iterate through each position of each string. If that character has not been seen at this position, then NT is modified with the value of nodecnt (line 12). Each time a new entry is placed in NT, the nodecnt is increased by 1 (line 13).

An example is shown in Code 6.9, where lines 1 and 2 establish the data set and the alphabet. These are passed to **NodeTable**, and it returns a matrix which is shown. Each row is associated with a letter in the alphabet, and each column is associated with a position in the data. Any cell with a −1 represents a letter and

---

Code 6.8 The **NodeTable** function.

```
# hmm.py
def NodeTable( sts, abet):
    L = len( sts )   # the number of strings
    D = len( sts[0] )    # length of string
    A = len( abet )
    NT = np.zeros( (A,D),int )-1
    nodecnt = 0
    for i in range( D ):
        for j in range( L ):
            ndx = abet.index( sts[j][i] )
            if NT[ndx,i] ==-1:
                NT[ndx,i] = nodecnt
                nodecnt +=1
    return NT
```

---

position which was not seen. The only other value in the first column is 0 on the third row, representing a node identified as 0, in the first position, with a state of 'G'. The current **nodecnt** is placed in this location of the matrix, and **noddecnt** is increased in preparation for the next iteration.

Code 6.9 Using the **NodeTable** function.

```
data =  ['GTATC', 'GTTTC', 'GT-AC']
abet = 'ACGT-'
nodetab = hmm.NodeTable( data, abet )
print(nodetab)
[[-1 -1  2  6 -1]
 [-1 -1 -1 -1  7]
 [ 0 -1 -1 -1 -1]
 [-1  1  3  5 -1]
 [-1 -1  4 -1 -1]]
```

In a similar fashion, the only non -1 value in the second column is associated with a T, and thus the number 1 is placed in the fourth row. The process continues. Each non -1 value has a unique identifying number, and these are the nodes for the HMM. The result is represented in Figure 6.6. The nodes are known, but not yet connected.

Connecting the nodes is performed in two steps. The first is to collect the data, and the second is to normalize the data. The first step is accomplished by the **MakeNodes** function shown in Code 6.10. It receives the data, the alphabet, a set of weights, and the node table. The weights relate to the number of times a data string was seen. In our example, the third string was observed to occur twice. Thus, the weights for

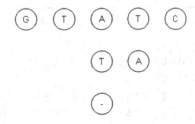

Figure 6.6: An unconnected HMM from Code 6.8.

the example are [1, 1, 2]. The program counts the number of each type of transition. For example, the letter T in the second position had transitions to the letters A, T, and gap in the data set, but the last transition was seen twice in the database.

Code 6.10 The **MakeNodes** function.

```python
# hmm.py
def MakeNodes( sts, abet, weights, nodet ):
    L = len( sts )
    D = len( sts[0] )      # length of string
    net = {}
    for j in range( D-1):
        for i in range( L ):
            clet = sts[i][j]
            nlet = sts[i][j+1]
            cnode = nodet[ abet.index(clet), j ]
            nnode = nodet[ abet.index(nlet), j+1]
            if cnode in net:
                if nnode in net[cnode][1]:
                    net[cnode][1][nnode] += weights[i]
                else:
                    net[cnode][1][nnode] = weights[i]
            else:
                net[cnode]= ( clet ,{ nnode: weights[i] })
    return net
```

Code 6.11 shows the result of using the **MakeNodes** function. Line 1 establishes the weights for each data vector. This can be the number of observances or the percentage of observations. Line 2 calls the **MakeNodes** function, and line 3 prints. The entry 1: ('T', 2: 1, 3: 1, 4: 2) indicates that node 1 can connect to three other nodes (2, 3, or 4), and associated with each is the number of times that this transition was observed in the data.

The count of observances, though, needs to be modified since some of the values exiting the node do not add up to 1. The **Normalization** function shown in Code 6.12 converts the counts to probabilities. The **for** loop starting in line 4 considers

Code 6.11 Results from the **MakeNodes** function.

```
1  weights = [1,1,2]
2  net = hmm.MakeNodes(data, abet, weights, nodetab)
3  print(net)
4  {0: ('G', {1: 4}), 1: ('T', {2: 1, 3: 1, 4: 2}), 2: ('A',
       {5: 1}), 3: ('T', {5: 1}), 4: ('-', {6: 2}), 5: ('T',
       {7: 2}), 6: ('A', {7: 2})}
```

each entry in the dictionary. Lines 5 through 7 collect the data from each dictionary entry and sums the data values. Lines 8 and 9 uses this sum to convert these values to probabilities.

Code 6.12 The **Normalization** function.

```
1  # hmm.py
2  def Normalization( net ):
3      t = net.keys()
4      for i in t:
5          sm = 0
6          for j in net[i][1].keys():
7              sm += net[i][1][j]
8          for j in net[i][1].keys():
9              net[i][1][j] /= sm
```

The nodes of the HMM are now established. The next step is to affix the *begin* and *end* nodes. Code 6.13 displays the **Ends** function which attaches these two nodes. It receives the HMM, the data strings, the alphabet, the weights, and the node table. Lines 5 through 13 construct the *begin* node. It must go through all strings to determine which nodes are associated with the first letters of the data strings, and then attach the *begin* node to those nodes. The variable T is the dictionary that will be contained inside the *begin* node. It collects the probability of each string in lines 10 through 13. Creating the *end* node is easier and is performed in lines 16 through 19.

Code 6.14 shows all steps in the process. Many of these have been seen in previous Codes. Lines 1 through 3 establish the data. Line 4 creates the node table, and line 5 attaches the end nodes. Line 6 normalizes the data. The last line shows the network. Each node is connected to others with probabilities totally one. The **TProb** function is employed to return the probability of a given string. The result is shown in Figure 6.7.

6.3 A RECURRENT HMM

In both the emission and transition HMMs the information flowed from the beginning to the end of the network only in a forward direction. In a *recurrent* HMM information

Code 6.13 The **Ends** function.

```
1  # hmm.py
2  def Ends( net, sts, abet, weights, nodet ):
3      T = {}
4      L = len( sts )
5      for i in range(L):
6          clet = sts[i][0]
7          nlet = sts[i][1]
8          idt = nodet[ abet.index(clet) ,0]
9          if idt != -1:
10             if idt in T:
11                 T[ idt] += weights[i]
12             else:
13                 T[ idt] = weights[i]
14     net['begin'] = ( '', T )
15     net['end'] = ('',{} )
16     for i in range( L ):
17         clet = sts[i][-1]
18         idt = nodet[ abet.index(clet) ,-1]
19         net[idt] = (clet,{'end':1})
```

Code 6.14 The completion of the transition HMM.

```
1  data = ['GTATC', 'GTTTC', 'GT-AC']
2  abet = 'ACGT-'
3  weights = [1,1,2]
4  nodetab = hmm.NodeTable( data, abet )
5  net = hmm.MakeNodes(data, abet, weights, nodetab)
6  hmm.Ends( net, data, abet, weights, nodetab )
7  hmm.Normalization( net )
8  print(net)
9  {0: ('G', {1: 1.0}), 1: ('T', {2: 0.25, 3: 0.25, 4: 0.5}),
      2: ('A', {5: 1.0}), 3: ('T', {5: 1.0}), 4: ('-', {6:
      1.0}), 5: ('T', {7: 1.0}), 6: ('A', {7: 1.0}), 'begin':
      ('', {0: 1.0}), 'end': ('', {}), 7: ('C', {'end':
      1.0})}
```

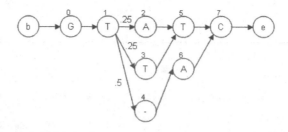

Figure 6.7: The constructed HMM.

can flow backward, and a node can even feed itself as shown in Figure 6.8. This system can emit strings such as ABD, ACD, ABCD, ABBBD, ABBBBBCD, etc. In fact, there is technically an infinite number of strings that this system can produce.

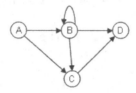

Figure 6.8: The HMM for Figure 6.8.

A program for a recurrent HMM can actually be quite easy to create. Consider the system shown in Figure 6.9 which can emit DNA strings. Every node is connected to every other node and to themselves. This looks complicated but can be realized with a single 4×4 matrix. In this matrix the M[i,j] element is the transition probability from node-i to node-j. The probability of the system is computed by considering consecutive letters in the string and finding the appropriate transition in the matrix M.

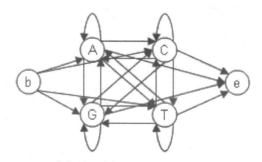

Figure 6.9: A recurrent HMM for DNA strings.

However, there is a problem with such networks in that the probabilities are highly sensitive to the string length. Very long strings will produce a very long sequence of probabilities, each less than 1.0, that are multiplied together. This will create an extremely small number. Consider a case in which the network has uniform probabilities. Since each node connects to four nodes the transition probability for each connection is 0.25. Strangely, this network which has uniform connections is called a 'random network' because it represents the network constructed from an infinite set of randomly generated strings. The problem is that a string of length 4 will have a probability of about 0.004. A string of length 10 will have a probability of 9×10^{-7}. The computation is 0.25^N where N is the length of the string. Obviously, the computer will have problems with strings of length of several hundred bases. The solution is to replace probabilities with log odds.,

$$l = \log \left(\frac{p}{q} \right), \tag{6.1}$$

where p is the probability of a transition, and q is the probability of a random network value. For example, if the probability of the transition A:C was 30%, the log odds would be $\log(0.3/0.25)$.

The odds ratio is greater than 1 if the transition is seen more often than the random case and less than 1 if the transition is rarely seen. The log of these values are positive for common transitions and negative for rare transitions. The log odds are additive as opposed to the probabilities which are multiplicative.

To realize this network in code, a matrix containing the log odds is created. The values from each transition in an input string are then summed. If the state string consists of very popular transitions then there will be many log odds values that are greater than 1, and thus the result will be a positive number. If the sequence contains many rare transitions then the results will be negative. The resultant calculation is more dependent on the content of the string and less so on the length of the string.

6.4 CONSIDERATIONS

The previous sections demonstrate the basic HMMs. However, there are problems that can quickly arise that should be noted or mitigated.

6.4.1 Assuming Data

Consider a case in which a data set has 1000 strings, and 99% of the strings start with 'A.' 10% of the data is selected for training, and they all start with the letter 'A.' The HMM is constructed without the possibility of a 'T' being in the first position. It is possible that rare transitions are not represented in the training data.

An easy method of handling this situation is to assume one more string. In this case if 100 strings start with 'A' and it is known that there is a possibility of starting with a 'T', then one more string starting with 'T' is assumed. Thus, the emission probability of an 'A' becomes 100/101 and the emission probability of a 'T' becomes 1/101. The error induced by this method decreases as the data set increases.

6.4.2 Spurious Strings

The methods above do build an HMM, but is it the correct HMM? Consider the data set "AGCTG", "ACCTA", and "CGGTA" which constructs the HMM shown in

Figure 6.10. Indeed this network will produce the correct probabilities for the strings as given. However, it will also produce probabilities for strings not in the training data such as "CGCTA". If it is desired that the HMM produces only the strings used in training then this method did not produce the correct HMM. The restrictive HMM is shown in Figure 6.11. Building this network is more involved. There are two instances where there are two nodes with the same emission at the same position. In the previous case the fourth position 'T' relied on only the immediate previous position. In this new construction the 'T' now relies on the entire string.

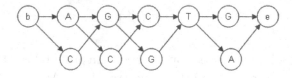

Figure 6.10: The HMM construct from the three strings.

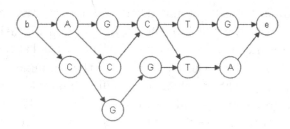

Figure 6.11: The HMM that prevents spurious states.

6.4.3 Recurrent Probabilities

In the recurrent network a similar problem arises. The network shown in Figure 6.9 has a single transition probability for 'C' feeding into itself. It will not be capable of handling cases in which it is more probable to see "CCC" and "CCCCC" than it is to see "CCCC".

6.5 SUMMARY

The Hidden Markov Model is an algorithm which contains probabilities of emissions or transitions between states. From this information, it can calculate the probability (or log odds) of given data streams. The next few chapters will explore specific applications.

PROBLEMS

1. Given the HMM shown in Figure 6.12, compute the probability for the strings ABCD.

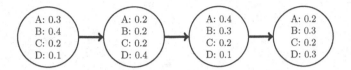

Figure 6.12: An emission HMM.

2. What are the values of x, y, and z for the HMM shown in Figure 6.13?

3. Modify the function **TrialSystem** to create the HMM shown in Figure 6.12.

4. Write a program that computes the probabilities for all possible strings for the HMM in Figure 6.12. Compute the sum of these probabilities.

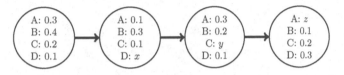

Figure 6.13: An emission HMM.

5. Given the following data, build a node table. Data: 'actg', 'acct', 'tgac', 'tggt', 'cgta'.

6. Given the following data and the number of observations for each, create the transition HMM. Data: 'actg' (43), 'acct' (41), 'tgac' (93), 'tggt' (11), 'cgta'(49).

## CHAPTER 7

Identification of Start Codons

I N THE EARLY DAYS of DNA sequencing, one of the biggest tasks was to identify locations of the coding DNA (cDNA) within a the DNA stream. The cDNA is the portion of DNA which is eventually used as the template for creating genes. This has been complicated because there isn't a single rule which identifies where cDNA is located. Genes can vary greatly in size, and many genes are generated from splices of DNA instead of a contiguous segment.

A protein is a chain of amino acids, and each amino acid is created by reading three nucleotides. These three letter combinations of cDNA are named *codons*. A significant number of coding regions start with ATG, thus qualifying for the name of *start codon*. However, many more ATG sequences exist in the data which are not start codons.

Yin *et al.* [3] created a transmission HMM that attempted to identify which ATGs are start codons based on the idea that nucleotides preceding a start codon must have structural qualities to begin the process of transcribing codons into amino acids. This chapter will replicate the process by training on known starting codons, and then testing on other start codons and ATG regions which are not start codons.

7.1 BRIEF BIOLOGICAL BACKGROUND

A DNA strand is constructed from a series of nucleotides, of which there are types (adenine, guanine, cytosine, and thymine) represented by their first letters: A, G, C, and T. A single strand of DNA can have millions of nucleotides. Some locations of the DNA are responsible for the creation of proteins. These locations are called coding regions, and a gene is created from one or more coding regions. In this process, the gene exits the nucleus of the cell and goes through a transition. The thymines are converted to uracils, and thus the character strings replace T with U.

Many cDNA (coding DNA) regions begin with ATG, earning this combination the name of *start codon*. However, most of the ATG combinations in the DNA are not a start codon. The transcription process involves the attachment of a RNA polymerase to the DNA strand. This acts as a machine which reads the DNA, collects amino acids floating about the cytoplasm, and connects them to make the protein. The polymerase needs to find locations to attach to the DNA, which are in front of the start codons. Thus, the theory is that there must be statistical properties of the DNA in front of the start codon which differ from the properties in front of nonstart codons.

Yin *et al.* [3] explored this by training an HMM on known start codons, and then testing it to other known regions in the DNA. Since the theory involves DNA before and after the ATG, their DNA snippets were 19 bases long with the ATG located at positions 14 through 16. Each layer of the HMM represented one location in the DNA, and the architecture is shown in Figure 7.1

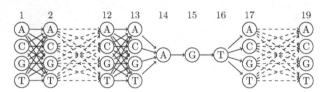

Figure 7.1: The architecture of Yin's HMM.

7.2 IMPLEMENTATION INTO PYTHON

The regularity of this problem allows for a more efficient implementation in Python compared to the code used in the previous chapter. The transition from one layer to another (excepting the ATG region) connects four nodes to four nodes. These connections can be represented by a 4×4 matrix. The HMM is thus a series of 4×4 matrices.

7.2.1 Data

Bacterial genomes are used for this example, and these can be collected from NIH. However, the necessary data is contained in a Genbank file format. Another program is needed to extract the pertinent information [4]. Sequences which had letters other than ACGT were excluded, as were sequences which were close too close to the beginning of the files to provide enough data before the ATG.

This data created over 31,000 start strings and 1,300,000 nonstart strings.[1] The list of strings were separated into two files:

- *starts.txt* collected the start ATG sequences, and

- *nonstarts.txt* collected the non-starting ATG regions.

- *bacteriafiles.txt* contains information about each file.

The files collected the data are in order. In this case, the first 1377 start strings belong to the first genome, the next 681 start strings belong to the second genome, etc.

The function **GatherData** in Code 7.1 reads these two files and separates the

---

[1]These files are available from the author or the book's accompanying website.

strings into three groups. One of these will be used for training and the others for testing. The inputs to the function are the names of the two files and the value pct. This is the percentage of strings from the starts collection which will be used for training. This value is between 0 and 1, and for demonstration it will be set to 0.1, thus designating 10% of the start strings as training data.

Code 7.1 The **GatherData** function.

```
1  # yin13.py
2  def GatherData(sname,nname,pct):
3      with open(sname) as f:
4          data = f.read().splitlines()
5      np.random.shuffle(data)
6      N = int(pct*len(data))
7      trainstarts = data[:N]
8      notrainstarts = data[N:]
9      with open(nname) as f:
10         nonstarts = f.read().splitlines()
11     np.random.shuffle(nonstarts)
12     return trainstarts, notrainstarts, nonstarts
13
14 datadir = # your data directory
15 np.random.seed( 279 )
16 starts1, starts2, nostarts = GatherData(datadir+'starts.
       txt', datadir+'nonstarts.txt', 0.1)
17 print(len(starts1), len(starts2), len(nostarts))
18 3152 28374 1315428
```

Line 4 reads the data from the files. The data was collected from multiple genes, but the first few thousand entries belong to one genome. In this experiment, 10% of the files will be used for training, and they should come from all genomes. Thus, the order of the data is shuffled in line 5. The value of N in line 6 is the number of strings to be in the training set, and the start strings are separated as such in lines 7 and 8. The output are three lists, each containing strings of 19 elements long with the target ATG at positions 14 through 16. The use of **np.random.seed** is used solely for the ability to replicate the results below. In normal use, this line would be omitted.

7.2.2   Probabilities and Log Odds

The HMM will provide a score for any input string. For a given string, a single probability value is collected from each transition matrix. These values are multiplied together to provide a HMM score for the string. As stated before, this leads to very small values.

Another issues it that probabilities do not treat common transitions in the same manner as rare transitions. Again, if the data was random, then the transition probability from an 'A' to another letter would be 0.25. Now, consider a case in which the data is not random. As we have seen, the transition from 'A' to 'G' at one position could be 0.5. This means that the 'AG' transition was twice as common as would be seen in random data. The difference between the observed value and the random data value is $0.5 - 0.25 = 0.25$. Now consider a case in which a transition was seen only have as frequent as would be seen in random data. The probability would be 0.125. The difference between this and the probability from random data is $0.25 - 0.125 = 0.125$. In one case, the twice as common transition changed the value by 0.25, and the twice as rare transition changed the value by only 0.125. They common and rare transition are not treated equally.

The log odds resolves this situation. Consider again the case in which one transition occurs twice as frequently as random and another half as frequently as random. In the first case, the probability is 50%, the odds is 2, and the log odds is 0.693. In the second case, the probability is 12.5%, the odds is 1/2, and the log odds is -0.693. The log odds values are equidistant to 0, which means that the two cases are now being weighted equally.

7.2.3 Building the Matrices

The strings in **starts1** will be used to create the HMM. Code 7.2 shows the **Build4Mat** function, which constructs just one of the 18 matrices. The inputs are the training strings and K the value of the identity of the matrix begin constructed. The output is both the probability and the log odds matrices.

Code 7.2 The **Build4Mat** function.

```python
# yin13.py
def Build4Mat( stdata, K, abet='acgt' ):
    N = len( stdata )
    mat = np.zeros( (4,4) )
    for i in range( N ):
        k1 = abet.index( stdata[i][K] )
        k2 = abet.index( stdata[i][K+1] )
        mat[k1,k2] += 1
    mask = mat==0
    mat = mask*1 + (1-mask)*mat
    for i in range( 4 ):
        mat[i] /= mat[i].sum()
    probs = mat + 0
    mat /= 0.25
    mat = np.log(mat )
    return probs, mat
```

The matrix is created in line 4. Lines 5 through 8 count the number of the occurrences for each transition. For the case of the first matrix (K=0), this program transitions from the first letters in the strings to the second letters. By line 9, this matrix is the counts of the 16 possible transitions. Line 9 finds the locations where the count is 0. These values are converted to 1 in line 10 for two reasons. One is that this transition is possible but just not seen, and for large data sets this is an acceptable practice. The second is that 0's will cause errors in line 15. In reality, a count of 0 for large data sets is not expected. Lines 11 and 12 convert the counts to probabilities. Lines 14 and 15 convert the probabilities to log odds.

An example is shown in Code 7.3. The value of K is set to 0, so this computes the transitions from the first letter in the strings to the second letter. Lines 4 through 7 show the probabilities of the transitions occurring. The sum of each row is 1. The first row corresponds to the first letter which was defined by the **abet** variable in line 2 of Code 7.2. The first column also corresponds to the first letter. Thus, the value of 0.354 indicates that if a string in the training data had an 'A' in the first position, then there is a 35.4% chance that there is an 'A' in the second position.

Code 7.3 Matrices of probabilities and log odds.

```
1  np.set_printoptions(precision=3)
2  probs, logodds = Build4Mat(starts1, 0)
3  print(probs)
4  [[0.354 0.122 0.351 0.173]
5   [0.306 0.204 0.276 0.214]
6   [0.325 0.12  0.418 0.138]
7   [0.304 0.134 0.251 0.311]]
8
9  print(logodds)
10 [[ 0.347 -0.715  0.34  -0.369]
11  [ 0.203 -0.206  0.098 -0.153]
12  [ 0.261 -0.737  0.514 -0.596]
13  [ 0.194 -0.624  0.006  0.218]]
```

This computation was just for the transition from the first position in the strings to the second position. The computation is repeated for all positions, as seen in the function **BuildHMM** in Code 7.4. Basically, it calls **Build4Mat** for each position in the strings except for the last one. The output consists of two arrays, each $18 \times 4 \times 4$. The first contains the probability matrices, and the second contains the log odds matrices.

Line 1 in Code 7.5 calls the **BuildHMM** function. The ensuing code prints the probabilities for the fourth matrix. Recall, the goal is to determine if the nucleotides before a start codon are indicative of a start codon. If the data were truly random, then the probability values would be 0.25. However, the first row of this matrix shows an interesting quality. This matrix corresponds to the transition from the fourth to the fifth letters in the strings. This is the activity eight positions in front of the ATG. If this position has an 'A', then the probability of the next nucleotide being a 'G' is just over 50%. This is significantly different than random chance.

Code 7.4 The **BuildHMM** function.

```
1  # yin13.py
2  def BuildHMM( stdata ):
3      N = len( stdata[0] )
4      probs = np.zeros( (N-1, 4,4 ) )
5      logodds = np.zeros( (N-1, 4,4 ) )
6      for i in range( N-1):
7          probs[i], logodds[i] = Build4Mat( stdata, i )
8      return probs, logodds
9
10 probs, logodds = BuildHMM( stdata )
```

Code 7.5 The largest probability before the ATG.

```
1  probs, logodds = BuildHMM(starts1)
2  print(probs[3])
3  [[0.254 0.085 0.512 0.15 ]
4   [0.28  0.189 0.28  0.252]
5   [0.315 0.073 0.461 0.151]
6   [0.24  0.137 0.337 0.286]]
```

It is possible that this 'AG' transition is common in front of all ATGs. The same function can be applied to the nonstart data, and the result is that the 'AG' transition for nonstart strings is 20%. The hypothesis that the structure in front of a start codon gains some support.

7.2.4 A Query

Both the probabilities and log odds are available for use. To compute the probability of a sequence the **SingleProbQuery** function is used (Code 7.6). The input `hmms` is the $18 \times 4 \times 4$ probability matrices, and the input `query` is the sequence. The values are extracted from locations in each matrix (lines 6 through 8) and multiplied together.

A similar function (not shown here) for the computation of the log odds is the **SingleQuery** function. The only difference in the two functions is the name and that in line 8 the values are added instead of multiplied.

Examples are shown in Code 7.7. The probabilities of a randomly selected training sequence and non start sequence are computed in lines 1 through 4. The start sequence produced a higher probability, but both values are low and the interpretation of the magnitudes is not immediately obvious. Lines 6 through 9 compute the log odds for the same sequences. Again, the training sequence produced a higher value, but by simply looking at the sign, it is obvious that one sequence was commonly seen and the other was not. In terms of detecting a start ATG in a stream of DNA, this

Code 7.6 The **SingleProbQuery** function.

```
# yin13.py
def SingleProbQuery( probs, query, abet='acgt' ):
    sc = 1
    N = len( probs ) # number of matrices
    for i in range( N ):
        k1 = abet.index( query[i] )
        k2 = abet.index( query[i+1] )
        sc *= probs[i][k1,k2]
    return sc
```

is critical. The start ATG produced a positive value and the non start produced a negative value.

Code 7.7 Query results for both the starts and non starts.

```
print(SingleProbQuery(probs[:9], starts1[3][:10]))
5.3387314384859895e-06
print(SingleProbQuery(probs[:9], nostarts[3][:10]))
4.117690334819816e-07

print(SingleQuery(logodds[:9], starts1[3][:10]))
0.33612675852943685
print(SingleQuery(logodds[:9], nostarts[3][:10]))
-2.226153993056577
```

7.2.5 Testing Queries

To complete the test, the log odds scores for many sequences need to be collected. The **ManyQueries** function shown in Code 7.8 receives the log odds matrices and a list of sequences. The score for each sequence is stored in the **answ** array and returned by the function.

All parts are in place. Code 7.9 shows the **TestHMM** function which receives input data and the log odds matrices. The input data is a list which contains the strings separated into their categories. Line 10 creates this data from the previously loaded list of strings. For each category, the function computes the scores from the log odds HMM and computes the mean and standard deviation for each category. The average HMM score for a training sequence is 5.38 with a standard deviation of 1.84.

The hypothesis was that the sequences before a start codon contained clues that the ATG is a start codon and not another instance of an ATG. If this is true, then the log odds score for the start sequences should be significantly higher than those for the nonstart sequences. The training starts produced an average value of 5.38.

Code 7.8 The **ManyQueries** function.

```
# yin13.py
def ManyQueries( logodds, queries ):
    N = len( queries )
    answ = np.zeros( N )
    for i in range( N ):
        answ[i] = SingleQuery( logodds, queries[i] )
    return answ
```

Code 7.9 The **TestHMM** function.

```
# yin13.py
def TestHMM(data, logodds):
    means, stds = [],[]
    for i in range(len(data)):
        scores = ManyQueries(logodds,data[i])
        means.append(scores.mean())
        stds.append(scores.std())
    return means, stds

data = [trainstarts, notrainstarts, nonstarts]
means,stds = TestHMM(data,logodds)
print(means)
[5.379286907995218, 5.359024441221441, 3.3073736971097927]

print(stds)
[1.8495644126175277, 1.8667411938143943,
    1.5373294284482257]
```

The nontraining starts produced a value of 5.36, and the nonstarts produced a much lower average of 3.31.

These values are meaningful only if the standard deviations are low enough. Figure 7.2 shows the distributions for the three cases, but two of them are so similar that they are not visibly separated. On the right are two overlapping curves which correspond to the training and nontraining start sequences. The left curve corresponds to the nontraining sequences. If the sequences before the ATG were completely indicative of the presence of a start codon, then these two curves would have minuscule overlap. However, they have a nontrivial overlap, which means that other evidence is needed to classify an ATG as a start codon. The hypothesis, though, is upheld. There is separation between the peaks of the curve. The HMM reacts differently to the start codons than it does to the nonstart ATGs.

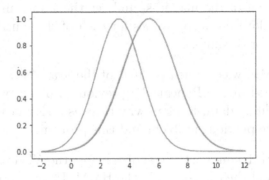

Figure 7.2: Distributions of the start and nonstart results.

7.3 SUMMARY

Yin *et al.* created a transition HMM system which provided evidence that an ATG region could be classified as a start codon. Their process had some success, but other evidence would be needed to declare an ATG to be a start codon or not. This conclusion is typical of methods attempting to recognize regions in DNA.

Replicating their system is easily performed, and this chapter provided the functions to create and use this HMM. Data gathering programs were not shown here. The results were similar to Yin *et al.*

PROBLEMS

Many problems require the use of data files, which include 19 length strings for start and non-start ATGs. While the bacteria data is available through the accompanying website, these problems can be pursued using your data sets.

1. Generate 10,000 random strings of length 19, and change all so that 'ATG' exists at Python positions 13, 14, and 15. Compute the HMM for this data set. Print the first HMM matrix and show that the values do not vary far from 0.25.

2. Compute the average and standard deviation for each of the first 12 matrices created in Problem 1. Print these values.

3. Using the data from the bacterial files (or data from your chosen source), create the HMM following the procedures in the chapter. Compute the standard deviation for each of the 18 matrices. The standard deviation in the ATG region will be high but not important to this question, so set those three values to 0. Create a plot of the standard deviation values. How does this plot indicate which regions in front of the ATG are more important than the others in the context of the HMM.

4. The HMM was trained on 10% of the available start strings. Create 10 HMMs, each with a different 10% of the training data. For each HMM, compute the standard deviation of the matrices, and set the values in the ATG region to 0. Plot the standard deviation values for each of the ten HMMs. Explain why they are similar or dissimilar.

5. The original HMM was trained on 10% of the available start strings after the order was shuffled order. Repeat the previous problem without shuffling the order of the training data. Explain why there is a significant different between the results of the previous problem and this problem.

6. Consider the HMM values in the matrices before the ATG region. Find the seven highest values and their locations in the HMM. Using the locations, determine what the transitions are. Example, if the highest value was in the 5th matrix at location (0,1), then it is the transition at the 5th location in the data for 'A' to 'C'. Print out, in order, the seven highest values, their matrix location (which matrix and location), and the transition letters. What conclusions can you draw from this?

7. Repeat the previous problem, except in this case, find the seven lowest values in the matrices before the ATG region. What conclusions can you draw from this?

8. As seen in the chapter, some nonstart sequences produced a high HMM response. In this problem, do not shuffle the nonstart strings. Find the five nonstart strings with the highest HMM score. Using the gene counts in the file *bacteriafiles.txt* determine which genomes these came from.

9. Do not shuffle the nonstart data. Compute the HMM response for all nonstart strings. Name this output vector with over 1,300,000 values as **scores** Plotting these would not be informative because there are too many value. Since there are thousands of genes in most files and the data is organized by genome, it is possible to retrieve information from a smoothed plot. Apply the **scipy.ndimage.gaussian_filter1d(scores, 800)**. Plot the output of this function. What does this plot indicate?

10. Reload the start data, but do not shuffle the vectors. Repeat the previous problem for this start data. What does this plot indicate?

11. Do the genomes have unique combinations of nucleotides in front of the ATG region? To answer this question, gather the HMM scores for each of the first five genomes in the database. (Use the gene counts in file *bacteriafiles.txt*) For each of these genomes, compute the average and standard deviation of the HMM scores for the start sequences. Use these results to answer the question: Do the genomes have unique combinations of nucleotides in front of the ATG region?

## CHAPTER 8

HMM Application in Baseball

S PORTS ANALYTICS has become a fertile ground for data science. Baseball, of all the major sports, offers a most expansive plethora of metrics, which could fill volumes of textbooks. This chapter will pick just one application. It will build an HMM based on state transitions of many baseball games. From this HMM it will be possible to find the rare events and innings.

8.1 JUST ENOUGH BASEBALL

The MLB rulebook is 184 pages of details for the game. These won't be explained here, but the major concepts need to be reviewed to understand the computational problem. Each team takes a turn in an inning to score runs. A run is scored when a player safely runs from the home base (bottom square in Figure 8.1), to the numbered bases (first, second, third), and then back to the home base. Events may move the player any number of bases. However, events can also lead to *outs*. The team's turn ends when they have accumulated three outs. The major league game consists of nine innings, and more are incrementally added if the score is tied after the ninth inning. Leagues for younger players use fewer innings.

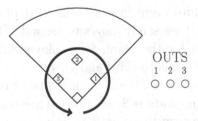

Figure 8.1: A baseball field with four bases. The teams attempt to score runs my moving players around the bases before they accumulate three outs.

While the goal of the game is to score more runs than the opponent, the goal of this chapter is to calculate the probability of transitioning from one state to another. Thus, the score is not important. The data of use is the number of outs and the bases which are occupied by players (runners) attempting to score runs. A team may have

DOI: 10.1201/9781003226581-8

0, 1, 2, or 3 outs, with the last value automatically ending a team's turn. Each base can be occupied by a single runner.

The state of the game at any moment is represented by a four character string. The first character is the number of outs and the other three are either a dash (no player on base) or a number (a player is on base). As seen later, this encoding is used by the data source, and is thus adopted here. An inning, consists of a sequence of events which alters the state until the three outs are reached. An example is shown in Figure 8.2. Initially, a team starts with no outs and no players on the bases. This is shown in Figure 8.2a, and this state is represented by the code 0---.

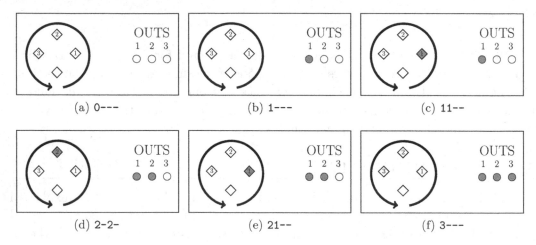

(a) 0---   (b) 1---   (c) 11--

(d) 2-2-   (e) 21--   (f) 3---

Figure 8.2: A sequence of events for a single inning.

In this example inning, the next event is a player recording an out. Thus the state changes to 1--- and is depicted in Figure 8.2b. In the second event, a player safely reaches first base. The code becomes 11-- (Figure 8.2c). This can be accomplished through several types of actions (hit a single, a walk, an error, interference, etc.). For this analysis, the event which caused the state to change is not recorded. The example continues to the third event in which the next player records an out, but in doing so, the player on first base safely moves to second. The new state is then 2-2-. The fourth event is a boon for the team, for a player safely reaches first, and the player on second base safely runs to third and then to the home base, thus scoring a run for the team. The new state is 21--. The next player records an out, thus ending the team's turn, and the final state is 3---. Players are removed from the bases, and the other team begins their turn to attempt to score runs.

8.2   BASEBALL HMM

A Hidden Markov Model for the transition of one state to another [5] is shown in Figure 8.3. Each node represents the state of outs and players on base. The connections are not shown because the image then becomes a mess. Not all connections are allowed. It is not possible to reduce the number of outs in an inning, and thus

Table 8.1: Events that follow 0---.

Event	Count	Probability
01--	136	0.195
1---	502	0.720
0---	27	0.038
0-2-	28	0.040
0--3	3	0.004
3---	1	0.001

the transition 1--- → 0--- is not possible. Some connections are bidirectional. Both 11-- → 1--- and 1--- → 11-- are possible.

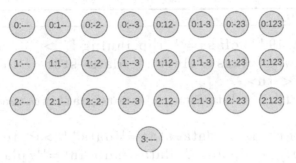

Figure 8.3: The nodes in a transition HMM.

The calculation in this chapter gathers data from several games and counts the number of instances for each transition. For example, in the 2019 playoffs, the events following 0--- are shown in Table 8.1. The first column contains the events following a 0---, the second column is the number of times the event occurred, and the final column is the probability. The HMM is constructed by placing the probabilities of all transitions between the nodes.

8.3 GATHERING DATA

Descriptions of baseball game data are readily available. The *Baseball Reference* [6] contains play-by-play lists for decades of games. Shown in Figure 8.4 is a portion of the last game of the World Series for 2019. There are many rows not shown before this inning and after this inning. The entries in the first column are "t7" which indicates these plays occur in the top of the seventh inning. The second column displays the pitch count when the event occurred, but neither of these columns are used for this project. Of interest are the third and fourth columns which list the number of outs and the runners on base. The state at the beginning of the inning is 0--- which means 0 outs and no runners on base. This batter (A. Eaton) grounded out which changed the state to 1---. There is now one out and still no runners on base.

For a single game there are usually 70 to 90 events. These events are stored in the a comment section of the HTML script. An example is shown in Code 8.1. This is event 49, which is the first row shown in Figure 8.4, and this is only a portion of

Top of the 7th, Nationals Batting, Behind 0-2, Astros' Zack Greinke facing 2-3-4											
						Jake Marisnick moves from PH to CF					
						George Springer moves from CF to RF					
t7	0-2	0	---	6,(2-2)	O	WSN	Adam Eaton	Zack Greinke	-4%	16%	Groundout: SS-1B
t7	0-2	1	---	2,(1-0)	R	WSN	Anthony Rendon	Zack Greinke	11%	27%	Home Run (Fly Ball to Deep LF Line)
t7	1-2	1	---	5,(3-1)		WSN	Juan Soto	Zack Greinke	5%	32%	Walk
						Will Harris replaces Zack Greinke pitching					
t7	1-2	1	1--	2,(0-1)	RR	WSN	Howie Kendrick	Will Harris	33%	65%	Home Run (Fly Ball to Deep RF Line); Soto Scores

Figure 8.4: Inning 7 from World Series game 7 of 2019.

the information available for this event. Of importance to this project are the last two lines. Line 4 contains the information for the outs, and line 4 contains the tt — for the state of the runners on base.

Code 8.1 Event 49.

```
1 <tr id=''event_49'' class='' top_inning '' >
2 <th scope=''row'' class=''left '' data-stat=''inning '' csk
     =''49'' >t7</th>
3 <td class=''left '' data-stat=''score_batting_team '' >0-2</td
     >
4 <td class=''right iz'' data-stat=''outs '' >0</td>
5 <td class=''left endpoint'' data-endpoint=''/play-index/def.
     cgi?html=1&game-event=HOU201910300-49-post '' data-stat=''
     runners_on_bases_pbp '' csk=''0.000'' >——</td>
```

The *lxml* package in Python provides tools which can access this data. Code 8.2 shows the **GetOutsBases** function. This function will read in an HTML page stored on a local computer. The data sought is contained within HTML comments, and these have to be removed in order for the *lxml* functions to extract the data. The comments are removed in lines 7 and 8.

The function **ToInnings** (Code 8.3) converts the pertinent data to a Python string which matches the HMM nodes. Code shows the function which performs this conversion. The first string is constructed in line 5 which concatenates the event from each list. Subsequent strings are created in line 12. However, at the end of the inning the string needs to be 3--- instead of the first event of the following inning. Lines 7 through 10 perform this replacement. The output is a list of lists, which each of these containing the strings for the events for one team in one inning.

An example is shown in Code 8.4. Line 1 loads the data from an HTML file named **fname**. The outputs are the two lists, of which the first four are shown (lines 2 through 6). The function **ToInnings** is called in line 9 which creates the strings and separates the events into innings. The first two of these are shown in line 10. The first team starts with 0---, and the first event puts a player on first base without an out: 01--. The following event creates an out but also moves the player from first to second: 1-2-. The next event moves that player to third and the batter gets on

Code 8.2 The **GetOutsBases** function.

```python
# baseball.py
from lxml import html

def GetOutsBases(fname):
    with open(fname) as f:
        page = f.read()
    page = page.replace('<!--','')
    page = page.replace('-->','')
    tree = html.fromstring(page)
    outs = tree.xpath('//td[@data-stat="outs"]/text()')
    onbase = tree.xpath('//td[@data-stat="runners_on_bases_pbp"]/text()')
    outs = outs[5:]
    onbase = onbase[5:]
    return outs, onbase
```

Code 8.3 The **ToInnings** function.

```python
# baseball.py
def ToInnings(outs,onbase):
    innings = []
    N = len(outs)
    st = [outs[0] + onbase[0]]
    for i in range(1,N):
        if outs[i]=='0' and outs[i-1]!='0':
            st.append('3---')
            innings.append( st )
            st = ['0---']
        else:
            tostring = outs[i] + onbase[i]
            st.append(tostring)
    st.append('3---')
    innings.append(st)
    return innings
```

first: 11-3. The next batter hits into a double play in which two players are out, thus bringing the total outs to three and removing all players from the bases: 3---.

In this particular game, there are 18 lists inside of `innings` which corresponds to a turn for each team in nine innings. A game can be shorter. If the second team is ahead in the score going into their turn of the ninth inning, then the game ends. They don't need to score any more runs. Rain can also shorten a game. A game can end inside of the second part of the ninth inning. If the second team gains the lead in the last inning, then the game immediately ends. A game can also be longer. If the score is tied after nine innings, then the game will play one more inning. They will keep playing innings until the score is not tied. Some historic games have gone into 20 innings, but this is an extremely rare occurrence.

Code 8.4 Data collected into innings.

```
1  outs, onbase = GetOutsBases( fname )
2  print( outs[:4] )
3  ['0', '0', '1', '1']
4
5  print( onbase[:4] )
6  ['---', '1--', '-2-', '1-3']
7
8  innings = ToInnings( outs, onbase )
9  print( innings[:2] )
10 [['0---', '01--', '1-2-', '11-3', '3---'], ['0---', '01--'
   , '11--', '1-2-', '11--', '21--', '21-3', '3---']]
```

8.4 COUNTING EVENTS

Constructing the HMM is performed in two steps. The first is to count the number of occurrences of each transition, and the second is to convert that information into probabilities. All possible events are shown in Figure 8.3, and the first task is to count the number of transitions from one node to another.

A dictionary is used to collect this information. The keys to the dictionary are the *from* events, and the data for each entry will eventually be the count of the *to* events. The **AddEvent** (Code 8.5) adds a single event to the dictionary. The inputs are the `fromstring`, the `tostring`, and the dictionary which initially is empty. Line 3 determines if the `fromstring` is currently in the dictionary. If it is not, then it needs to be created. Since it hasn't been seen before, this is the first transition for this state. Lines 4 and 5 create the event dictionary which this transition, and line 6 adds it to the main dictionary. If the `fromstring` has been seen before, then the program determines if the transition to the `tostring` has been encountered (line 8). If it has, then the counter is incremented (line 11), and if this is a new transition, then the event dictionary is created (line 9).

Code 8.5 The **AddEvent** function.

```
# baseball.py
def AddEvent( fromstring, tostring, dct):
    if fromstring not in dct:
        d = {}
        d[tostring] = 1
        dct[fromstring] = d
    else:
        if tostring not in dct[fromstring]:
            dct[fromstring][tostring] = 1
        else:
            dct[fromstring][tostring] += 1
```

Of course, a game consists of many events, usually somewhere between 70 and 90. The repetition of the adding events is handled in the **EventCounts** shown in Code 8.6. This function receives the `innings` created by **ToInnings**, and the main dictionary, `dct`. Initially, this dictionary is empty. However, as many games may use to populate this dictionary, it could not be created anew inside of this function.

Code 8.6 The **EventCounts** function.

```
# baseball.py
def EventCounts( innings, dct):
    NI = len(innings) # number of innings
    for i in range(NI):
        fromstring = innings[i][0]
        for j in range(1,len(innings[i])):
            tostring = innings[i][j]
            AddEvent(fromstring,tostring,dct)
            fromstring = tostring
```

The final step is to count the events for all games in a given directory. Code 8.7 shows the **GetCounts** function gathering information for a large collection of games. The `mydir` string is the directory in which the HTML files are stored. Line 3 calls the **GetGames** function which gathers the file names from a given directory. This function returns a list of strings of these file names including their directory structure. It also excludes file that do not end with ".shtml."

Line 4 creates an empty directory which will collect the counts of the events. In a given season, a team is scheduled to play 162 games. This can decrease if there is a late-season rain-out which the league decides not to make up. It can increase if two teams are tied at the end of season and they are vying for a playoff position. A 163rd game will be added for these two teams. Playoff games add even more games. For now, the directory used in this example contained 162 games from the 2019 Washington Nationals.

Code 8.7 The **GetCounts** function.

```
1  # baseball.py
2  def GetCounts(mydir):
3      games = GetGames(mydir)
4      dct = {}
5      for i in range(len(games)):
6          outs, onbase = GetOutsBases(games[i])
7          innings = ToInnings(outs,onbase)
8          print(games[i],len(outs))
9          EventCounts(innings,dct)
10     return dct
11
12 dct = GetCounts(mydir)
13 dct['0--3']
14 Out[]: {'1---': 6, '01--': 6, '0-2-': 2, '1--3': 12, '01-3
      ': 4, '0---': 1}
```

Lines 6 through 9 collect the data from the individual games using the **GetOuts-Bases**, **ToInnings**, and **EventCounts** functions. Line 8 prints the progress to the console, listing the file name and the number of events in that game. These range from the high 60's to the 90's, with the occasional game extending to over 100 events due to extra innings.

The output is the dictionary which contains 24 event dictionaries. The call to the function is shown in line 12. Line 13 retrieves the event dictionary for 0--3. In this situation, there are no outs and a player is on third base. This situation was rare, occurring only 31 times in a season with 12,824 events. The most popular ensuing state was 1--3 which occurred 12 out of 31 times. In this situation, the next batter achieved an out, and a player still remained at 3rd base.

8.5 CREATING THE TRANSITION HMM

All events have been counted, and the HMM can be constructed by converting the counts to probabilities, which is accomplished by the **ToProbs** function (Code 8.8). Line 3 creates a copy of the dictionary so the original data is preserved. The dct dictionary has 24 entries corresponding to the 24 nodes in Figure 8.3. For each of these, lines 5 through 7 compute the sum of the transitions in the event dictionary. Lines 8 and 9 then divide the event counts by the sum.

An example call to the function is shown in Code 8.9. The results for the state 0--3 are shown. Given the event 0--3, the event 1--3 followed it 12 out of 31 times. Thus, the probability is $12/31 = 0.387$.

Consider the most common inning, in which three consecutive batters achieve an out. The probability of each transition is shown in the first six lines in Code 8.10.

Code 8.8 The **ToProbs** function.

```python
# baseball.py
def ToProbs(dct):
    probs = copy.deepcopy( dct )
    for k in probs.keys():
        sm = 0
        for k2 in probs[k].keys():
            sm += probs[k][k2]
        for k2 in probs[k].keys():
            probs[k][k2] = probs[k][k2] / sm
    return probs
```

Code 8.9 Examining the transitions from one event.

```python
probs = ToProbs( dct )
probs['0--3']
Out[]:
{'1---': 0.1935483870967742,
 '01--': 0.1935483870967742,
 '0-2-': 0.06451612903225806,
 '1--3': 0.3870967741935484,
 '01-3': 0.12903225806451613,
 '0---': 0.03225806451612903}
```

The HMM value for a 123 inning is the multiplication of these values which is 0.3206. Thus, according to the HMM, the probability of this inning is 32%.

Code 8.10 The probabilities of a sequence of events.

```
1   print(probs['0---']['1---'])
2   0.6829349269588313
3   print(probs['1---']['2---'])
4   0.6933035714285715
5   print(probs['2---']['3---'])
6   0.6771523178807947
7
8   p = probs['0---']['1---']
9   p *= probs['1---']['2---']
10  p *= probs['2---']['3---']
11  print(p)
12  0.32061890824631145
```

This can be confirmed by returning to the original data and counting the number of 123 innings. This is divided by the total number of innings as shown in Code 8.11. The data is loaded and the variable ct collects the number of 123 innings. The results show that there were 916 occurrences of the 123 inning and a total of 2874 innings. Thus, the actual probability was 31.9%, which is quite close to the estimate by the HMM.

Code 8.11 The probabilities of a sequence of events.

```
1   games = baseball.GetGames( datadir )
2   NG = len( games)
3   N = 0
4   ct = 0
5   for i in range(NG):
6       outs, onbase = baseball.GetOutsBases(games[i])
7       innings = baseball.ToInnings(outs,onbase)
8       for j in innings:
9           N += 1
10          if j==['0---','1---','2---','3---']:
11              ct += 1
12  print( ct, N, ct/N)
13  916 2874 0.3187195546276966
```

8.6 ANALYSIS

This section will consider a few questions that can be asked of the HMM.

1. What is the probability of a user selected inning?

2. What is the rarest event?

3. Which inning was the most unusual?

8.6.1 The User-Selected Inning

The probability of a selected inning is merely the multiplication of the probabilities of the transitions in that inning. Code 8.12 shows a sequence from the National's 7th inning in the final game of the World Series. Each transition is a probability, and these are multiplied to get the small number shown in line 7. This sequence of events was a rarity.

Code 8.12 The value for the Nationals' 7th inning of the 7th game in the World Series.

```
trail = ('0---','1---','1---','11--','1---','11--','112-',
    '212-','3---')
NT = len(trail)
pb = 1
for i in range(NT-1):
    pb *= probs[trail[i]][trail[i+1]]
print(pb)
2.2093752566156523e-06
```

8.6.2 Rarest Transition

The second question is to find the rarest transition in the HMM. In order to explore this question, a different set of games is used because of an oddity that occurs in this data set that does not occur in the one used on the previous sections. For this data, all games with an American League team in the year 2015 are used. The HMM has the same nodes but altered transitions. This data set includes multiple teams, and it includes the games in which an American League team played a National League team. More than 1400 games are contained in this data set. The common events, such as the 123 inning, have the same probability of occurring.

An oddity can be seen in considering the rarest event. Code 8.13 finds the event with the smallest probability. The variables dct15 and probs15 are the dictionaries for this new data set. It goes through all entries in the probs dictionary and finds the smallest probability value. It is printed to the screen and is associated with the transition from 1--- to 3---. This could occur is a team is batting in the bottom of the ninth or later. They have one out and no one on base. The next batter hits a home run to win the game, and the state of the game goes to 3--- because the inning has ended. Indeed it is a rare event. Code 8.14 shows that this transition occurred 4 times in those 1400 games with over 120,000 events. The rarity of this transition is confirmed.

Code 8.13 Finding the smallest probability.

```
1  pb = 11111
2  for i in probs15:
3      for j in probs15[i]:
4          if probs15[i][j] < pb:
5              pb = probs15[i][j]
6              print(i,j,pb)
7
8  # last item printed
9  1--- 3---  0.00020945698277216316
```

Code 8.14 This event occurred 4 times in the season.

```
1  print(dct15['1---']['3---'])
2  4
```

However, it is not the rarest event. Code 8.15 counts the number of transitions that occurred only once in the season. There are 13 such events, and one is shown in the last line. The team had a runner on first and second. In the next event, the team had one out an no runners on base. This event occurred in a game between the Detroit Tigers and Chicago White Sox on October 2, 2015. Chicago had two runners on base, the batter hit a double, and the two runners came in to score. However, the batter ran to third base with dreams of turning that double into a triple. He was tagged out at third. When the dust settled, Chicago had no runners on base and an additional out.

Code 8.15 The events which occurred only once during the season.

```
1  solos = []
2  for i in dct15:
3      for j in dct15[i]:
4          if dct15[i][j] == 1:
5              solos.append((i,j))
6  print(len(solos))
7  print(solos[0])
8  13
9  ('012-', '1---')
```

Thus, the transition with the smallest probability is not the rarest event. At issue is the definition of the probability. This is not the measure of the probability of a transition occurring in the database. Recall that they probabilities exiting a node must sum to 1. These are probabilities of an event occurring given an initial event. The probability of 0.000209 is the probability of the 3--- occurring after the 1---.

Let's consider an opposite, theoretical case in which the transition is from event A to event B. This event occurs only once in the database. However, the event A also occurs only once in the database. Thus, the probability of this transition is 100% even though the event occurred only once. Given A, there is a 100% chance that the next event is B.

The answer to the question is that there were 13 transitions which were seen only once. These are the rarest.

8.6.3 Unusual Inning

Which inning was the most unusual? This is not asking which is the rarest, but the one with the most unusual sequence of events. This would be the inning with the lowest probability.

Code 8.16 shows the **StrangeInning** function. The variable `least` will keep track of the smallest probability value, so it is initially set to a large value. Each game is loaded and processed in lines 7 and 8. Each inning is considered in line 10, and the events in these innings are considered in lines 12 through 15. The event is defined as a transition from an event, `fromstring`, to another event, `tostring`. The probability of this transition is obtained in line 15 and multiplied into the `pb` variable.

Code 8.16 The **StrangeInning** function.

```
1  # baseball.py
2  def StrangeInning(datadir, probs):
3      least = 999999
4      strange = []
5      games = GetGames(datadir)
6      for i in range(len(games)):
7          outs, onbase = GetOutsBases(games[i])
8          innings = ToInnings(outs,onbase)
9          print('.',end='')
10         for j in range(len(innings)):
11             pb = 1
12             for k in range(len(innings[j])-1):
13                 fromstring = innings[j][k]
14                 tostring = innings[j][k+1]
15                 pb *= probs[fromstring][tostring]
16             if pb == least:
17                 strange.append(innings[j])
18             if pb < least:
19                 least = pb
20                 strange = [innings[j]]
21     return least, strange
```

By line 16, the probability of one inning is calculated. If this value matches the `least` value then the inning is appended to the list `strange`. If the probability is lower than the `least` (line 18), then the value of `least` is changed and the `strange` list is reset to contain this one inning. In this manner, all innings with the lowest probability are collected in `strange`.

Code 8.17 runs this function in line 1 using the data from 2019. The lowest inning probability was 5.47×10^{-14} and it occurred once. That inning is shown. It contained many events, which is an expected result.

Code 8.17 Finding the most unusual inning.

```
pb, strange = baseball.StrangeInning(datadir, probs)
print(pb, len(strange))
5.4718816383802395e-14 1
print(strange)
[['0---', '1---', '11--', '112-', '112-', '212-', '21-3',
    '2-23', '2123', '2--3', '2-2-', '21-3', '2--3', '3---'
    ]]
```

8.7   SUMMARY

This chapter creates an HMM based on events of events from an entire season of baseball games. The only data measured is the number of outs and positions of runners on base. The HMM contains the probabilities of transitions from one state to another. From this HMM a few of the many possible queries were explored.

PROBLEMS

The problems below assume that the season's worth of data is available in a single directory.

1. What is the average number of events per game?

2. Which game had the most number of events? Using the file name of this game and the *Baseball Reference* website to identify who won the game, the final score, and the number of innings.

3. Identify the inning(s) with the largest number of events. Print the number of events and the file names of the games.

4. What are the three most common event transitions. Write the two events involved in the transition and the number of times the transition occurred.

5. How many transitions were seen only once during an entire season?

6. Create a bar chart for the number of times each transition occurred. The x-axis corresponds to each transition, and the y-axis corresponds to the count of those

events. Sort the data such that bars go from low to high as the chart goes from left to right.

7. Double plays occur when two outs are created in one play. Thus, the out count goes from 0 to 2 or from 1 to 3. How many double plays occurred during the season?

8. Using the HMM, estimate the probability of the sequence 0---, 0-2-, 1-2-, 2--3, 3---.

9. Compute the probability of the sequence 0---, 0-2-, 1-2-, 2--3, 3--- from the game data (not using the HMM).

10. The 123 inning was the most common inning at just under 33% of the innings. What was the second most common inning, and what was the percentage of its occurrence?

## CHAPTER 9

Hidden Shakespeare Model

S HAKESPEARE'S writings different significantly from the modern-day texts. Readers can easily detect differences between centuries-old musings from today's prose. The differences in the two styles can also be picked up by a properly trained HMM.

In this chapter, an HMM will be trained on Shakespeare's texts, and it will be used to generate new text. As the HMMs become more complicated, the generated text displays the qualities of English, Shakespearean English, and finally content which makes sense. In the final example, an HMM is trained on a play (*Romeo and Juliet*), and generated text will display the structure of a written play versus a written sonnet. Then of course, the finale is an attempt to break the whole system.

9.1 BUILDING THE HMM

The Hidden Markov Model (HMM) is based on the probabilities of sequential letters. Consider the text, "So long lives this and this gives life to thee." The letter 'l' occurs three times. Twice the letter 'l' is followed by the letter 'i', and once it is followed by an 'o'. Thus, for this tiny bit of data, the probability of an 'o' following an 'l' is 33%.

In the DNA example, the HMM was built from a series of 4×4 matrices, and all 16 elements of the matrices had significant values (excepting the ATG region). In this Shakespeare case, there are 26 lowercase letters, 26 uppercase letters, and punctuation. Thus, such a matrix would be about 55×55, but the matrix would be sparsely populated. For example, only three letters follow the letter 'z' in the text. To reduce the complexity, the text is converted to lowercase, which still leaves 39 unique characters.

Another modification is that the DNA HMM had several matrices because the probabilities changed relative to the position of the ATG. This is not the case here. Only one matrix will be needed. Thus, a different representation of the data is warranted. Instead of creating a matrix, the same information will be contained in a dictionary. Such a change in variable type is common when dealing with sparse matrices.

The consideration begins with the simplest HMM. The *Hidden Shakespeare Model* (HSM) will store the gathered statistics in a Python dictionary. For the small example, the information for the letter 'l' would be stored as l: [['o','i'], [1,2]]. The

DOI: 10.1201/9781003226581-9

key is a letter, and the data is two lists. The first is the following letters, and the second is the count of those letters following the key.

This idea is applied to the sonnets data, finding the percentage of two letter combinations. The construction of this network is performed in the following steps:

1. Load and clean the data,

2. Count the events, and

3. Convert to probabilities.

Shakespeare's sonnets are contained in a file named *sonnets.txt*[1] containing more than 96,000 characters. The function **Read** (Code 9.1) loads this data and converts all characters to lowercase.

Code 9.1 The **Read** function.

```
# shakespeare.py
def Read( fname ):
    a = open( fname, encoding = "ISO-8859-1" ).read()
    a = a.lower()
    return a
```

The second step is to count the events. For every letter, this system will count the number of times other letters follow it. To be clear, the first letter is called the *key letter* since it will be used as the key in a dictionary. The following letter is called the *retral letter*. Code 9.2 shows the **MakeDict** function which creates this dictionary. The inputs are the text strings (Shakespeare's sonnets), the WL is the word length which is set to 1, and a flag used to return probabilities (**True**) or counts (**False**). The WL variable will be discussed later.

The dictionary is started in line 4. The for loop started on line 5 gathers the counts of the unique pairings of keys and retral letters. It considers consecutive letters through the whole input string except for a few characters at the end. The variable keyl is the key letter, and the retral is the retral letter. Three options occur in the program: this is a new key, this is a previously seen key but a new retral letter, or this is a previously seen key and previously seen retral letter. If the key has not been seen before, then line 16 is used. It creates a new entry in the dictionary. The value of the entry is a list which contains the list of retral letters and their counts. For this case, there is only this one retral letter with a count of 1. If the key has been seen before but the retral letter is new, then the program uses lines 13 and 14. The new retral letter is appended to the list of retral letters (line 13) and the count of 1 is appended to the list of counts. Finally, if both have been seen before, then lines 10 and 11 are used. Line 10 finds the location of the retral letter in the list of retral letters, and line 11 increases its count by 1. By line 17, all occurrences have been counted. Lines 18 through 21 convert these counts to probabilities. In this process, the list of counts is

---

[1] While this is available from the author, this is an easy file to obtain from web resources.

Code 9.2 The **MakeDict** function.

```
1   # shakespeare.py
2   def MakeDict( instr, WL=1, retprobs=True ):
3       L = len( instr )
4       dct = {}
5       for i in range( L-WL ):
6           keyl = instr[i:i+WL]
7           retral = instr[i+WL]
8           if keyl in dct:
9               if retral in dct[keyl][0]:
10                  ndx = dct[keyl][0].index( retral )
11                  dct[keyl][1][ndx] +=1
12              else:
13                  dct[keyl][0].append( retral )
14                  dct[keyl][1].append( 1 )
15          else:
16              dct[keyl] = [[retral],[1]]
17      K = list(dct.keys())
18      if retprobs:
19          for i in K:
20              vec = np.array( dct[i][1] )
21              vec = vec/vec.sum()
22              dct[i][1] = vec
23      return dct
```

converted to a vector of floats. Line 19 checks the input flag and selects whether to return counts or probabilities.

Code 9.3 shows the process so far. Line 2 loads the data, and line 3 creates the dictionary. Line 5 is the output when the key is 'z'. As seen, only three unique letters follow the letter 'z'. The letter 'a' was seen 17 times, the letter 'i' was seen 4 times, and the letter 'o' was seen once. Thus, the probability of seeing an 'a' following a 'z' is $17 / 22 = 0.77$.

Code 9.3 Examining the output of the **MakeDict** function.

```
1   datadir = # Your data directory
2   sonnets = shakespeare.Read( datadir + 'sonnets.txt')
3   dct = shakespeare.MakeDict(sonnets)
4   print(dct['z'])
5   [['e', 'i', 'o'], array([0.77272727, 0.18181818,
        0.04545455])]
```

This dictionary represents the HMM. For any two letter combination the transition probability can be retrieved.

9.2 CREATING NEW STRINGS

The goal of this section is to build a new string based on the transitions seen in the sonnets. The process starts with a random letter, for example 'z', and then it uses the collected information to determine the next letter in the string. For the sake of argument, let's use the case in which the letter 'e' is chosen. The constructed string is now 'ze.' In the second iteration, the process would determine which letter should follow 'e' based on the data contained in dct['e']. This process continues for the user-defined number of iterations.

The **BuildString** function shown in Code 9.4 creates the string. The input dct is the dictionary built in **MakeDict**. The value L is the desired length of the output string, which is solely at the user's discretion. In the more complicated HMMs developed later, it is possible for the HMM to get stuck when a search string is not in the dictionary. In those situations, a random letter is chosen from the input alphabet abet. This is a string defined by the user which can include the entire English alphabet or selected letters. The value WL is the same as the one used in **MakeDict** and is currently set to 1.

Code 9.4 The **BuildString** function.

```
1   # shakespeare.py
2   def BuildString( dct, L, abet, WL ):
3       keys = list(dct.keys())
4       stng = np.random.choice(keys)
5       for i in range( L ):
6           preced = stng[-WL:]
7           if preced in dct:
8               newlett = np.random.choice(dct[preced][0], p=
                    dct[preced][1])
9               stng += newlett
10          else:
11              r = int( np.random.ranf()*len(abet) )
12              stng += abet[r]
13      return stng
```

Lines 3 and 4 initialize the string by randomly choosing one of the keys. The for loop begins the process of adding to this string. Line 6 gets the last entry in the string, which at the beginning is the full string. Lines 7 through 9 determine which retral letter will be used through the **choice** function. It receives two inputs. The first is the list of retral letters, and the second is the probabilities. As this is an optional argument to the function the p= is needed. This function will select one letter from the retral list based on the given probabilities. This letter is appended to the string in line 9. Line 11 and 12 are used if the key letter does not exist in the dictionary. In this case, a random letter is selected from **abet** and attached to the string.

Lines 9 and 12 add letters to a string, but in reality, they create a new string with the attached letter. This process of creating new strings can become slow if the string is very long. To speed up the process, the code should be replaced with the construction of a list which is united by the **join** function. However, for modest strings, this savings in computation is negligible.

The function is called in Code 9.5. The output string is 100 characters long and is based on the probabilities inherent in Shakespeare's sonnets. The third argument is the list of letters available in case the system gets stuck, but that doesn't happen when WL = 1. The output, as seen, is garbage. While it does depend on the statistics of the sonnets, the output doesn't replicate any sonnet phrase. In fact, it doesn't have any semblance of English – either modern or Shakespearean. More work needs to be done.

Code 9.5 The first generated string.

```
1  output = shakespeare.BuildString(dct, 100, 'abcdefgh', 1)
2  print(output)
3  ngord st w s no pile thind thanoy ndequpr adeiss thto we
     apaliveththeenes me, me t orey t tofaplorise
```

9.3 DISCOVERING A NEW SHAKESPEARE

The HMM did provide a text string based on the statistics from a large segment of Shakespeare's work. However, the generated text was pure unpronounceable babble. The idea of using a single letter as a key was not strong enough. So, the improvement is to use two-letter keys. From the phrase "so long lives this and this gives life to thee", the keys would be "so", "o ", " l", etc. The spaces inside the quotes represent the spaces in the original string. In this example phrase, the key "th" occurs three times and the retral letters would be "i" and "e".

The two functions are already built for handling this situation. The only change is to set the word length to WL = 2 as seen in Code 9.6. The output is on multiple lines because there are newline characters in the output. While this output is still heavy on the babble, there are combinations which present English words. Furthermore, the components which are not words are mostly pronounceable. Thus, this increase in word length has improved the results.

The next obvious step is to continue to increase the world length. The only change to the code is to alter the value of WL in line 1. The outputs for different cases are:

- **3**:

  etly audit feath think on me roof the havers argetfull stain-top of trare, and with so vex'd; potion of

Code 9.6 The second generated string.

```
1  WL = 2
2  dct = shakespeare.MakeDict(sonnets,WL)
3  output = shakespeare.BuildString(dct, 100, 'abcdefgh', WL)
4  print(output)
5  oand me, frow one true,
6  myseet.
7
8  hat me theartas fors wee to rhy ith's to reed my love
      thatumb
9  whead h
```

- **4**:

  serving thy face a tyrantique perful tastering so the increasure of man weep
  doth hence of your with po

- **5**:

  al his sick of new pay the prevenues over every had stol'n from far more shall
  summer's jaws,
  and there;

- **6**:

  zings hymns did shine
  with swift messengers return in hue
  could my pain.
  if i could he living in seeming;

- **7**:

  c-mad with me, then did feel
  needs must ne'er love looks fair, no beauty, like her i sometime absent in the

- **8**:

  oth
  and to be praise confounding age's cruel hand.
  is it thy will thy image should my heart;
  another white

- **9**:

  s despised every where.
  you to your fair no painting thy outward part,
  and thither hied, a sad distemper'd gu

- **10**:

  It, thou art old,
  and rather make them cruel;
  for well thou know'st to my dear doting heart
  thou art all the w

- **12**:

  gilded tomb,
  and to be praised of ages yet to be.
  then do thy office, muse; i teach thee wit, better it were,
  th

As the value of WL increases, so does the readability of the generated text. The text becomes pronounceable, English-like, Shakespearean-like, and finally a replication. Clearly, the increase in WL improves the performance, but a problem emerges. With an increase in WL comes an increase in the size of the dictionary. For WL = 1 the dictionary had 39 entries. These are the 26 letters and punctuation characters. When WL = 2 the maximum possible number of entries is $39^2 = 1521$. However, the dictionary has only 656 entries. Many possible combinations of two letters are not seen in the text. For example, "qq" does not exist in the text.

Figure 9.1 shows the increase in dictionary size as the word length increases. Initially, there is exponential growth less than O^2. However, the growth curve flattens. The cause of this problem is two-fold. First the data set (which is almost 100,000 characters) is too small. Most 12 letter keys have only one retral letter. The second is that the combinations have less variance. Even if the data set were enormous, there would still be a flattening of the curve because there is a finite set of combinations seen in English text.

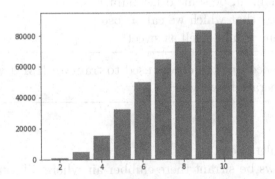

Figure 9.1: Growth of the dictionary with respect to the increase in WL.

The problem of the limited data size is quite apparent in the case of WL = 12. The actual text from one sonnet is:

> To make him much outlive a gilded tomb,
> And to be praised of ages yet to be.
> Then do thy office, Muse; I teach thee how
> To make him seem long hence as he shows now.

As seen much of the generated text is a copy of the original text. This occurs when the keys have only one retral letter. Most of the keys were seen only once in the sonnets, and thus there is only one choice but to copy the actual text. In this case, there is a deviation when the key is " teach thee " (with spaces at each end of the string). This string appears twice in the sonnets and the retral letters were "h" and "w". This process selected the "w" and the phrase "teach thee w" came from a different sonnet.

9.4 STRUCTURE

A stage play script has a structure different than prose. Speech for each character is preceded by the character's name. In the previous case, the HMM could replicate . In this section, the HMM replicates structure.

A famous part of the play *Romeo and Juliet* is shown. Each speech starts with the character's name in all capitals and a colon. Directions for the character are enclose in square braces.

JULIET: O Romeo, Romeo! wherefore art thou Romeo?
    Deny thy father and refuse thy name;
    Or, if thou wilt not, be but sworn my love,
    And I'll no longer be a Capulet.

ROMEO: [Aside] Shall I hear more, or shall I speak at this?

JULIET: 'Tis but thy name that is my enemy;
    Thou art thyself, though not a Montague.
    What's Montague? it is nor hand, nor foot,
    Nor arm, nor face, nor any other part
    Belonging to a man. O, be some other name!
    What's in a name? that which we call a rose
    By any other name would smell as sweet;

The script for *Romeo and Juliet* was used to train an HMM with a key length of 3. The result of a generated text was:

---

    then spiteouse.

romeo: what it i capulet keeps
    so like, i'll wereflows be sirrant there clubber air where, i'll reparis: i
        nepheturney
    breast above be my love; not not is exeunt such much an

Again, the **Read** function converts text to lowercase. The play structure appears in this sample. Although, the phrase "reparis: i" shows that the structure is not perfect. As Paris is a character in the play, the text and structure of the generated text is mixed. However, the key length was only 3.

The following text was generated from a HMM which used a key length of 7. The structure of the play seems to be intact. The phrase "art poor:" has a colon which is indicative of a speaking character. However, this phrase with colon is part of Romeo's speech when Romeo is buying poison at the end of the play. Similarly, the colon for the phrase "thou art taken:" is part of Benvolio's speech.

---

mercutio: good prudence; smatter than in words,
    which you from the face of him.

benvolio: he ran this,——thou art poor:
    that i yet know not
    her nurse,
    thou art taken: hence from thy heart

A HMM with the key length of 8 was trained. The length of the play string is about 150,000 and the number of entries in the dictionary was 102,000. Thus, the average number of choices for a key was slightly less than 1.5. A segment of generated text for Benvolio is shown. The phrase "upon thy fortune" appears once in the play. This is from a quote by Friar Laurence, and it is shown as well.

Generated Text
benvolio: what, art thou fall upon thy fortune in my misery.

Actual Text
FRIAR LAURENCE:
...
    But, like a misbehaved and sullen wench,
    Thou pout'st upon thy fortune and thy love:
    Take heed, take heed, for such die miserable.
...

Even with a key length of 8, the text of a speaker is from mixed sources. Thus, the HMM does generate new text, and it also follows a play script structure.

The final test considers non-Shakespearean text. From the same country, perhaps the script that is most opposite of the style of Shakespeare comes from Monty Python's *Holy Grail*. A sample of generated text using WL = 10 is shown.

[music stops]

black knight: none shall pass.

arthur: he is the keepers of the saxons, sovereign of all england!

soldier #2: well, simple! they'd just use a strand of creeper!

soldier #1: pull the other one!

arthur: how do you know she is a witch!

The script has less than 70,000 letters, and thus a HMM with a key length of 10 provides cases in which very keys have more than one option. Yet, the generated script is mixed up. Each speaker's line is intact, but the lines are out of order. Consider the line from Soldier #2. In the original play, Soldier #1 does speak after the "creeper" line, but he doesn't say "Pull the other one!" That script is elsewhere.

Code 9.7 shows the possible transitions for the end of the "creeper" speech. Line 2 of the Code shows that there is only one possible transition, to the letter 's'. The process continues in lines 4 and 5 which show that the next possible letter can be only 'o'. This process is building up the next speaker "Soldier #1". However, the name of the character is more than 10 letters. Line 7 shows the possible first letters for a speech by Soldier #1. Here, the network has several choices. More importantly, is that the key is "ldier #1: ". This key has no information about the previous line from the play. Thus, there is no link between the speech of one person to the other. The only link is that after Soldier #2 speaks his "creeper" line, the next speaker is Soldier #1, but his speech can be any line he has in the play.

Code 9.7 Possible transitions for the *Holy Grail* using a key length of 10.

```
1  dct['creeper!\n\n']
2  Out[]: (['s'], [1])
3
4  dct['reeper!\n\ns']
5  Out[]: (['o'], [1])
6
7  dct['ldier #1: ']
8  Out[]:
9  (['h', 'p', 'w', 'y', 'f', 'a', 'i', 'l', 'o', 'b', 's', '
      n'],
10   [1, 1, 5, 2, 1, 2, 1, 1, 1, 1, 1, 1])
```

9.5 MIDSUMMER MADNESS

This section's title comes *Twelfth Night*, and it is an indication of what is to come. An HMM has been used to replicate the Shakespearean text, and another has been created to replicate script from *Romeo and Juliet*. The final presentation of this chapter is an attempt to explore how this process can go far afield.

Consider a new HMM which is trained on two plays. The first is *Romeo and Juliet*. The second comes from the same country, but is perhaps the most opposite of Shakespeare – *Monty Python and the Holy Grail*. An example, with key length of 10 is:

---

lady capulet: what, art thou drawn among these heartless hinds?
    turn to another deed,
    or my true heart with the men, i will tell her, sir, that will find you a
shrubbery?

[dramatic chord]

old crone: who sent you?

As seen, the generated script mixes characters from the two plays and speech from the plays. Most assuredly, Lady Capulet did not say, "find you a shrubbery" in *Romeo and Juliet*. The Old Crone is a character from the *Holy Grail*, and thus this segment of generated code also shows a mixing of the characters.

When the key length is 12, however, this mixing vanishes. Large segments of generate text come from one play only. Although, the order of speaking can change if the character's name (plus a colon and a space) is more than 11 letters long. Furthermore, the speech of the characters does mix on occasion. The switch between the plays though is quite rare. At a key length of 12, the HMM is able to distinguish between the two plays, mostly due to the small size of the data.

9.6 SUMMARY

In this chapter, an HMM based on Shakespearean text was created. The previous chapter used matrices to contain the HMM information, but that approach would be less effective in this application due to the sparseness of the information. Instead, dictionaries were employed to provide efficient recall of HMM information. This chapter described the method of creating the dictionary and how to use it to create new data strings. In this application, a single variable, word length, was used to control the training, and its effect on creating readable or meaningful phrases was explored. The created HMM demonstrated the ability to recreate Shakespeare-like text up to the limit of the size of the training data.

PROBLEMS

These problems rely heavily on the Shakespeare sonnets text, which is available through the author. However, creating this file is easy as the sonnets are readily available from many websites. These problems can also be applied to other text files with at least 100,000 characters.

1. Load the sonnets and convert to lowercase. Count the occurrences for each of the 26 letters of the alphabet. Sort and print the counts and the associated letters from high to low. (You can compare your results to those printed at `http://letterfrequency.org/`.)

2. Generate a 1000 letter-length sentence using the sonnets HMM with WL = 1. Count the letter frequency using the process from the previous question. Sort and print the results. Are there significant differences in the order of the letter popularity compared the output from the previous question?

3. Create a sonnets HMM with WL = 7, but use the letter counts instead of the letter frequencies. (This can be accomplished by commenting out a few lines

of code in MakeDict.) Print out the five most popular keys words (keys of the dictionary) and their counts.

4. The previous problem returned the most popular keys. However, each key as several retral letters, thus creating several key/retral letter pairs. Each one of these has a count for the number of times it appeared in the text. Print out the ten most popular key/retral letter pairs and their counts.

5. Write a Python script to return the average and standard deviation of the word lengths from the sonnets file.

6. Repeat the previous problem for strings generated by **BuildString**. Compute the average and standard deviation of word lengths for cases in which $WL = 1$, 3, 5, 7, and 9. Print the results for each.

7. Large values of WL will extract larger contiguous regions from the sonnets. For example, a generated string was "O truant and crooked knife" which contains two phrases which are contiguous segments from the sonnets data "O truant " and " and crooked knife". The lengths of these matching segments are 9 and 18.

   Build a function that will that will return the lengths of all matching segments from a generated string (length 1000) when compared to the entire sonnets file.

   For values of $WL = 5$, 7, 9, 11, and 15, print out the top three lengths. If the hypothesis is correct, then the values should increase as WL increases.

8. This problem will explore the uniqueness of the last sonnet when compared to the others. Build an HMM with $WL = 4$ for the counts of the retral letters instead of the frequencies. (This was accomplished in a previous problem.) For every 4 letter segment in the last sonnet, retrieve the count value for the ensuing retral letter. Print the sum of these values.

   Repeat this process except that the last sonnet is excluded from the training of the HMM. Print the sum of the counts. (In this case, it is possible that there are 4 letter keys in the last sonnet but not in the dictionary. It is also possible that the key phrase exists in the training data, but the retral letter does not. Skip over these cases.)

   The two cases should provide similar values. Repeat the experiment for $WL = 7$, and now the values of the two cases are vastly different. Explain why this is so.

## CHAPTER 10

Connected Data

S AMPLES within a data set often have connections. A popular example is the Kevin Bacon Effect which connects actors through the movies they have been in. Actors A and B are in a movie together, and actors B and C are in a movie together, thus A and C are connected through B. This is a single step. The Kevin Bacon Effect is that any two actors are no more than six steps apart.

The connectedness of data provides rich information concerning group behavior and underlying commonalities within a data set. Often the data is represented in graphical form, and the field of study is call *graph theory*. This chapter will review the basics of this field and present Python scripts to store the data and retrieve various types of information.

10.1 MOVIES DATABASE

The Kevin Bacon Effect requires that the shortest possible path between any two actors be determined. To explore this concept, a small database is needed. Netflix does offer a movie and actor database, but the size of the database causes issues in memory space and computational load. Thus, demonstration of the algorithms will be performed with a smaller database.

This database contains names of movies and actors as well as their connections. Only a few actors are listed for each movie, and only a few movies are listed for each actor. This database is significantly abridged, but that actually supports the proof of concept. If the Kevin Bacon Effect is achieved in an abridged database, then it can certainly be achieved in a complete database.

It is possible to store movie and actor data in a flat file such as:

```
``The Man Who Shot Liberty Valence'' : 1962 : 9.4 : James
    Stewart, John Wayne, John Carradine
``It's a Wonderful Life'' : 1946 : 8 : Jimmy Stewart, Lionel
    Barrymore
``The Last Hurrah''        1958 : 7 : John Caradine, Spencer
    Tracy
```

This contains the data necessary to make the connected, but there are issues of concern. The first issue is that data is duplicated. The same actor is listed more

DOI: 10.1201/9781003226581-10

than once, and this is a waste of memory. The second issue is that this format is not amenable to some searches. Asking the question: "Who is in a specific movie?" is easy to answer. However, the question: "Which movies was a specific actor in?" requires a loop through all movies, and within that a loop through all actors. This is inefficient and avoidable. The third issue is that the data has some legitimate alternative data. The actor James Stewart was often referred to as Jimmy Stewart. Both are correct, but a search on one name will not find all of the movies for this actor. The fourth issue is that of incorrect data. What is the correct spelling: John Carradine or John Caradine? One of these entries is wrong. If a name has duplicate appearances in the database, then it is necessary to find all of those instances to correct.

The point is that a flat file is not a good way to store linked data. Instead, the data needs to be placed into multiple tables. The chosen format for this data is to use three tables. Two contain the movie and actor data, and the third provides the connections between the movies and the actors. In this manner, data is listed only once, searches can query both the actors and the movies with the same efficiency, and corrections are much easier to make. The three tables are:

- Movies: List of movies, year released, and quality.

- Actors: List of first and last names of actors.

- Isin: The connection between the movies and the actors.

Figure 10.1a shows a bit of the *movies* table. It contains the name of the movie, the year of release, and a quality rating. The design is such that this table contains only those items which occur once for each movie. Each movie has one title (although this is not actually true). Each movie can contain several actors, and thus, that data is not contained here. Figure 10.1b shows a bit of the *actors* table. Each actor has one first name and one last name (although again there are exceptions). In these two tables, each movie is listed only once and each actor is listed only once. Figure 10.1c shows a bit of the third table which links the actors and movies. Each actor and movie had a unique identifier which are now used. Each row of this table connects one actor with one movie. A movie with multiple actors will have multiple rows in this table. Likewise, an actor with multiple movies will also appear multiple times in this table.

To find which actors are in a movie, the query converts the name of the movie to the `mid` (the movie identifier), uses the *isin* table to find which actor identifiers are associated with this movie identifier, then it uses the *actors* table to retrieve the names of those actors. A query to find the movies of a particular actor uses the same logical but in a reversed path. Either query has the same level of effort. If an actor's name is found to be misspelled or an actor changes their name, then the repair is to a single entry in the *actors* table.

This database is contained in a file named *movies1100ma.xlsx*.[1] It contains 1100 movies and 855 actors. Each movie has a title, a year of release, and a quality rating based on external resources. Each actor has a data field for a first name, a last name,

---

[1]These files are available from the author or the book's accompanying website.

	A	B	C	D
1	mid	title	year	grade
2	1	A Face In the Crowd	1957	8.2
3	2	A Perfect Couple	1979	6
4	3	Touch of Evil	1958	8
5	4	Across the Universe	2007	7.4
6	5	Amadeus	1983	8.3

(a)

	A	B	C
1	aid	firstname	lastname
2	1	Leonardo	DiCaprio
3	2	Andy	Griffith
4	3	Walter	Matthau
5	4	Orson	Welles
6	5	F. Murray	Abraham

(b)

	A	B	C
1	id	mid	aid
2	1	3	4
3	2	2	2
4	3	2	3
5	4	5	5
6	5	6	6
7	6	6	7
8	7	7	8

(c)

Figure 10.1: Samples of the three tables.

a birth date, and death date. Some actors (Madonna, Andre the Giant, etc.) have their names contained in just the last name field, and, of course, actors still alive do not have a death date.

10.2 PYTHON QUERIES

Connections between movies and actors are now possible, but first, the data needs to be read into a Python data structure. Code 10.1 shows the **ReadMovies** function which uses functions from the *pandas* module to read data from an Excel spreadsheet. The input is the filename and the output contains three arrays. Each row in the arrays is a row from the spreadsheet.

The *movies3.py* module contains several functions to query the data. These have similar interfaces and are organized within the file. The name of each query function has three parts: Output – From – Input. Thus, a query to return the mid value from the title of a movie is **MidFromTitle**. The inputs to the function usually have two arguments. The first is the table to be used, and the second is the input data. Some queries require more than one input variable. For example, the retrieval of an actor's aid value from his name requires two input strings. Some queries receive a single input but produce multiple outputs. If an actor is in several movies then the query with the input aid value will retrieve multiple mid values. For these cases,

---

Code 10.1 The **ReadMovies** function.

```
1   # movies3.py
2   import pandas
3   def ReadMovies(fname):
4       df = pandas.read_excel(fname,sheet_name='movies')
5       movies = df.values
6       df = pandas.read_excel(fname,sheet_name='actors')
7       actors = df.values
8       df = pandas.read_excel(fname,sheet_name='isin')
9       isin = df.values
10      return movies, actors, isin
11
12  mdir = # your data directory
13  import movies3 as mvs
14  movies,actors,isin = mvs.ReadData(mdir+'movies1100ma.xlsx'
        )
15  print(movies[:3])
16  [[1 'A Face in the Crowd' 1957 8.2]
17   [2 'A Perfect Couple' 1979 6.0]
18   [3 'Touch of Evil' 1958 8.0]]
```

---

the function name has a plural, as in **MidsFromAid**. Likewise, some queries receive multiple inputs to retrieve multiple outputs. The function **MidsFromAids** has two plurals because it receives a list of `aid` values and returns a list of `mid` values. The functions are sorted by this pluralism.

The use of this convention allows the user to correctly guess at the function they will need. The first example is to retrieve the title of a movie given an `mid` value. The function is this **TitleFromMid** shown in Code 10.3. The inputs are the `movies` table and the desired `mid` value. The output is the title of the movie. Of course, this can be confirmed by examining the data in the spreadsheet.

Code 10.2 Retrieving a movie by `mid`.

```
1   print( mvs.TitleFromMid(movies,731) )
2   Rebecca
```

The case of finding the title of a movie from its `mid` value is simple in concept. Each row of the *movies* table is searched for the given `mid` value. This does require a `for` loop, but since the data is stored as an array, the loop does not have to be explicit in the Python script. Efficiency is gained by using *numpy* tools. Line 3 establishes the default answer as an empty string. Line 4 searches the first column of the `movies` array for a match with the input `mid` value. The variable `ndx` is the index of the location of this matching row. Line 6 uses **ndx** to retrieve the movie's title, which is returned in line 7.

Code 10.3 The **TitleFromMid** function.

```
# movies3.py
def TitleFromMid( movies, mid ):
    tt = ''
    ndx = (movies[:,0]==mid).nonzero()[0]
    if len(ndx)>0:
        tt = movies[ndx[0]][1]
    return tt
```

Many of the functions in *movies3.py* follow this same format, and thus they will not be printed here. The available functions are:

- **TitleFromMid**
- **MidFromTitle**
- **AidFromName**
- **NameFromAid**
- **AidsFromMid**
- **MidsFromAid**
- **NamesFromAids**
- **TitlesFromMids**
- **AidsFromMids**
- **MidsFromAids**

As stated earlier, some functions deviate from the convention. To obtain an actor's aid value from his name, it is necessary to have two strings as the input. Code 10.4 shows a call to the **AidFromName** function which receives two strings for the actor's name and returns the aid value.

Code 10.4 Retrieving an actor's aid from an input name.

```
mvs.AidFromName(actors,'Jeff','Goldblum')
Out[]: 36
```

Some functions receive a single input value and return multiple values. The example is to return the mid values for a single actor. The input is the aid value and, the output is an array of the mid values. The call to the **AidsFromMid** function

Code 10.5 Retrieving multiple `aid` values from a single `mid`.

```
1  aids = mvs.AidsFromMid( isin, 647 )
2  aids
3  Out[]: array([688., 285., 36., 290., 123., 686., 689.,
      690.])
```

is shown in Code 10.5. It receives 647 as the input `mid` value and returns eight `aid` values.

These numbers do not reveal the actor's names, which is usually the goal of such as query. The **NamesFromAids** function has two plurals in the name. It receives several `aid` values and returns the associated actor's names. The example is shown in Code 10.6. Now the names associated with the movie 647 are known.

Code 10.6 Retrieving a list of names from several `aid` values.

```
1  mvs.NamesFromAids(actors,aids)
2  Out[]:
3  [('Tom', 'Berenger'),
4   ('Marlee', 'Matlin'),
5   ('Jeff', 'Goldblum'),
6   ('William', 'Hurt'),
7   ('Kevin', 'Kline'),
8   ('Mary Kay', 'Place'),
9   ('Meg', 'Tilly'),
10  ('JoBeth', 'Williams')]
```

Not all queries have functions in *movies3.py*. However, the functions therein can make creating new functions simple. Consider the case of finding the movie with the most actors listed in the database. No such function exist, but there is a function which returns the `aid` values for a single `mid` value. The length of this output is the number of actors. Code 10.7 shows the approach. A `for` loop considers each movie. The **AidsFromMid** function is called for each. The length of the output in line 4 is the number of actors. Lines 5 through 7 seek the movie with the largest value of N. The results show that the movie *It's a Mad Mad Mad Mad World* has 17 actors listed in this database.

10.3 CONNECTIONS

Connections between actors are defined by being in a common movie. Figure 10.2 shows a few connections for this database. Barbara Stanwyck is in two movies. Fred MacMurray was in *Double Indemnity* with Stanwyck, thus they are connected. Jack Lemmon and MacMurray were in *The Apartment*. In this database, Lemmon and Stanwyck do not appear in the same movie, thus there are two connections required

Code 10.7 Retrieving the movie with the most actors.

```
mostmid, mostct = 0,0
for i in range(1,1001):
    aids = mvs,AidsFromMid(isin,i)
    N = len(aids)
    if N > mostct:
        mostct = N
        mostmid = i

print( mvs.TitleFromMid(movies, mostmid) )
It's a Mad Mad Mad Mad World
print(mostct)
17
```

to go from Lemmon to Stanwyck. This chart does not show all connects for this group of actors because the diagram can become easily crowded.

The building of this chart starts with retrieving the movies for a single actor, Stanwyck. Code 10.8 retrieves the titles of the movies Stanwyck was in. The process requires three steps: convert her name to an `aid` value, find the `mid` values associated with this `aid` value, and retrieve the titles of the movies with those `mid` values. Three movie are retrieved: *Double Indemnity*, *The Strange Love of Martha Ivers*, and *The Stolen Jools*.

Code 10.8 Retrieving the movies of Barbara Stanwyck.

```
aid = mvs.AidFromName(actors,'Barbara','Stanwyck')
mids = mvs.MidsFromAid(isin,aid)
titles = mvs.TitlesFromMids(movies, mids)
print(titles)
['Double Indemnity', 'The Strange Love of Martha Ivers', '
    The Stolen Jools']
```

Likewise, a series of functions retrieve the actor's names from a movie title, as shown in Code 10.9. In this case, the title of the movie was converted to its `mid`. The `aid` values associated with this were retrieved, and finally the names of the actors were obtained. In this abridged database, three actors were listed for this movie.

Finding movies common to a pair of actors is an extension of this process. The **MoviesOfTwoActors** shown in Code 10.10 receives the *actors* table, the *isin* table, and the names of two actors. Lines 3 and 4 obtain the `aid` and `mid` values for the first actor, and lines 5 and 6 obtain these values for the second actor. Line 7 calls the **CombineLists** function which creates one list from the intersection of two lists. This function is shown in Code 10.11. It receives two lists, converts them to sets, computes the intersection of these sets, and then returns the data as a list.

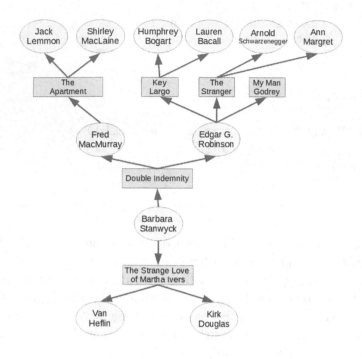

Figure 10.2: The connections between movies and actors.

Code 10.9 Retrieving the actors of *Double Indemnity*.

```
1  mid = mvs.MidFromTitle( movies, 'Double Indemnity')
2  aids = mvs.AidsFromMid(isin, mid)
3  names = mvs.NamesFromAids( actors, aids )
4  print(names)
5  [('Fred', 'MacMurray'), ('Barbara', 'Stanwyck'), ('Edward
     G.', 'Robinson')]
```

Code 10.10 The **MoviesOfTwoActors** function.

```
1   # movies3.py
2   def MoviesOfTwoActors(actors,isin,f1,l1, f2, l2):
3       aid1 = AidFromName(actors,f1,l1)
4       mids1 = MidsFromAid(isin,aid1)
5       aid2 = AidFromName(actors,f2,l2)
6       mids2 = MidsFromAid(isin,aid2)
7       mids = CombineLists(mids1,mids2)
8       return mids
9
10  mids = mvs.MoviesOfTwoActors(actors,isin,'Barbara','
        Stanwyck','Van','Heflin')
11  print( mids )
12  [812]
13
14  mids = mvs.MoviesOfTwoActors(actors,isin,'Fred','MacMurray
        ','Van','Heflin')
15  print( mids )
16  []
```

Code 10.11 The **CombineLists** function.

```
1   # movies3.py
2   def CombineLists( list1, list2 ):
3       s1 = set(list1)
4       s3 = s1.intersection( list2 )
5       outlist = list( s3 )
6       return outlist
```

Line 10 requests the `mid` values of the movies with both Stanwyck and Heflin. One movie was returned. This confirms the entry in the chart. Line 14 requests the common movie for MacMurray and Heflin, and the function returns an empty list which means that these two are not in a common movie in this database. The shortest path between MacMurray and Heflin is two steps because they both share a common movie with another actor, and there is not direct path from MacMurray to Heflin.

The number of possible paths, though, grows exponentially as actors are added to the database. Finding the shortest path between two actors becomes involved because there are many paths which connect two actors. Thus, an efficient algorithm is needed.

10.4   FLOYD-WARSHALL ALGORITHM

The Floyd-Warshall algorithm is a popular solution for finding the shortest path between any two nodes. The computation involves a triple-nested loop which will be slow in Python. Thus the size of the function will be increased to make use of *numpy* functions so the computation can be efficient. The algorithm creates two matrices, one which contains information of distances of connectivity and the other which encodes the shortest path. Before the algorithm is reviewed, the matrices are discussed to understand how they are used to retrieve the desired information.

10.4.1   The B and P Matrices

The Floyd-Warshall algorithm creates two matrices. The **B** matrix will contain distance information, and the **P** matrix will contain connection information. To demonstrate the construction of these matrices, a ten node example (Figure 10.3) will be used. This is a *directed graph* because the connections have direction. The connections between D and G are two-way, but the weights are different in each direction.

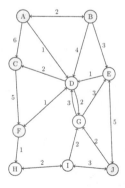

Figure 10.3: A graph with ten nodes.

The weights are similar to the distance between the nodes. One path from A to E is A:D:G:E with a distance of 6. As the number of nodes increase, so does the complexity of the system and the number of possible paths.

This graph differs from the actors graph in two manners. First this is a directed graph whereas the actors graph is an *undirected graph*. All connections in the actors graph are two-way. The second is that all connections in the actors graph have a length of 1. Either the actors are in a movie together or they are not. However, the methods developed here work on both types of graphs.

The **G** matrix for Figure 10.3 is:

$$
\mathbf{G} = \begin{pmatrix}
0 & 2 & 3 & 1 & 5 & 2 & 3 & 3 & 5 & 8 \\
2 & 0 & 5 & 3 & 3 & 4 & 5 & 5 & 7 & 10 \\
6 & 8 & 0 & 7 & 11 & 5 & 9 & 6 & 8 & 11 \\
6 & 4 & 2 & 0 & 5 & 1 & 2 & 2 & 4 & 7 \\
7 & 5 & 3 & 1 & 0 & 2 & 3 & 3 & 5 & 8 \\
14 & 12 & 10 & 8 & 8 & 0 & 5 & 1 & 3 & 6 \\
9 & 7 & 5 & 3 & 3 & 4 & 0 & 5 & 7 & 10 \\
3 & 11 & 9 & 7 & 7 & 8 & 4 & 0 & 2 & 5 \\
11 & 9 & 7 & 5 & 5 & 6 & 2 & 7 & 0 & 3 \\
11 & 9 & 7 & 5 & 5 & 6 & 2 & 7 & 3 & 0
\end{pmatrix}.
\tag{10.1}
$$

This matrix contains the distances of the shortest paths between any two nodes. Each row and each column is associated with a node in alphabetical order. The first row and first column are associated with the node A, and the last row and column are associated with the node J. For example, $G[1,2]$ contains the distance of the shortest path from B to C, and the path has a length of 5.

The final **P** matrix contains information of the actual path and it is:

$$
\mathbf{P} = \begin{pmatrix}
0 & 0 & 3 & 0 & 1 & 3 & 3 & 5 & 7 & 8 \\
1 & 1 & 3 & 0 & 1 & 3 & 3 & 5 & 7 & 8 \\
2 & 0 & 2 & 0 & 1 & 2 & 3 & 5 & 7 & 8 \\
1 & 3 & 3 & 3 & 6 & 3 & 3 & 5 & 7 & 8 \\
1 & 3 & 3 & 4 & 4 & 3 & 4 & 5 & 7 & 8 \\
1 & 3 & 3 & 6 & 6 & 5 & 8 & 5 & 7 & 8 \\
1 & 3 & 3 & 6 & 6 & 3 & 6 & 5 & 7 & 8 \\
1 & 3 & 3 & 6 & 6 & 3 & 8 & 7 & 7 & 8 \\
1 & 3 & 3 & 6 & 6 & 3 & 8 & 5 & 8 & 8 \\
1 & 3 & 3 & 6 & 6 & 3 & 9 & 5 & 9 & 9
\end{pmatrix}.
\tag{10.2}
$$

There is no direct transition between B and C, intermediate nodes are required to make this path. Once again, the rows and columns are associated with the nodes in alphabetical order. Thus, the second row (and column) are associated with the B node. The encoding of the path uses only the row of the first element in the path. In this case, the goal is to find the path from B to C, thus the second row will be used. The last node in this this path is C, thus the value in third column is considered. Python begins indexes at 0, so the first row and second column are $P[1,2]$. This is where the pertinent information starts.

This process builds the path backwards, from last node to first. The information in a cell indicates the next previous element in the path. In this case, $P[1,2]$ is 3, which is associated with D. Thus, the last bit of the path is D:C. The next cell to examine is the one associated with the D, P[1,4]. The element in this position is 0, which indicates that the next previous node is A. The path is A:D:C. The value at P[1,0] is 1, which is associated with B, which is also the first node in the path. Thus, the shortest path is known, B:A:D:C. The length of the path is known to be 5.

10.4.2 Creating the G and P Matrices

The process of making these two matrices joins known sequences by considering each node as a possible intermediate node. From Figure 10.3 some connections are known such as (AB, BA, BD, BE, etc.). The initial **G** matrix contains just these connections, as in,

$$
G = \begin{pmatrix}
0 & 2 & 6 & 1 & \infty & \infty & \infty & \infty & \infty & \infty \\
2 & 0 & \infty & 4 & 3 & \infty & \infty & \infty & \infty & \infty \\
6 & \infty & 0 & \infty & \infty & 5 & \infty & \infty & \infty & \infty \\
\infty & 4 & 2 & 0 & \infty & 1 & 2 & \infty & \infty & \infty \\
\infty & \infty & \infty & 1 & 0 & \infty & 3 & \infty & \infty & \infty \\
\infty & \infty & \infty & \infty & \infty & 0 & \infty & 1 & \infty & \infty \\
\infty & \infty & \infty & 3 & 3 & \infty & 0 & \infty & \infty & \infty \\
\infty & \infty & \infty & \infty & \infty & \infty & \infty & 0 & 2 & \infty \\
\infty & \infty & \infty & \infty & \infty & \infty & 2 & \infty & 0 & 3 \\
\infty & \infty & \infty & \infty & \infty & \infty & 2 & \infty & 3 & 0
\end{pmatrix}
\tag{10.3}
$$

The ∞ is used for nodes which currently have no transition path. The rows of the **P** matrix initially contain the index of the row,

$$
P = \begin{pmatrix}
0 & 0 & 0 & 0 & 0 & 0 & 0 & 0 & 0 & 0 \\
1 & 1 & 1 & 1 & 1 & 1 & 1 & 1 & 1 & 1 \\
2 & 2 & 2 & 2 & 2 & 2 & 2 & 2 & 2 & 2 \\
3 & 3 & 3 & 3 & 3 & 3 & 3 & 3 & 3 & 3 \\
4 & 4 & 4 & 4 & 4 & 4 & 4 & 4 & 4 & 4 \\
5 & 5 & 5 & 5 & 5 & 5 & 5 & 5 & 5 & 5 \\
6 & 6 & 6 & 6 & 6 & 6 & 6 & 6 & 6 & 6 \\
7 & 7 & 7 & 7 & 7 & 7 & 7 & 7 & 7 & 7 \\
8 & 8 & 8 & 8 & 8 & 8 & 8 & 8 & 8 & 8 \\
9 & 9 & 9 & 9 & 9 & 9 & 9 & 9 & 9 & 9
\end{pmatrix}.
\tag{10.4}
$$

In this matrix, any the path of any node is a direct connection. For example, P[1,2] is 1, which indicates that the currently known best transition from B to C is a direction connection BC, but G[1,2] indicates that this path length is ∞.

Each iteration finds paths in which the use of the intermediate node finds a shorter path. The first step in the process considers all possible paths which could use A as an intermediate node. The known paths with A as the beginning node are A:B, A:C, and A:D. The known paths with A as an ending node are B:A. Thus, there are three new paths to consider B:A:B, B:A:C and B:A:D. The first is not necessary since the beginning and ending nodes are the same. The path B:A:D has a length of 3. The cell G[1,3] indicates that the current known path B:D is 4, thus the new path of B:A:D is shorter. The value of G[1,3] is replaced with 3. The value of P[1,3] is replaced with 0, since the segment of the path is now A:D.

By considering A as an intermediate node, the **G** and **P** matrices are changed to,

$$G = \begin{pmatrix} 0 & 2 & 6 & 1 & \infty & \infty & \infty & \infty & \infty & \infty \\ 2 & 0 & 8 & 3 & 3 & \infty & \infty & \infty & \infty & \infty \\ 6 & 8 & 0 & 7 & \infty & 5 & \infty & \infty & \infty & \infty \\ \infty & 4 & 2 & 0 & \infty & 1 & 2 & \infty & \infty & \infty \\ \infty & \infty & \infty & 1 & 0 & \infty & 3 & \infty & \infty & \infty \\ \infty & \infty & \infty & \infty & \infty & 0 & \infty & 1 & \infty & \infty \\ \infty & \infty & \infty & 3 & 3 & \infty & 0 & \infty & \infty & \infty \\ \infty & \infty & \infty & \infty & \infty & \infty & \infty & 0 & 2 & \infty \\ \infty & \infty & \infty & \infty & \infty & \infty & 2 & \infty & 0 & 3 \\ \infty & \infty & \infty & \infty & \infty & \infty & 2 & \infty & 3 & 0 \end{pmatrix} \quad (10.5)$$

and

$$P = \begin{pmatrix} 0 & 0 & 0 & 0 & 0 & 0 & 0 & 0 & 0 & 0 \\ 1 & 1 & 0 & 0 & 1 & 1 & 1 & 1 & 1 & 1 \\ 2 & 0 & 2 & 0 & 2 & 2 & 2 & 2 & 2 & 2 \\ 3 & 3 & 3 & 3 & 3 & 3 & 3 & 3 & 3 & 3 \\ 4 & 4 & 4 & 4 & 4 & 4 & 4 & 4 & 4 & 4 \\ 5 & 5 & 5 & 5 & 5 & 5 & 5 & 5 & 5 & 5 \\ 6 & 6 & 6 & 6 & 6 & 6 & 6 & 6 & 6 & 6 \\ 7 & 7 & 7 & 7 & 7 & 7 & 7 & 7 & 7 & 7 \\ 8 & 8 & 8 & 8 & 8 & 8 & 8 & 8 & 8 & 8 \\ 9 & 9 & 9 & 9 & 9 & 9 & 9 & 9 & 9 & 9 \end{pmatrix}. \quad (10.6)$$

Four new paths have been created, B:A:C, B:A:D, C:A:B, and C:A:D. Each of these have lengths shorter than their predecessors. The algorithm then considers B as an intermediate node. The results are,

$$G = \begin{pmatrix} 0 & 2 & 6 & 1 & 5 & \infty & \infty & \infty & \infty & \infty \\ 2 & 0 & 8 & 3 & 3 & \infty & \infty & \infty & \infty & \infty \\ 6 & 8 & 0 & 7 & \infty & 5 & \infty & \infty & \infty & \infty \\ 6 & 4 & 2 & 0 & 7 & 1 & 2 & \infty & \infty & \infty \\ \infty & \infty & \infty & 1 & 0 & \infty & 3 & \infty & \infty & \infty \\ \infty & \infty & \infty & \infty & \infty & 0 & \infty & 1 & \infty & \infty \\ \infty & \infty & \infty & 3 & 3 & \infty & 0 & \infty & \infty & \infty \\ \infty & \infty & \infty & \infty & \infty & \infty & \infty & 0 & 2 & \infty \\ \infty & \infty & \infty & \infty & \infty & \infty & 2 & \infty & 0 & 3 \\ \infty & \infty & \infty & \infty & \infty & \infty & 2 & \infty & 3 & 0 \end{pmatrix} \quad (10.7)$$

and

$$P = \begin{pmatrix} 0 & 0 & 0 & 0 & 1 & 0 & 0 & 0 & 0 & 0 \\ 1 & 1 & 0 & 0 & 1 & 1 & 1 & 1 & 1 & 1 \\ 2 & 0 & 2 & 0 & 2 & 2 & 2 & 2 & 2 & 2 \\ 1 & 3 & 3 & 3 & 1 & 3 & 3 & 3 & 3 & 3 \\ 4 & 4 & 4 & 4 & 4 & 4 & 4 & 4 & 4 & 4 \\ 5 & 5 & 5 & 5 & 5 & 5 & 5 & 5 & 5 & 5 \\ 6 & 6 & 6 & 6 & 6 & 6 & 6 & 6 & 6 & 6 \\ 7 & 7 & 7 & 7 & 7 & 7 & 7 & 7 & 7 & 7 \\ 8 & 8 & 8 & 8 & 8 & 8 & 8 & 8 & 8 & 8 \\ 9 & 9 & 9 & 9 & 9 & 9 & 9 & 9 & 9 & 9 \end{pmatrix}. \tag{10.8}$$

The matrices indicate three new shorter paths have been identified, each with B as an intermediate node: A:B:E, D:B:A, and D:B:E. This process continues by considering the other nodes as intermediate nodes, eventually, producing the matrices in Equations (10.1) and (10.2).

10.4.3 Creating the Matrices in Python

These matrices are created by the Floyd-Warshall algorithm, which in theory, is quite simple, and it is shown in Code 10.12. This algorithm is only a few lines long, but it has a three-nested loop. In Python, this can be devastating to computational speed. The first loop is the one that considers each node as the intermediate node. The inner two loops perform the task of consider the possible combinations created by this inner node. It does this by adding values in the G array.

Code 10.12 Altering the **G** matrix.

```
1  for k in range( N ):
2      for i in range( N ):
3          for j in range( N) :
4              if G[i][j] > G[i][k] + G[k][j]
5                  G[i][j] = G[i][k] + G[k][j]
```

These inner two loops can be replaced by the **numpy.outer.add** function, which performs the same math, but uses the efficient codes within the *numpy* module. Thus, the algorithm uses only one Python loop as seen in Code 10.13. The **FastFloydP** function receives the initial G and P arrays. Line 7 considers each node to be an intermediate node. Line 8 just prints out the progress for every 50 nodes. Line 9 performs the inner 2 loops of the algorithm. Line 10 finds those cases in which the intermediate node found a shorter path. The `mask` is binary-value where a `True` value indicates that a shorter path has been found. Lines 11 and 12 replace the G values, and line 14 replaces the P values.

Code 10.13 The **FastFloydP** function.

```
1   # floyd.py
2   def FastFloydP( ing, inp ):
3       d = ing + 0
4       N = len( d )
5       oldd = d + 0
6       p = inp + 0
7       for k in range( N ):
8           if k%50==0: print (k,end=' ')
9           newd = np.add.outer( oldd[:,k], oldd[k] )
10          mask = np.less( newd, oldd )
11          mmask = 1-mask
12          g = mask*newd + mmask * oldd
13          oldd = g + 0
14          p = (1-mask)*p + mask * p[k]
15      return g, p
```

10.4.4 Finding the Shortest Path

Once the matrices are created, the task is then to find the shortest path between any two selected nodes. For example, what is the shortest between A and J? Node A is associated with 0 and node J is associated with 9. Thus, the length of the shortest path is G[0,9] which is 8. The path is built by using the data in the first row. It begins with the last column, P[0,9] which has a value of 8. The next value is thus P[0,8], and the process repeats until the value reaches 0, which is associated with the first letter in the sequence.

The process is encapsulated in the **FindPath** function shown in Code 10.14. It receives three variables. The P is the matrix generated by **FastFloydP**, and the K and L are the starting and ending nodes. Line 3 defines the pth list which builds the path from ending node to beginning node. The first element is the ending node, L. Line 4 defines n which is the value from P that indicates the next column to be used. The process then iterates until n is equal to K, which means that an entry in P is equal to the starting node. During the iterations, the path continues to add intermediate nodes (line 6). The beginning node is appended to the list in line 8. The pth was built backwards, so the order of the elements are reversed in line 9.

A test program is shown in Code 10.15. Lines 2 through 8 establish the initial connections from Figure 10.3, where a large number is used to represent ∞. Lines 9 and 10 ensure that that diagonal elements are 0, because the distance on any node to itself in this system is 0. Lines 11 through 13 create the initial **P** matrix. Line 14 calls the **FastFloydP** function to compute the final values of **G** and **P**.

Line 1 in Code 10.16 runs the **TestFloyd** algorithm to create the matrices. The first test is to find the shortest path between nodes A and C. The call to **FindPath** is shown in line 2 and the result is shown in line 3. This indicates that the path

Code 10.14 The **FindPath** function.

```
1  # floyd.py
2  def FindPath( P, K, L ):
3      pth = [ L ]
4      n = P[K,L]
5      while n != K:
6          pth.append( int(n) )
7          n = int(P[K,n])
8      pth.append( K )
9      pth.reverse()
10     return pth
```

Code 10.15 The **TestFloyd** function.

```
1  def TestFloyd():
2      G = np.zeros((10,10))+ 999999999
3      G[0,3]= G[3,5]= G[4,3]=G[5,7] = 1
4      G[0,1] = G[1,0]= G[3,2] =G[3,6]=G[7,8]=G[8,6] =G[9,6]=
           2
5      G[1,4] = G[4,6]=G[6,3]= G[6,4]= G[8,9]=G[9,8]=3
6      G[1,3] = G[3,1] = 4
7      G[2,5] = 5
8      G[0,2] = G[2,0] = 6
9      for i in range(10):
10         G[i,i] = 0
11     p = np.zeros((10,10),int)
12     for i in range( 10 ):
13         p[i] = i
14     G2,P = FastFloydP(G,p)
15     return G2,P
```

is A:D:C. The test to find the path from node A to J is shown in lines 5 and 6. The shortest path is A:D:H:I:J. This is a directed graph, which means that some connections are one-way. Thus, the shortest path from J to A can be different than the path from A to J. Indeed, this is born out in lines 8 and 9. The shortest path from J to A is J:G:D:B:A. The value of G[9,0] is 11 which is the distance of this path.

Code 10.16 Example use of the Floyd-Warshall algorithm.

```
1  gg,pp = TestFloyd()
2  print( FindPath(pp,0,2) )
3  [0, 3, 2]
4
5  print( FindPath(pp,0,9) )
6  [0, 3, 5, 7, 8, 9]
7
8  print( FindPath(pp,9,0) )
9  [9, 6, 3, 1, 0]
```

Quick examinations of these matrices provide other types of information. Lines 1 and 2 in Code 10.17 show that the average length of the paths is 5.7. The sum of the matrix is divide by 90 instead of 100, to exclude the diagonal elements which represent the case of the beginning and ending nodes being the same node. Lines 4 and 5 show that the longest path has a length of 14. Lines 7 and 8 show the location of this max, and lines 9 and 10 retrieve the path. The shortest path from F to A is, FHIEDBA. Finally, line 12 sums the rows. The largest value is 7.1 in the third position, which indicates that node C tends to have longer paths than other nodes.

Code 10.17 Extracting information from the matrices.

```
1   gg.sum()/(100-10)
2   Out[]: 5.7
3
4   gg.max()
5   14.0
6
7   divmod(gg.argmax(),10)
8   Out[]: (5, 0)
9   FindPath(pp,5,0)
10  Out[]: [5, 7, 8, 6, 3, 1, 0]
11
12  gg.mean(1)
13  Out[]: array([3.2, 4.4, 7.1, 3.3, 3.7, 6.7, 5.3, 6.6, 5.5,
           5.5])
```

10.5 APPLICATION OF FLOYD-WARSHALL TO ACTORS

The parts are built to analyze the connections among the actors in the given database. The first step is to create the **G** matrix, which is performed by function **MakeG** shown in Code 10.18. This receives the `isin` table. The `for` loop started in line 8 uses the **MidsFromAid** function and the **AidsFromMids** function to get all co-actors, those that are in the same movie. The index i loops through each actor, and for each actor, the `aids2` are the `aid` values of the actors at one degree of separation (those that are in the same movie with actor i). The -1 values in line 12 are necessary since the database starts the index at 1 and Python starts the index at 0.

Code 10.18 The **MakeG** function.

```python
# bacon.py
def MakeG( isin ):
    mat = np.array( isin )
    t = mat[:,2]+0
    aids = np.array(list(set(t)))
    N = len(aids)
    G = np.zeros((N+1,N+1))
    for i in aids:
        mids = MidsFromAid(isin, i)
        aids2 = AidsFromMids( isin, mids )
        for a in aids2:
            G[i-1, a-1] = 1
    return G
```

The **RunFloyd** function shown in Code 10.19 finishes the task. It receives the output from **MakeG**. In this case, actors are either connected (a value of 1) or not connected. Currently, the latter has a value of 0, but it is necessary to convert those to large values to represent ∞. This is done in lines 3 and 4. The **FastFloydP** function is called to produce the final values of **G** and **P**. The last two lines run the codes.

Code 10.20 finds the shortest path from Kevin Bacon to Charles Chaplin. Chaplin retired long before Bacon started working in movies, yet the path is surprisingly short. Since functions are contained in different modules, they are imported as shown in lines 1 and 2. Lines 3 and 4 get the actor `aid` values, but these are slightly larger than needed since Python starts indexing at 0. Thus line 5 subtracts 1 from these values. These `aid` values have been converted to row and column indices v and h (vertical and horizontal). As seen in line 7, the distance between actors is only 2.

Line 9 retrieves the path for these two actors, which are the values in line 10. Code 10.21 reveals the names of the actors. This states that Bacon and Matthau were in a movie together, and Matthau and Chaplin were in a movie together.

To confirm this finding, the movies are retrieved from the database as seen in Code 10.22. Bacon and Matthau were in *JFK*, and Matthau and Chaplin were in a movie named *Chaplin*, which was made well after the actor Chaplin had passed away.

Code 10.19 The **RunFloyd** function.

```
1  # bacon.py
2  def RunFloyd( G ):
3      GG = np.zeros( G.shape )
4      GG = G + (1-G)*9999999
5      ndx = np.indices( GG.shape )
6      pp = (G * ndx[0]).astype(int)
7      g,p = FastFloydP( GG,pp )
8      return g,p
9
10 G = MakeG( isin )
11 G,P = RunFloyd( G )
```

Code 10.20 The path from Bacon to Chaplin.

```
1  import movies as mov
2  import floyd, bacon
3  aid1 = mov.AidFromName(actors,'Kevin','Bacon')
4  aid2 = mov.AidFromName(actors,'Charles','Chaplin')
5  v,h = aid1-1,aid2-1
6  print('Distance',G[v,h])
7  Distance 2.0
8
9  path = floyd.FindPath(P,v,h)
10 print('Path',path)
11 Path [142, 2, 467]
```

Code 10.21 The actors in the path from Bacon to Chaplin.

```
1  for i in path:
2      print( mov.NameFromAid(actors,i+1))
3
4  ('Kevin', 'Bacon')
5  ('Walter', 'Matthau')
6  ('Charles', 'Chaplin')
```

Movies that use older clips still give credit to the actors in those clips, which occurred in this movie. Thus, Chaplin was in a movie after he died.

Code 10.22 The common movies of the actors.

```
1  mids = MoviesOfTwoActors(actors,isin,'Kevin','Bacon','
      Walter','Matthau')
2  print( mov.TitlesFromMids(movies,mids) )
3  ['JFK']
4
5  mids = MoviesOfTwoActors(actors,isin,'Charles','Chaplin','
      Walter','Matthau')
6  print( mov.TitlesFromMids(movies,mids) )
7  ['Chaplin']
```

This process can be applied to any two actors in the database. Consider the path from Dennis Weaver and Myrna Loy. The process is shown in Code 10.23. The program, however, does not return a meaningful result. As seen in lines 5 the distance between Weaver and Loy is the large value representing no connection. Indeed, in this database, Dennis Weaver is not connected to the main group of actors. A path between Weaver and Loy does not exist. Of course, a database listing all actors in the movies, and all movies for each actor, would have found a path from Weaver to Loy.

Code 10.23 The path between Weaver and Loy does not exist.

```
1  aid1 = mov.AidFromName(actors,'Dennis','Weaver')
2  aid2 = mov.AidFromName(actors,'Myrna','Loy')
3  v,h = aid1-1,aid2-1
4  print('Distance',G[v,h])
5  Distance 9999999.0
```

10.6   BEYOND CONNECTIONS

The matrices offer other information besides the shortest paths. For example: which actor has the most connections?

The elements in G are either 1 or large. Thus, the number of direction connections an actor has is the number of 1's in their row in **G**. For this task, the **MakeG** function is called in line 1 in Code 10.24. The resultant matrix uses 0's for disconnections. Thus the number of connections is simply the sum of a row (line 2). The rest of the code finds that Dan Aykroyd has 25 connections, which is the largest value. This process does not indicate if he is the only actor with 25 connections.

The next quest is to find the path with the longest length. Since all connections are 1, the longest path is also the longest chain of actors. The result is shown in Code

Code 10.24 Aykroyd has the most connections.

```
1  g = bacon.MakeG( isin )
2  vec = g.sum(1)
3  ag = vec.argsort()
4  print(ag[-1])
5  25
6
7  mov.NameFromAid(actors,26)
8  Out[]: ('Dan', 'Aykroyd')
```

10.26. Line 1 converts the final **G** matrix to binary values. Thus, the longest path is also the highest value in **G**. This is shown to be 7. This goes from Denzel Washington to Mads Mikkelsen.

Code 10.25 Longest connection.

```
1  Gdist = (G<99999)*G
2
3  mx = Gdist.max()
4  print(mx)
5  7.0
6
7  v,h = (Gdist==mx).nonzero()
8  print(v[0],h[0])
9  156 692
10
11 print(mov.NameFromAid(actors,v[0]+1))
12 ('Denzel', 'Washington')
13 print(mov.NameFromAid(actors,h[0]+1))
14 ('Mads', 'Mikkelsen')
```

Most importantly, Code 10.26 confirmed the Kevin Bacon Effect. In this mostly incomplete, abridged data set, the number of degrees of freedom is 7. This is a tad higher than theory, but if all of the actors in each movie were included, then this calculated value would go down. It can't go up by adding completeness for the movies in the database.

Lines 10 through 12 indicate that there are 72 entries in the **G** matrix with the value of 7. Thus, the Washington to Mikkelsen path is not the only one with a length of 7. However, this is an undirected graph. Each connection goes both ways. Thus, the Mikkelsen to Washington path is also 7. The number of unique paths is half of 72.

Code 10.26 Longest connection.

```
1  ('Denzel', 'Washington')
2  ('Chris', 'Pine')
3  ('Bill', 'Pullman')
4  ('Tom', 'Hanks')
5  ('Ed', 'Harris')
6  ('Robbie', 'Coltrane')
7  ('Shirley', 'Henderson')
8  ('Mads', 'Mikkelsen')
9
10 v,h = (Gdist==mx).nonzero()
11 len(v)
12 Out[]: 72
13
14 len(v)//2
15 Out[]: 36
```

10.7 SUMMARY

Connected data can be represented by connected graphs. This chapter demonstrates the representation of such connections by a matrix. Once established, this graph can then be searched for answers for a variety of queries. This chapter also presented a method to realize the Floyd-Warshall algorithm to find the shortest path between any two selected nodes. This was used to support the Kevin Bacon Effect with a limited database.

PROBLEMS

These problems are designed to use the movies database provided by the author.

1. Write a Python script to return the aid value for Kim Crosby.

2. Write a Python script to return the mid values for all movies with Amy Irving.

3. Write a Python script that returns the titles of the movies that Lena Horne is in.

4. Write a Python script to return the names of the actors in *Inherit the Wind*.

5. Write a Python script to return the aid values that are in the shortest path from Spencer Tracy to Lena Horne.

6. Write a Python script to find the titles of the movies that are in the shortest path from Aidan Quinn to Anthony Quinn.

7. Write a Python script to find the shortest path from Kevin Bacon to another actor that is longer than any other path from Kevin Bacon to another actor. Print the actors and movie titles that are in this path.

8. In this database, most of the actors are connected to each other. There are others such as Dennis Weaver, which are not. One of the actors in this large group is Leonardo DiCaprio. Write a Python script to find the number of actors in this connected group.

9. Mads Mikkelsen has been identified as an actor that is a chain of 7 handshakes with another actor. How many chains of length 7 is he in?

## CHAPTER 11

Gene Expression Arrays

G ENE EXPRESSION arrays (also known as microarrays) can aid in the identification of thousands of genes in a single experiment. A set of known DNA sequences are attached to a substrate (often a glass slide). A dye (call it red) is attached to a DNA sample, and this sample is smeared onto the plate. If the DNA in the sample has sequences similar to those on the plate, then the DNA (and thus the dye) will stick to the plate at the locations of those samples. An image of this slide would should several red dots where DNA adhered to samples and several locations without the red dye where the DNA on the slide and in the sample are dissimilar.

The absolute magnitude of the dye is hard to control, making it difficult to quantify the results. So, a second DNA sample with a second dye (green) is smeared on the same plate. It also sticks to some places and not to others. In reality, the dyes are sensitive to infrared radiation, but their responses are digitally represented as red and green on the computer screen.

Consider a simple experiment in which the red sample is for a sick patient and the green sample is for a healthy patient. There are four basic scenarios for the spots on the plate.

- At a location, both the red and green dyes are not present in a significant amount. This means that the DNA on the plate is not present in either patient.

- At a location, both the red and green dyes are present in a significant amount. This means that the DNA in both patients matches that at the location on the plate.

- At a location, the green is significantly higher than the red. This means that the DNA appears in one patient but not the other.

- At a location, the red is significantly higher than the green. This means that the DNA appears in one patient but not the other.

Consider an over-simplified task of finding out which part of the DNA is responsible for an illness. The researcher would search the responses of several patients, seeking those DNA strands which readily appear in the sick patients and not in the healthy patients, or vice versa. The spots on the slides which are *differentially expressed* are of keen interest to the researcher.

DOI: 10.1201/9781003226581-11

Like any experiment, it is much harder to implement than to visualize. Significant biases occur in the process of collecting data. For example, the sample with the red dye may simply better adhere to the slide than does the green sample. This causes a bias which needs to be removed. Real experiments will use several slides, and each of these slides will have their own response properties. This is another bias which needs to be removed.

This chapter will start with expression data from the repository of National Library of Medicine. Raw and processed data are provided in spreadsheets. This chapter will review a standard normalization process and apply to the raw data contained in these files. Small examples of extracting information from the files will be provided at the end of the chapter.

11.1   THE DATA

The National Libraries of Medicine at the NIH provides data from a vast number of experiments. The one chosen to be used here (mostly as a random choice) is GSE6553 "Natural variation in gene expression between normal human individuals studied using Hu800 cDNA microarrays" from `https://www.ncbi.nlm.nih.gov/geo/query/acc.cgi?acc=GSE6553`.

This experiment has files for several microarray slides. These slides use the same arrangement of DNA samples. Thus, there is one file which explains the architecture of the slide. This platform is denoted as HU800 and the website has a file named GPL4671 for this array.

The other files are the data from the expression array trials. Each of these are provided as a spreadsheet. Each spreadsheet has three sections: metadata, analysis, and raw data. The goal of this chapter is to demonstrate a normalization process applied to the raw data to present results similar to the processed data.

There are 800 DNA samples used in this experiment, but each DNA sample is duplicated on the slide. So, there are 1600 spots on the slide. The raw data starts on line 1650 of the spreadsheet because there are 50 lines of metadata and 1600 rows of analyzed data. A small portion of the spreadsheet is shown in Figure 11.1. The spots are placed on the slide in sets of blocks. Each block is a rectangle and within this block there are several DNA samples. So the location of a single spot is given in terms of the location of the block (columns B and C), and the location within that block (columns D and E). The (x, y) coordinates are also given in columns G and H. Column F provides the name of the gene.

Number	Array Row	Array Col	Row	Column	Name	X Location	Y Location	ch1 Intens	ch1 Back	ch1 Intens
1650 Begin Data										
1	1	1	1	1	phosphod	3170	4730	3077.652	1083.672	1964.162
2	1	1	1	2	phosphod	3370	4730	3353.428	1280.672	2610.696
3	1	1	1	3	butyrophil	3570	4700	2507.094	995.6875	1629.222
4	1	1	1	4	butyrophil	3780	4700	3911.974	1371.094	1084.669

Figure 11.1: A sample from the raw data.

The two channels (referred to as red and green above) are denoted as Channel 1 and Channel 2. Both channels have several measurements, but only the intensity and background intensity are used here. Column I in the spreadsheet shows the measured intensity of the first channel. Column J is the measured background. In the early days of expression experiments, the background could be significant and varied across the plate. Other measurements include geometric qualities of the spot. The intensity and background for channel 2 are in columns W and X.

11.2 READING THE SPREADSHEET

The Anaconda installation of the Python comes with the *pandas* package which does have a function to read in spreadsheet information. Line 1 in Code 11.1 imports this module for use. Line 2 uses the **read_excel** function to read data directly from the spreadsheet. As the spreadsheet has only one page, there is no need to specify the page during this process.

Code 11.1 Loading the original data.

```
1  import pandas
2  data = pandas.read_excel('/../GSM151667.xls')
3  dv = data.values
4  print( dv[1650,:9] )
5
6  array([1, 1, 1, 1, 1,
7         'phosphodiesterase I/nucleotide pyrophosphatase 2 (
             autotaxin)',
8         3170, 4730, 3077.651611], dtype=object)
```

Line 3 extracts the data into an array which is named dv. This step is merely for convenience. Line 4 prints out the data for row 1650 up to column 9. However, this data is slightly off from the spreadsheet, as these values are in row 1652. Recall Python begins counting at 0 whereas the spreadsheet begins counting rows at 1. Furthermore, the first row is not converted in line 3 as **read_excel** considers it to be a header line. Thus, the row values between the data and Python differ by 2. The intensity for channel 1 is in row I which is the 9th letter of the alphabet. Again, Python begins counting at 0, and so this intensity information is in position 8 in dv. Thus, the intensity for channel 1 for the first gene is in dv[1650,8].

11.3 PROTOCOL

The normalization process was presented by Yang *et al.* [7] which eliminates the biases within a single slide and those across slides. This section will review and implement those steps along with a small analysis of the data. The tasks before us are:

1. Subtract the background,

2. Compute R/G and I,

3. Compute M and A,

4. Apply LOWESS normalization,

5. Repeat for all files, and

6. Query the data.

11.3.1 Background Subtraction

The data for the channel 1 intensity starts in row 1650 and ends at row 1650+1600. It is in column 8 and the background is in column 9. The *pandas* function conveniently returns the data as Python arrays, so the first step of subtracting the background from the signal is easy to accomplish as in line 1 of Code 11.2. Lines 2 through show a few of the results. Line 7 performs the subtraction for Channel 2.

Code 11.2 Subtraction of the channel data.

```
1  ch1 = dv[1650:1650+1600,8] - dv[1650:1650+1600,9]
2  ch1[:4]
3  Out[]:
4  array([1993.9797359999998, 2072.756592, 1511.40625,
       2540.880615],
5       dtype=object)
6
7  ch2 = dv[1650:1650+1600,20] - dv[1650:1650+1600,21]
```

The first few values of `ch1` are printed to the console. These values are also in column M starting in row 48 of the spreadsheet. As stated earlier, the process reviewed in this chapter replicates some of the analyzed data in the second part of the spreadsheet. Column N has the background subtracted data for the channel 2.

Code 11.3 creates the plot shown in Figure 11.2. This is the R vs G (red vs green) information. The biologist seeks those cases in which the R is significantly higher than the G, or vice versa. If $R = G$ for all cases, then the scatter plot would have all of its points along a 45° line. As seen, this is not the case. In fact, the overall shape of the points have a swoop to it. This indicates that the ratio R/G has some other influences which affect the result. This is a clear indication of at least one bias.

Code 11.3 Creating Figure 11.3.

```
1  import matplotlib.pyplot as plt
2  plt.scatter(ch1,ch2)
```

11.3.2 Ratios and Intensities

The second step is to compute the red/green ratio (R/G) and the intensity (I). Code 11.4 shows one line of Python for each computation.

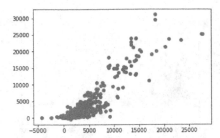

Figure 11.2: A plot of R vs G.

Code 11.4 Calculating R/G and I.

```
1  rgratio = ch1/ch2
2  intensity = (ch1 + ch2)/2
```

Code 11.5 creates the plot of R/G vs I. The data has some extreme outliers. The **xlim** and **ylim** functions are used to limit the range of the x and y axes, so a few data points are not seen in this chart. Figure 11.3 shows the data with limits on the plotting function. The vertical axis is the ratio of red to green, and the horizontal axis corresponds to the intensity of the spot. Any relationship between the ratio and intensity is difficult to see in this plot, which requires more steps in the analysis.

Code 11.5 Plot of R/G vs I.

```
1  import matplotlib.pyplot as plt
2  plt.scatter(intensity,rgratio)
3  plt.xlim(-10,8000)
4  plt.ylim(-5,30)
5  plt.show()
```

11.3.3 M and A

Using the ratio of R/G presents a problem. Consider a case in which the red channel and the green channel have the same intensity. Then $R/G = 1$. Now, double the intensity of the red channel and $R/G = 2$, but if the green channel was the channel doubled then $R/G = 0.5$. Herein lies the problem. The difference from the uniform case to the red-doubled case is 1, but the difference from the uniform case to the green-doubled case is only 0.5. The red channel and the green channel are not treated in the same manner. The goal is that is that the double of channel or the other should produce the same value (excepting a minus sign). The common way to achieve this goal is to convert the data to log scales. In this case, $M = \log_2(R/G)$ and $A = \log_2(I)$.

Step 3 is shown in Code 11.4 which computes these values and plots the data.

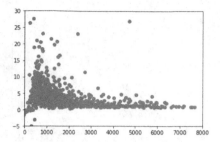

Figure 11.3: A plot of R/G vs I.

The result is shown in Figure 11.4. Now the value of ratio x is equal to the negative of the ratio of $1/x$. Both channels are on the same scale.

Code 11.6 Plot of M vs A.

```
1  M = np.log2(rgratio.astype(float))
2  A = np.log2(intensity.astype(float))
3  plt.scatter(A,M)
```

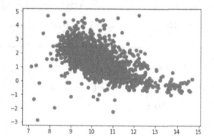

Figure 11.4: A plot of M vs A at a different scale.

There are 1600 spots on the slide. With this large number of spots, the red and green channels should have the same statistics. There should be a similar number of points in which $R > G$ and $R < G$. The average ratio should then be $R/G = 1$, and the log of this should be 0. Thus, the expectation is that this plot should have roughly the same number of points above and below $y = 0$ for all ranges of x.

This chart reveals two problems. The first is that most of the points are above $y = 0$, thus there is a global bias for the red channel. However, even if the data were lowered such that the average was $y = 0$ there would still be biases for different intensities. Points for lower x values would be above $y = 0$ and larger intensities would be below $y = 0$. The second bias seen here is dependent on the intensity of the spot.

The normalization goal is to move the cloud such that there are (about) the same number of points above $y = 0$ as below for all intensities.

11.3.4 LOWESS

The LOWESS (locally weighted estimated scatterplot smoothing) will perform the needed task. Basically, it considers a column of points and removes the average. For example, it takes the first 50 points (lowest x values) and subtracts the average from these points. Then it takes the next 50 points and removes the average. This is step 4 from the above list.

Fortunately, the *statsmodel* package contains the **lowess** function, which is imported in line 1 of Code 11.7. Line 2 determines the sort order of the data so it can be cast with the points associated with the lowest values of x at the beginning of the array. This is not a necessary step for the **lowess** function, but it will be useful later. Lines 3 and 4 create new arrays for sorted data. Line 5 calls the **lowess** function and returns filtered data. The first two inputs are the x and y data. Since the data is sorted, the `is_sorted` flag is set to `True`. The `frac` variable is the fraction of data which is in each column of the computation. In the example above, each column of data contained 50 of 1600 data points. The fraction is computed by $50/1600 = 0.03125$. The `it` variable is the number of re-weightings to perform, and it is set to 0.

Code 11.7 Sorting the data before calling the function.

```
1  from statsmodels.nonparametric.smoothers_lowess import
       lowess
2  ag = A.argsort()
3  A2 = A[ag]
4  M2 = M[ag]
5  filtered= lowess(M2,A2,is_sorted=True,frac=0.03125,it=0)
```

The result of the computation is `filtered` which is the local average of the data. In the example, it would be the average for every column of 50 data points. In order to modify the 1600 data points, this average needs to be subtracted from the data. To demonstrate this, the `filtered` data is plotted on top of the 1600 data points. Code 11.8 creates the plot shown in Figure 11.5.

Code 11.8 Plotting the average on the data.

```
1  plt.scatter(A,M)
2  plt.scatter(filtered[:,0],filtered[:,1])
3  plt.show()
```

The next step is to remove the average from the data. Once again, Python performs this step in a single command. As noted before, the size of `filtered` and M2 are not the same. The first gene in M is in position 942 in M2, but it is in position 930 in `filtered`. Thus, the subtraction requires the trimming and alignment of M2. The result of Code 11.9 is shown in Figure 11.6.

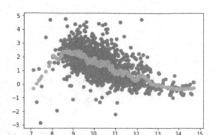

Figure 11.5: The local average overlain on the M vs A data.

Code 11.9 The normalized data.

```
1 genex = M2[12:-10] - filtered[:,1]
2 plt.scatter(filtered[:,0], genex)
```

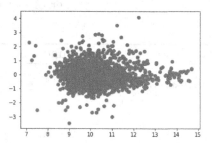

Figure 11.6: The normalized expressed data.

The x-axis is associated with the intensity of the spot. The y-axis is associated with the ratio of R to G. However, the number of plotted points above $y = 0$ is about the same as below. Furthermore, this is now true for all intensity levels. Thus, the normalization process is complete.

Biologists would then look for genes which are differentially expressed. In other words, genes that have a high value in one channel compared to the other. These are now easy to find as these are the points with high or low values in the vertical axis. For example, if the task is to find genes which are 4 times more intense in one channel then the other, then the points selected would be those with $y > 2$ or $y < -2$ (since the y-axis is on a $\log_2$ scale).

11.4 MULTIPLE FILES

The previous process operated on a single file, and it can be applied to multiple files. This normalization is intra-file, dealing only with the data of a single file. However, there are inter-file biases which also need to be removed.

The **NormGeneExp** function (Code 11.10) automates the processes. The input is a file name, and line 3 reads in the data from that file. Some of the data points will have failed, as the data does not exist or is impossible to use. These need to be removed. They can occur in either channel, and since the purpose is to compute ratios of the two channels, but both channels need to be removed if the data in one channel is bad. This check occurs in lines 7 through 10. The list, glist, gathers the good data, and the background is subtracted in lines 15 and 16. The RG ratio is computed in line 19, and lines 20 through 25 compute the M and A values. The LOWESS is computed in line 14 and applied in lines 26 and 27. The output is the data after the normalization processes.

Code 11.10 The **NormGeneExp** function.

```
1   # marray.py
2   def NormGeneExp(fname):
3       data = pandas.read_excel(fname)
4       dv = data.values
5       ch1 = dv[1650:1650+1600,8] - dv[1650:1650+1600,9]
6       ch2 = dv[1650:1650+1600,20] - dv[1650:1650+1600,21]
7       glist = []
8       for i in range(len(ch1)):
9           if ch1[i] > 0 and ch2[i]>0:
10              glist.append(( dv[i+1650,5],dv[i+1650,8],dv[i
                    +1650,9],dv[i+1650,20], dv[i+1650,21],i))
11      N = len(glist)
12      ch1 = np.zeros(N)
13      ch2 = np.zeros(N)
14      i = 0
15      for k in range(len(glist)):
16          ch1[i] = glist[k][1]-glist[k][2]
17          ch2[i] = glist[k][3]-glist[k][4]
18          i += 1
19      rgratio = ch1/ch2
20      intensity = (ch1 + ch2)/2
21      M = np.log2(rgratio.astype(float))
22      A = np.log2(intensity.astype(float))
23      ag = A.argsort()
24      A2 = A[ag]
25      M2 = M[ag]
26      filtered = lowess(M2,A2, is_sorted=True, frac=0.03125,
                it=0)
27      lowessdata = M2 - filtered[:,1]
28      return lowessdata,glist
```

One of the first issues to face is the removal of bad data points. Each file will have a few points which are removed, but these aren't the same points in every file. Furthermore, each file will have a different number of valid genes. To keep this straight, the list glist in **NormGeneExp** contains more than just the intensity and background of a point. Each item in glist is a tuple with two items. The first is a data tuple, and the second is the integer which indicates the gene. Since all experiments use the same Hu800 slide, then gene n in one file is the same as gene n in another. The tuple contains the gene name and the intensities and background for both channels.

Code 11.11 collects the data from all files in this data set. The variable `indir` is the data directory for the user. The list `lds` collects the LOWESS filtered data for each file. Thus, it is a list of vectors, but the vectors are not the same length. The `dcts` is a list of dictionaries which are returned by **NormGeneExp**.

Code 11.11 Gathering the data.

```
1  fnames = ['GSM151667.xls','GSM151668.xls','GSM151669.xls',
       'GSM151670.xls',\
2          'GSM151671.xls','GSM151672.xls','GSM151673.xls',
           'GSM151674.xls',\
3          'GSM151675.xls','GSM151676.xls']
4  lds = []
5  dcts=[]
6  for i in range( len( fnames )):
7      name = indir + fnames[i]
8      y,dct = NormGeneExp(name)
9      lds.append( y+0 )
10     dcts.append(dct)
```

Lines 1 and 2 in Code 11.12 show that of the 1600 original points, 22 failed to be gathered because of the channels had bad data. Each file produced a different number of valid data points. Lines 4 and 5 show that the mean of the data from the first file is 0. This is as expected since LOWESS does remove this bias. However, the standard deviation is not controlled. Lines 7 and 8 show the standard deviation of the first file, and lines 10 and 11 show standard deviation of the data from the second file.

Code 11.12 Statistics from the filtered data.

```
1  print( len(lds[0]) )
2  1578
3
4  print( lds[0].mean() )
5  -0.0007938121085207652
6
7  print( lds[0].std() )
8  0.7813116822472366
9
10 print( lds[1].std() )
11 0.6738991150423048
```

Each experiment has slightly less than 1600 data points, which is a considerable number. If the experiments were exactly the same, then we'd expect that the standard deviation values would be similar. Of course, this is not a reality when performing experiments. For one experiment, the data was spread out more than another. This is a bias that needs to be removed. The standard procedure in these cases is to force all files to have a 0 mean and a standard deviation of 1. These are accomplished by,

1. Subtracting the mean, and

2. Dividing by the standard deviation.

While the first step is not necessary in this case because of LOWESS, it is still described as other applications will need this step. The process is shown in Code 11.13. Starting with a list of file names, this code runs from the loading of the file through all of the normalization.

Code 11.13 Normalizing the mean and standard deviation.

```
1  lds = []
2  glists=[]
3  for i in range( len( fnames )):
4      name = indir + fnames[i]
5      y,glist = NormGeneExp(name)
6      y = y-y.mean()
7      y = y/y.std()
8      lds.append(y)
9      glists.append(glist)
```

11.5   SIMPLE ANALYSIS

The goal of analyzing several files is to find genes that might be associated with a particular condition, be it an illness or other. Consider the case in which Bob has a genetic illness, but Alice and Fred do not, and that this illness is created by the presence of a gene. We expect that Bob has this gene and the others do not. Three tests are performed, each with two patients (Bob:Alice, Fred:Bob, and Fred:Alice). If the tests are successful, then the gene should be differentially expressed in the first two files, but not the third. The gene would be positively expressed in the first file, negatively expressed in the second, and not differently expressed in third.

The search for genes of interest reverses this logic. The process seeks genes expressed in multiple files, and determines if this expression is meaningful. If successful, the gene should be expressed for some patients and not for others.

Of course, an illness could be caused by the absence of a gene. In this case, the first file would have a negative expression, the second file would have a positive one, and the third file would still be neutral even though both genes are present in this third case.

For this data, the task is to find genes expressed in females but not males. The NLM data accompanying the spreadsheets signified the gender of the participants. The data is shown in Table 11.1. The first entry has the designation F51_M58 which signifies that the first channel was from a female (identified only as 51), and the second channel was from a male.

Table 11.1: File identification.

File	ID
GSM151667	F51_M58
GSM151668	M58_M57
GSM151669	M57_M56
GSM151670	M56_M55
GSM151671	M55_F53
GSM151672	F53_F52
GSM151673	F52_F51
GSM151674	F53_F51
GSM151675	F52_M57
GSM151676	M55_M58

Three files have a female/male combination, so these are used in the following examination. Code 11.14 shows the **ExpressedG** function. This receives the two outputs generated by **NormGeneExp** , and a threshold named gamma. This function searches the data for cases in which a gene is above the positive value of the threshold or below the negative of this value. These are the expressed genes.

Code 11.14 The **ExpressedG** function.

```
# marray.py
def ExpressedG(y,glist,gamma):
    answ = []
    for i in range(len(y)):
        if gamma>0 and y[i]>gamma:
            answ.append(glist[i][0])
        if gamma<0 and y[i]<gamma:
            answ.append(glist[i][0])
    return answ
```

The value of the threshold is up to the user. If the goal is to find only those genes which are expressed four times more in one channel then the other, then the threshold is set to the log of 4, since the data being used is in the log space.

A simple application is shown in Code 11.15. The three files which had mixed genders are used. The sign of the threshold depends on whether the female is the first or second participant. The results are converted to sets, and then the **intersection** function is applied to the sets to find the genes expressed high in the first and last cases and low in the second case, The set **ast** has 23 genes listed.

Code 11.15 Isolating expressed genes.

```
1  a = ExpressedG(lds[0],glists[0],1.5)
2  b = ExpressedG(lds[4],glists[4],-1.5)
3  c = ExpressedG(lds[8],glists[8],1.5)
4  ast = set(a)
5  bst = set(b)
6  cst = set(c)
7  ast = ast.intersection(bst)
8  ast.intersection(cst)
```

Much more analysis is needed. First, each gene was used twice on each array slide. Thus, if a gene is truly expressed then it is expected that it will be expressed twice for each case. This information is not available in **ast** since the **set** function removes duplicate data.

Second, this is a small data set, and there could be other reasons why these genes are expressed in these three females and not in these three males. The functions of these genes would need to be investigated to see if there is any link to gender, or more data would need to be gathered.

The computational task has been completed. The data has been normalized and a process established to extract genes which are expressed.

11.6 SUMMARY

This chapter considered data retrieved from gene expression arrays. Several normalization processes were employed to provide a uniform space to compare data within a file and data across multiple files. A single example of finding expressed genes for a certain population was provided, although the data set is too small to provide any meaningful answer.

PROBLEMS

These problems are designed to use the same database used in the chapter. See the link in Section 11.1. Other data sets may be used.

1. Write a Python *function* that will retrieve the raw data from a single column from a file such as GSM151667.xls. Use this function to retrieve the radii from channel 1. Print the average and standard deviation values for these radii. (Hint: You can confirm your result by using the spreadsheet to also compute the average and standard deviation.)

2. Compute the average and standard deviation values for the radii in channel 1. Use these values to create a plot a unit-height, Gaussian curve. Repeat this process for the radii in channel 2. Plot both Gaussian curves on the same graph.

3. Determine if there is a relationship between the radii in the two channels. Create

a scatter plot of the radius in channel 1 versus channel 2 on a log-log scale. View the plot without outliers by setting the range in channel 1 to 4.6 to 4.9 and the plotting range for channel 2 to 4.4 to 4.9. (These ranges are for the log-log space.) Use the chart to explain if there is or is not a relationship of the radii between the two channels.

4. Is there a relationship between channel 1 intensity and radius? Create a scatter plot of the radius versus the intensity. Interpret the plot to determine if a relationship exists.

5. Repeat the process to get to figure 2.4, but replace the **lowess** function with your own code, by computing the average for consecutive columns of 50 points each. Create a plot similar to figure 2.4 with the M vs A data points and your computed line overlain.

6. To test the effect of the `frac` variable in LOWESS, plot the average vector (orange vector in figure 2.4) for cases where `frac` = 0.01, 0.03, and 0.1. Create a single plot with all three vectors. Explain what this chart indicates.

7. Modify the process of Section 11.5 to identify genes that are differentially expressed in MY57 compared to M56 and M58.

8. Each gene had to locations on the slide. Thus, and expressed gene should have both spots on the slide providing a differential signal. For GSM 151667, find the genes which are expressed twice with a threshold of gamma = 1.2.

9. Find the genes where are differentially expressed in females compared to males, for only those cases in which both genes on the female slides were expressed beyond the gamma threshold. Set gamma to either 0.7 or −0.7 as appropriate. Exclude DMSO, EST, and ESTs from your results. There should be one gene left. Use the abstract from `https://pubmed.ncbi.nlm.nih.gov/27079296/` . Does this article confirm your findings?

## CHAPTER 12

Simultaneous Equations

C ONSIDER the case of two equations with two unknowns,

$$3x + 4y = 11 \tag{12.1}$$

and

$$x - y = -1. \tag{12.2}$$

This problem of finding the values of x and y can be solved easily without a computer. One equation is selected and then solved for one of the variables. Picking the easiest of these,

$$y = x + 1. \tag{12.3}$$

This is substituted back into the first equation to get,

$$3x + 4(x + 1) = 11. \tag{12.4}$$

This is one equation and one unknown and can be easily solved to give

$$x = 1, \tag{12.5}$$

The x value is plugged back into Equation (12.3) to find the value of y,

$$y = 2. \tag{12.6}$$

The final step is to check to ensure the values of x and y were calculated correctly. Using either Equation (12.1) or (12.2), the values are plugged into the equation to confirm the solution.

Two equations with two unknowns is easy to solve without mechanical assistance. Five equations, such as,

$$
\begin{aligned}
4x + y - z + 2w - v &= 7 \\
-3x + y + z - w + 2v &= -1 \\
x - 2y - 2w + 2v &= 4 \\
-2x - 3y + w + v &= 5 \\
-x + y + z - w - v &= 0
\end{aligned}
\tag{12.7}
$$

DOI: 10.1201/9781003226581-12

require tedium which many people do not wish to use. Real-world systems can have a much larger number of equations and variables. This chapter will present methods to solve simultaneous linear equations in Python for any reasonable number of equations. This chapter will also provide two ventures into the limitations of these computations.

12.1 A LINEAR ALGEBRA APPROACH

The efficient approach to solving simultaneous linear equations invokes linear algebra techniques. Equations (12.1) and (12.2) can be written in terms of a matrix-vector multiplication,

$$\begin{pmatrix} 3 & 4 \\ 1 & -1 \end{pmatrix} \begin{pmatrix} x \\ y \end{pmatrix} = \begin{pmatrix} 11 \\ -1 \end{pmatrix}. \tag{12.8}$$

The top row of the matrix in Equation (12.1) is multiplied by the vector to produce the top value in the vector on the right. Equation (12.2) uses the bottom row of the matrix and the bottom element in the vector on the right. Using the substitutions,

$$\mathbf{M} = \begin{pmatrix} 3 & 4 \\ 1 & -1 \end{pmatrix} \tag{12.9}$$

$$\vec{x} = \begin{pmatrix} x \\ y \end{pmatrix} \tag{12.10}$$

$$\vec{c} = \begin{pmatrix} 11 \\ -1 \end{pmatrix} \tag{12.11}$$

Equation (12.8) becomes,

$$\mathbf{M}\vec{x} = \vec{c}. \tag{12.12}$$

The matrix $\mathbf{M}$ and vector $\vec{c}$ have known values. Isolating $\vec{x}$ is performed by left-multiplying both sides of the equation by the matrix inverse $\mathbf{M}^{-1}$, to get,

$$\mathbf{M}^{-1}\mathbf{M}\vec{x} = \mathbf{M}^{-1}\vec{c}. \tag{12.13}$$

The $\mathbf{M}^{-1}\mathbf{M}$ is the Identity Matrix, and thus the problem becomes one of which a computer can solve,

$$\vec{x} = \mathbf{M}^{-1}\vec{c}. \tag{12.14}$$

12.2 IMPLEMENTATION INTO PYTHON

Line 3 of Code 12.1 creates the matrix from Equation (12.9). Equation (12.13) uses the inverse of the matrix $\mathbf{M}$, which can be computed by the **numpy.linalg.inv** function. If the **inv** provides the correct answer, then the output of this multiplication should be the Identity Matrix, which has a value of 1 in the diagonal elements and 0 in the off-diagonal elements. Line 10 multiples the matrix by its inverse, and as seen, the Identity Matrix is returned within the computer's precision.

Code 12.1 Inverting a matrix.

```
1  import numpy as np
2
3  M = np.array(((3,4),(1,-1)))
4  M
5  Out[]:
6  array([[ 3,  4],
7         [ 1, -1]])
8
9  Mi = np.linalg.inv(M)
10 Mi.dot(M)
11 Out[]:
12 array([[ 1.00000000e+00, -2.22044605e-16],
13        [ 0.00000000e+00,  1.00000000e+00]])
```

The error of the computation is the square of the sum of the differences in the calculated values and the desired values. Given two matrices **A** and **B** which are supposed to have equivalent values, the error is measured by,

$$E = \sum_{i,j}(A_{i,j} - B_{i,j})^2, \tag{12.15}$$

where the $\sum_{i,j}$ sums over all elements, and $A_{i,j}$ and $B_{i,j}$ represent the individual elements in the matrices. If $A_{i,j} = B_{i,j}$ for all elements, then $E = 0$. Code 12.2 shows the computation for the inverted matrix. The inverse is multiplied by the original matrix, and this result is compared to the Identity Matrix which is created using the **eye** function. The result is an incredibly small number, which is essentially 0. Thus, the computation is confirmed. This metric of performance will be used again in later computations.

Code 12.2 Computing the error in the computation.

```
1  ((Mi.dot(M) - np.eye(2))**2).sum()
2  Out[]:  4.930380657631324e-32
```

Equation (12.14) solves for the desired vector. It involves the multiplication of an matrix inverse with a vector. The process is shown in Code 12.3. Line 1 creates the matrix, and line 2 computes the matrix inverse. Line 3 creates the vector, and line 4 performs the matrix-vector multiplication. The result is shown in line 5. These results correspond to the solutions found in Equations (12.5) and (12.6).

They beauty of this method is that it can be applied to a problem with any number of simultaneous equations. Consider again the problem of Equation (12.7) which has five equations and five unknowns. Creating the matrix is more tedious as seen in line 1 of Code 12.4. However, the solution process is the same. Line 4 computes the matrix inverse, and line 5 multiplies this by a vector to produce the

Code 12.3 Solution to simultaneous equations.

```
1  M = np.array(((3,4),(1,-1)))
2  Mi = np.linalg.inv(M)
3  cvec = np.array((11,-1))
4  Mi.dot(cvec )
5  Out[]: array([1., 2.])
```

final answer. The result has values for all five variables. Line 7 puts these variables into the first equation in Equation 12.7, and the computed answer matches that of the original equation, thus confirming that the correct values of x, y, z, w, and v have been found.

Code 12.4 Solution to five simultaneous equations.

```
1  M = np.array(((4,1,-1,2,-1),(-3,1,1,-1,2),(1,-2,0,-2,2),
2    (-2,-3,0,1,1),(-1,1,1,-1,-1)))
3  cvec = np.array((7,-1,4,5,0))
4  Mi = np.linalg.inv(M)
5  x,y,z,w,v = Mi.dot(cvec )
6
7  4*x + y - z + 2*w - v
8  Out[]: 7.0
```

The *numpy* module does offer the **numpy.linalg.solve** function which performs the same computation as lines 3 and 4 from Code 12.4. It receives the matrix and vector, and it returns the values of the output vector as shown in Code 12.5. Most of the work for the user is creating the matrix and vector. Replacing lines 3 and 4 from Code 12.4 with line 1 of Code 12.5 does not provide any significant computational advantage.

Code 12.5 Using the **solve** function.

```
1  answ = np.linalg.solve( M, cvec )
2  print(answ)
3  [ 3.79104478 -2.07462687 12.2238806    4.1641791
     2.19402985]
```

12.3   LIMITS OF COMPUTATION

Code 12.4 successfully computed the values for five unknowns, and clearly the number of equations and unknowns can be increased. However, computational accuracy can be limited by a couple of factors. The first is the accuracy of computation versus the number of equations, and the second is the case of singularity.

12.3.1 Matrix Inversion Precision

The simultaneous equation solution consists of a matrix inversion and a matrix-vector multiplication. The inverse is the component that will cause problems, so the question basically is: how big of a matrix can Python successfully invert?

Code 12.6 creates a 1000×1000 matrix with random values in line 1. Line 2 computes the inverse, and line 3 computes the error as per Code 12.2. The value is very close to 0, thus the matrix inverse was successfully computed. This far exceeds the capacity of most applications. On a computer with 16 MB, Python can successfully invert a $10,000 \times 10,000$ matrix. However, the limits of the computer memory can prevent the computation of larger matrices. Some reports indicate that Python with sufficient memory will have issues inverting matrices larger than $48,000 \times 48,000$ due to computational precision.

Code 12.6 Successful inversion of a 1000×1000 matrix.

```
1  M = np.random.ranf((1000,1000))
2  Mi = np.linalg.inv(M)
3  ((Mi.dot(M) - np.eye(1000))**2).sum()
4  Out[]: 8.835215735500398e-21
```

12.3.2 Singularity

There is another issue of obtaining a proper solution which is related to the data content rather than the size of the arrays. In fact, this problem can occur with two equations and two unknowns. Consider these two equations,

$$2x - 3y = 5$$
$$-4x + 6y = -10. \tag{12.16}$$

The matrix for this equation is created in line 1 of Code 12.7. However, line 2 creates an error (most of which is not shown in this Code). The attempt to invert the matrix associated with these two equations results in a singularity error. The matrix does not invert. These reason is that these two equations are, in a sense, the same equation. The second equation is the first equation multiplied by -2. Thus, no new knowledge is gained by the second equation. In reality, there are two unknowns but only one equation.

The problem can be deceptively embedded in a system of equations. Consider a second example, with three equations,

$$x - y = 2$$
$$2x + 3y = 9 \tag{12.17}$$
$$-x - 4y = -7.$$

None of these equations can be obtained by multiplying a value by another equation. Yet, the matrix created from this system of equations provides the singularity error

---

Code 12.7 An unsuccessful attempt at inverting a matrix.

```
1  M = np.array(((2,-3),(-4.,6)))
2  Mi = np.linalg.inv( M )
3
4  Traceback (most recent call last):
5  . . .
6  LinAlgError: Singular matrix
```

---

when attempting to compute the inverse. The issue is that one equation is a weighted linear combination of the other two. Equation 3 is equation 1 minus equation 2. Thus, this system has three unknowns but only two equations.

No single equation is guilty of this infraction. Any of the equations is a weighted linear combination of the others. When this occurs, the matrix inversion creates a singularity. If the system had 100 unknowns and 100 equations, but one equation is a linear combination of some of the others, then the error will occur.

Code 12.8 shows the case of Equation (12.16), but one of the values in the matrix has a tiny addition. The second equation is no longer the same as the first equation with a multiplication of -2. The **inv** function does not return and error, and the matrix multiplied by its inverse returns the Identity Matrix.

Code 12.8 Successful inversion with a small adjustment.

```
1  M = np.array(((2,-3),(-4.000001,6)))
2  Mi = np.linalg.inv( M )
3  Mi.dot(M)
4  Out[]:
5  array([[ 1.00000000e+00,  0.00000000e+00],
6         [-4.65661287e-10,  1.00000000e+00]])
```

The values of the matrix inverse, though, are enormous as shown in Code 12.9. As the matrix in line 1 of Code 12.8 becomes closer to a singular matrix, the values in the matrix inverse tend toward infinity. While Python could mathematically solve this problem, the returned values are probably not useful. If a matrix is close to being singular, then the computations may not provide useful results.

Code 12.9 Values of the matrix inverse from Code 12.8.

```
1  Mi
2  Out[]:
3  array([[-1999999.99976502,  -999999.99988251],
4         [-1333333.66651001,  -666666.66658834]])
```

This *condition number* provides a measure of how close a matrix is to being singular. Matrices with low condition numbers will invert and provide useful results. The condition number is determined by,

$$\kappa = \parallel \mathbf{A} \parallel \parallel \mathbf{A}^{-1} \parallel, \tag{12.18}$$

where

$$\parallel \mathbf{A} \parallel = \left(\sum_{i,j} A_{i,j}^2 \right)^{1/2}. \tag{12.19}$$

The *numpy.linalg* module offers the **cond** function which computes the condition number. Condition numbers of the matrices used above are calculated in Code 12.10. Larger values indicate problems with singularity.

Code 12.10 The condition numbers of various matrices.

```
1  M = np.array(((2,-3),(-4,6)))
2  np.linalg.cond(M)
3  Out[]: 1.0045358665050384e+16
4
5  M = np.array(((2,-3),(-4,6.00001)))
6  np.linalg.cond(M)
7  Out[]: 3250005.9991313317
8
9  M = np.array(((3,4),(1,-1)))
10 np.linalg.cond(M)
11 Out[]: 3.5776280543736
```

12.4 WORD PROBLEMS

Word problems often plague students, and many of these are easily solved by simultaneous equations. For example: Given two integers. Their sum is 16 and one integer is 4 more than the other. What are the two integers?

This problem has three parts. First, given two integers. These can be named as x and y. Second, their sum is 16. Thus $x + y = 16$. Third, one integer is 4 more than the other. This gives either of two equations $x = y + 4$ or $x + 4 = y$. In this case, it doesn't matter which equation is used. For this example, the latter is chosen,

$$\begin{aligned} x + y &= 16 \\ x + 4 &= y. \end{aligned} \tag{12.20}$$

These create two equations and two unknowns which can be easily solved as seen in Code 12.11. The matrix is established in line 1 and the vector is established in line 2. The rest follows the protocol for solving simultaneous linear equations. The answers are $x = 6$ and $y = 10$. Had the $x = y + 4$ equation been used, then the results would have been $x = 10$ and $y = 6$. In either case, the problem is solved.

Code 12.11 Solving the first word problem.

```
1  M = np.array(((1,1),(1,-1)))
2  cvec = np.array((16,-4))
3  Mi = np.linalg.inv(M)
4  Mi.dot(cvec)
5  Out[]: array([ 6., 10.])
```

12.4.1 Amusement Park Fees

A second typical problem is: The entrance fee to a park is $10 for adults and $6 for children. There are 20 people in the park and $164 in the cash register. How many adults and children are in the park?

Simultaneous equations can solve this problem. There are two variables – the number of adults, a, and the number of children, c. The total number of people in park is 20, thus $a + c = 20$. The received cash begets $10a + 6c = 164$. The solution is shown in Code 12.12. The matrix and vector are established in lines 1 and 2. The answer is that there are 11 adults and 9 children.

Code 12.12 Solving the second word problem.

```
1  M = np.array(((1,1),(10,6)))
2  cvec = np.array((20,164))
3  Mi = np.linalg.inv(M)
4  Mi.dot(cvec)
5  Out[]: array([11., 9.])
```

12.4.2 Traffic Flow

Another problem is shown in Figure 12.1. Four one-way roads intersect at junctions labeled by capital letters. The arrows with numbers indicate how many vehicles travel through the intersection in a time window. The goal is to determine the number of cars traveling along the roads with lowercase letters.

The figure needs to be converted to equations. Consider the flow through junction 'A.' The number of cars going into the intersection needs to be the same as the number of cars leaving the intersection. If the number of cars entering the intersection is greater than the number leaving, then there will be a pile-up in the intersection. Thus, the equation for this junction is $a + b = 241 + 190$. Applying the logic to the four intersections, the following equations emerge,

$$a + b = 241 + 190$$
$$150 + 105 = a + c$$
$$280 + 236 = b + d$$
$$c + d = 110_230.$$

$$(12.21)$$

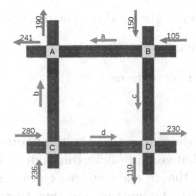

Figure 12.1: A traffic flow problem with four roads.

This provides four equations and four unknowns. However, this creates a singular matrix,

$$\begin{pmatrix} 1 & 1 & 0 & 0 \\ 1 & 0 & 1 & 0 \\ 0 & 0 & 1 & 1 \\ 0 & 1 & 0 & 1 \end{pmatrix}. \tag{12.22}$$

Any line is a linear combination of the other three lines. This makes sense. If the flow rate of three of the lanes are known, then the flow rate of the fourth can be determined. There is no variability, and thus there is no fourth equation.

Unfortunately, there are no more intersections, and thus a new equation is not available. To solve this situation, more information is needed. In this case, the word problem does not provide it. However, in a real-life situation, the lesson-learned is that the researcher needs to gather more data. For example, the researcher could learn that road d has a flow rate that is 1.5 times higher than road b. This provides a new equation $d = 1.5b$. Now, the problem has four equations and four unknowns. It is solved in Code 12.13. The flow rates for each road are determined.

Code 12.13 Solving the traffic problem with additional information.

```
1 M = np.array(((1,1,0,0),(1,0,1,0),(0,0,1,1),(0,-1.5,0,1)))
2 cvec = np.array((431,255,340,0))
3 Mi = np.linalg.inv(M)
4 Mi.dot(cvec)
5 Out[]: array([224.6, 206.4,  30.4, 309.6])
```

12.5 APPLICATION TO KIRCHHOFF'S LAWS

The final problem to consider is an electrical circuit which contains batteries and resistors. Given the voltage of the batteries and the values of the resistors, the task is to determine the current through each wire. This process relies on two Kirchhoff's rules:

1. At a junction in a circuit, the total current must be 0.

2. The total voltage through a loop in a circuit is 0.

These are explained in the next sections.

12.5.1 The Junction Rule

The formal explanation of the rule is that the total current at a junction is 0. The informal explanation is "What goes in – must come out." Figure 12.2 shows a junction with current coming in from the left and going out on two branches on the right. There are five electrons coming into the junction and thus there are five electrons coming out of the junction.

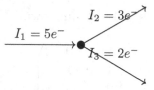

Figure 12.2: A junction in a circuit.

Mathematically, this is:

$$I_1 = I_2 + I_3. \tag{12.23}$$

12.5.2 The Loop Rule

The loop rule states that the total voltage around a loop must equal 0. Before this is explored, Ohm's law needs to be refreshed. This states that the voltage is equal to the current times the resistance,

$$V = IR. \tag{12.24}$$

Now consider the circuit in Figure 12.3. The black dots labeled a, b and c are not part of the circuit. They merely mark locations. This circuit has two resistors R_1 and R_2 and a battery which has a voltage V. There is a voltage drop across each resistor which obeys Ohm's law. Thus Kirchhoff's loop rule for this circuit is:

$$V - IR_1 - IR_2 = 0. \tag{12.25}$$

12.5.3 Creating the Equations

This section will present the steps necessary to use Kirchhoff's rules to compute the current in all parts of a circuit.

Consider the circuit shown in Figure 12.4. The values for the resistors and battery voltages are known. The first resistor is $57.5\,\Omega$ (where Ω represents the units of Ohms).

- $R_1 = 57.4\,\Omega$

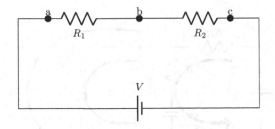

Figure 12.3: Circuit 1.

- $R_2 = 114.8\,\Omega$

- $R_3 = 172.2\,\Omega$

- $\mathcal{E}_1 = 3.22\,\mathrm{V}$

- $\mathcal{E}_2 = 3.22\,\mathrm{V}$

The goal is to find the current (Amperes) through each component. At first this seems as a daunting quest, but Kirchhoff's laws and simultaneous equations come to the rescue.

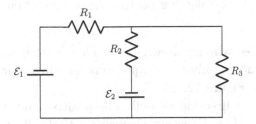

Figure 12.4: The initial circuit.

Figure 12.5 adds directional arrows for each loop. The user opted to make the arrows go in a clockwise direction. This is merely a random choice of establishing a convention. The user could choose the loops flowing in the other directions, and later rules will manage the sign conventions for these decisions. In short, the direction of the loops does not change the complexity of the computation.

The next step is to decide on which direction the current arrows should point (Figure 12.6). Again this is an arbitrary decision, and if the arrows were pointing in the opposite directions, then the computations would have negative signs in different locations.

The loop and current directions are established, so the next step is to build Kirchhoff's equations. There are two junctions in this circuit. They provide the same equation, so only one will be used here. Using the arrows in Figure 12.6 the equation for either junction is:

$$I_1 + I_2 = I_3. \tag{12.26}$$

There are three loops in this circuit. Only two will be needed to compute the

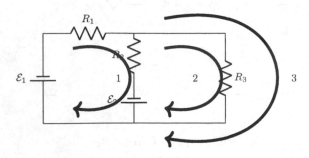

Figure 12.5: Identifying the loops.

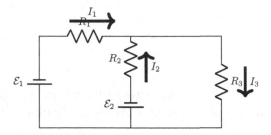

Figure 12.6: Selecting positive directions of current flow.

currents, but all three will be shown here. This system has three unknowns (the currents), and thus needs only three equations, of which one Equation (12.26). The first loop is shown in Figure 12.7.

Each battery has a direction as well. The positive end of the battery is the end shown with the longer bar. However, electrons actually flow out the negative end of the battery, so the direction is toward the smaller bar (negative node).

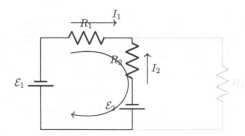

Figure 12.7: The first loop.

The loop contains two resistors and two batteries. Each will provide a positive or negative voltage. The rules for determining the sign of the voltages are:

- Battery: If the loop curve and positive node of the battery are in the same direction, then it contributes a positive voltage.

- Battery: If the direction of the battery (positive end) opposes the direction the loop arrow or the current arrow, then the voltage is multiplied by -1.

- Resistor: If the loop and arrow are in the same direction then the resistor provides a voltage drop $-IR$.

- Resistor: If the directions are opposite, then the resistor provides a positive value IR.

In the first loop the direction of the blue arrow through the battery $\mathcal{E}_1$ is in the same direction as positive node of the battery and the loop. Thus, the battery contributes $+\mathcal{E}_1$. For the second battery the arrow and loop are in opposite directions (multiply by -1), and the battery direction is in the opposite direction of the loop arrow (multiply by another -1). Thus it contributes $+\mathcal{E}_2$. The first resistor, R_1, has the loop arrow and the current arrow in the same direction. Thus it contributes $-I_1 R_1$. The second resistor has the loop and arrow in opposite directions, so it contributes $+I_2 R_2$.

The loop equation is the sum of these four components, and Kirchhoff's law states that this sum must be equal to 0, as in,

$$-\mathcal{E}_1 - I_1 R_1 + I_2 R_2 + \mathcal{E}_2 = 0. \tag{12.27}$$

The second loop is shown in Figure 12.8. It has one battery and two resistors. The equation for this loop is,

$$-\mathcal{E}_2 - I_2 R_2 - I_3 R_3 = 0. \tag{12.28}$$

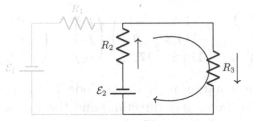

Figure 12.8: The second loop.

The final loop is shown in Figure 12.9 and it produces

$$-\mathcal{E}_1 - I_1 R_1 - I_3 R_3 = 0. \tag{12.29}$$

12.5.4 Computing the Currents

The loops and junctions have been identified, and they produce four equations,

$$I_1 + I_2 = I_3, \tag{12.30}$$

$$-\mathcal{E}_1 - I_1 R_1 + I_2 R_2 + \mathcal{E}_2 = 0, \tag{12.31}$$

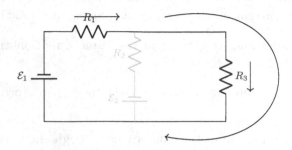

Figure 12.9: The third loop.

$$\mathcal{E}_2 + I_2 R_2 + I_3 R_3 = 0, \tag{12.32}$$

and

$$\mathcal{E}_1 + I_1 R_1 + I_3 R_3 = 0. \tag{12.33}$$

There are three unknowns I_1, I_2, and I_3. Thus, only three equations are needed. The following computation uses the first three.

These produce the following equation:

$$\begin{pmatrix} 1 & 1 & -1 \\ R_1 & -R_2 & 0 \\ 0 & R_2 & R_3 \end{pmatrix} \begin{pmatrix} I_1 \\ I_2 \\ I_3 \end{pmatrix} = \begin{pmatrix} 0 \\ \mathcal{E}_1 - \mathcal{E}_2 \\ -\mathcal{E}_2 \end{pmatrix}. \tag{12.34}$$

With the known values, the equation becomes,

$$\begin{pmatrix} 1 & 1 & -1 \\ 57.4 & -114.8 & 0 \\ 0 & 114.8 & 172.2 \end{pmatrix} \begin{pmatrix} I_1 \\ I_2 \\ I_3 \end{pmatrix} = \begin{pmatrix} 0 \\ 0 \\ -3.22 \end{pmatrix}. \tag{12.35}$$

The Python implementation is shown in Code 12.14. The results show that all current arrows were in the correct direction, and the values were $I_1 = 0.0102\,\text{A} = 10.2\,\text{mA}$, $I_2 = 0.0051\,\text{A}$, and $I_3 = 0.0153\,\text{A}$.

Code 12.14 Computing the currents.

```
1  import numpy as np
2  A = np.array(((1,1,-1),(57.4,-114.8,0),(0,114.8,172.2)))
3  Y  = np.array( (0,0,-3.22))
4  Ai = np.linalg.inv(A)
5  Ai.dot(Y)
6  Out[]: array([ 0.0102,   0.0051 0.0153])
```

To confirm the results, these values can be plugged into the fourth equation which was not used in the computation.

12.6 SUMMARY

Simultaneous equations can be solved by hand, but for systems with a few more equations, a computer program provides an easy channel for getting a solution. Python linear algebra scripts can be used to solve this system of multiple equations. There are limits to the computation, particularly if one of the equations is a weighted linear combination of the others. The condition number provides a measure which can validate the use of the Python script for a particular application.

PROBLEMS

1. Solve the following for x and y.

$$4x + 2y = 14$$

$$y - x = -5$$

2. Solve the following for x, y, and z.

$$1.1y - 3x - 0.9z = 3.61$$

$$4.7z - 4.1x - 0.17y = -42.527$$

$$2.9y + 2.2z - 1.1x = 3.87$$

3. Given the following equations.

$$ax + by = c$$

$$dx + ey = f$$

   (a) Randomly generate values for a, b, d, and e that are between -1 and 1.
   (b) Randomly generate values for c and f.
   (c) Compute x and y
   (d) Use the given two lines of code to print out the results.

4. Solve for x, y, and z in

$$4x + 6y - z = 0$$

$$-x + 2y - 2z = 2$$

$$3x + 8y - 3z = 1$$

5. The following situation creates a singular matrix. Can the problem be solved if we change the values on the right hand side of the equation. Explain your answer in one sentence.

$$4x + 2y - z = 0$$

$$x - 1y - 2z = 2$$

$$5x + y - 3z = 1$$

6. Georgina has 30 coins which consists of dimes and nickels. The total amount that she has is $2.45. How many dimes and how many nickels does she have?

7. Georgina is back again. This time she has pennies, nickels, dimes, and quarters. She has 30 coins. The total amount she has is $3.92. She has one more dime than she has pennies. The total number of dimes and quarters is 15. How many of each coin does she have?

8. In Section 12.5.4, the solution used the junction equation and the first two loop equations. Solve this same problem using the junction equation and the last two loop equations. Confirm your answer using the first loop equation.

9. Using $R_1 = 14$, $R_2 = 8$, $R_3 = 10$, $\mathcal{E}_1 = 40$, and $\mathcal{E}_2 = 22$ in Figure 12.10. Determine the current and direction for each component.

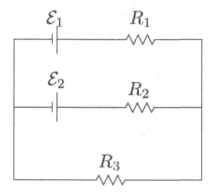

Figure 12.10: A circuit.

## CHAPTER 13

Simulations of Motion

M OTION is the fundamental theme of kinematics, and is often the second topic taught in physics courses (after units and estimations). Motion equations are rather simple and are therefore easy to implement. This chapter will explore basic theories of linear motion, accelerated motion, projectile motion, and the energies associated with these motions. Python simulations will be created, and a few examples will be provided.

13.1 LINEAR MOTION

Linear motion is the study of a mass moving in one direction at a constant velocity. An example is shown in Figure 13.1 in which the mass is a hockey puck moving in a single direction. The ice resembles a frictionless surface, and so theoretically the hockey puck would continue on at the same speed forever. This model does not take into account any acceleration to get the puck moving. It just starts moving at a single velocity. The original location of the puck is x_0 and the final position is x_1.

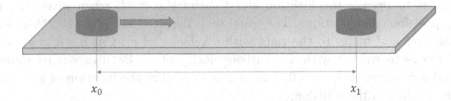

x_0 x_1

Figure 13.1: A mass (hockey puck) moves along the frictionless ice with a constant speed.

The equation to compute the final position is,

$$x_1 = x_0 + v\Delta t, \tag{13.1}$$

where v is the velocity and Δt is the amount of time required to travel this distance. Physicists will worry about the units of these variables, and so to placate their nervousness, the distances are measured in meters, the velocity is measured in meters per second, and the time is measured in seconds. Since the purpose of this text is modeling and simulation, the text will not consider motion using other units.

DOI: 10.1201/9781003226581-13

Equation (13.1) computes the new position given the old position, the speed, and the time. However, other questions might be asked of this situation. For example, if the two positions and speed are known, then the question can be to compute how much time is required to make the journey. To solve this problem, Equation (13.1) is rearranged to solve for Δt,

$$\Delta t = \frac{x_1 - x_0}{v}. \tag{13.2}$$

Code 13.1 shows an example of implementing this system. In this example, the puck starts at $x_0 = 0\,\text{m}$ and ends at $x_1 = 7\,\text{m}$. The velocity during the entire trip is $v = 1.3\,\text{m/s}$. The time of travel is computed to be $\Delta t = 5.38\,\text{s}$.

Code 13.1 Computing the travel time for linear motion.

```
x0 = 0
x1 = 7
v = 1.3
t = (x1-x0)/v
print('time = ',t)
time =   5.384615384615384
```

A standard convention for velocity is that a positive velocity represents movement to the right, and negative velocity represents movement to the left. Two cars moving at 20 m/s in opposite directions have the same speeds, but opposing velocities. One car has a velocity of $+20$ m/s and the other has a velocity of -20 m/s.

13.2 CAR CRASH

Consider a case in which two cars are racing toward each other and will soon crash. The task is to predict the location and time of the crash when given the initial starting positions and locations. The situation is depicted in Figure 13.2. Car A starts at position x_1 and moves to the right with a velocity of v_1. Car B starts at position x_2 and moves to the left with a negative velocity of v_2. Both cars start moving at $t = 0$ and for convenience $x_1 = 0$. The task is to predict the location of the collision, x_3, and the time of the collision.

In this case, the collision is when both cars are at the same place at the same time. Thus, both cars will be at x_3 at some time t. To begin the displacements are defined as,

$$\Delta x_A = x_3 - x_1$$
$$\Delta x_B = x_3 - x_2 \tag{13.3}$$

Solving both equations for x_3, they become,

$$x_3 = \Delta x_A + x_1 = \Delta x_B + x_2. \tag{13.4}$$

The travel time for each car is the same, thus $\Delta t = \Delta t_A = \Delta t_B$. The time equation for each car is,

$$\Delta t = \frac{\Delta x_A}{v_1} = \frac{\Delta x_B}{v_2}. \tag{13.5}$$

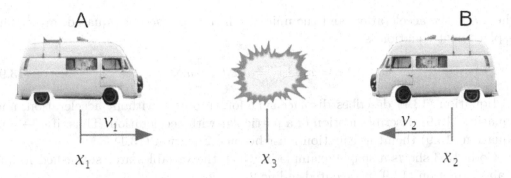

Figure 13.2: Two cars race toward each other and soon will collide.

Substituting the terms Δx_A and Δx_B become,

$$\frac{\Delta x_A}{v_1} = \frac{\Delta x_B}{v_2} = \frac{x_3 - x_1}{v_1} = \frac{x_3 - x_2}{v_2}. \tag{13.6}$$

All variables are known in the right two terms except x_3, thus these terms are rearranged to get,

$$x_3 = \frac{x_1 v_2 - x_2 v_1}{v_2 - v_1}. \tag{13.7}$$

All terms on the right are known, thus, the location of the collision, x_3, is determined. Once this is known, the time can be calculated by Equation (13.5). These steps are encapsulated in Code 13.2 through an example. Car A starts at $x = 0$ with a velocity of 3. Car B starts at $x = 25$ and moves to the left with a negative-valued velocity of -4. The collision occurs at $x = 10.7$ at a time of 3.57.

Code 13.2 Computing the location and time of the collision.

```
1   v1 = 3
2   v2 = -4
3   x1 = 0
4   x2 = 25
5   x3 = (x1*v2-x2*v1)/(v2-v1)
6   t = (x3-x1)/v1
7   print(x3,t)
8   10.714285714285714  3.571428571428571
```

13.3 ACCELERATED MOTION

In the previous sections, the objects were moving at a constant velocity. They didn't slow down or speed up. This section will consider the equations of motion for an object under the influence of acceleration. The change in velocity due to acceleration is defined as,

$$v_2 = v_1 + a\Delta t, \tag{13.8}$$

where a is the acceleration, and the units are meters per second squared, m/s^2. The displacement equation is,

$$\Delta x = x_2 - x_1 = v_1 \Delta t + \frac{1}{2} a \Delta t^2. \tag{13.9}$$

Equation (13.1) describes displacement for an object without acceleration, and Equation (13.9) describes motion of a particular with acceleration. Thus, if $a \to 0$ in Equation (13.9) then this equation must become Equation (13.1).

Code 13.3 shows a simple example in which the variables are established in line 1, and Equation (13.9) is executed in line 2.

Code 13.3 Displacement for an accelerating object.

```
1  x1=0; v1=1; a=3; t=0.3
2  x2 = x1 + v1*t + 0.5*a*t*t
3  print(x2)
4  0.435
```

Equation (13.9) can be rearranged to solve for other variables. For example, if the problem provides the initial position, the final position, the initial velocity, and the time, then the acceleration can be calculated by,

$$a = \frac{x_2 - x_1 - v_1 \Delta t}{\frac{1}{2} \Delta t^2}. \tag{13.10}$$

Given $x_1 = 0$, $x_2 = 0.435$, $v_1 = 1$, $\Delta t = 0.3$, Code 13.4 solves for the acceleration. The value is $3.0 \, \text{m/s}^2$.

Code 13.4 Solving for the value of the acceleration.

```
1  x1=0; x2=0.435; v1=1; t=0.3
2  a = (x2-x1-v1*t)/(0.5*t*t)
3  print(a)
4  3.000
```

Another example is to start with the values of position, velocity, and acceleration, and then compute the time. Equation (13.9) can be rearranged to be,

$$\frac{1}{2} a \Delta t^2 + v_1 \Delta t + (x_1 - x_2) = 0. \tag{13.11}$$

This is a second-order equation in the form of,

$$qx^2 + bx + c = 0, \tag{13.12}$$

where q, b, and c are coefficients. This equation can be solved by the quadratic equation,

$$x = \frac{-b \pm \sqrt{b^2 - 4qc}}{2q}. \tag{13.13}$$

The *numpy* module solves the quadratic equation through the **roots** function. An example is shown in Code 13.5. The function receives an argument which is a tuple. This tuple contains the coefficients in order from the highest power term to the lowest. This means that q is first since it is associated with x^2. The quadratic equation provides two answers and so does the **roots** function as seen in line 4.

Code 13.5 Solving the quadratic function.

```
x1=0; x2=0.435; v1=1; a=3
t1, t2 = np.roots((0.5*a, v1, x1-x2))
print(t1,t2)
-0.967    0.3
```

13.4 VERTICAL MOTION

For clarity, motion in the horizontal direction will be described by an x variable, and motion in the vertical direction will be described using a y variable. Movement to the right is a positive v_x, motion to the left is $-v_x$, motion upward is $+v_y$, and motion downward is $-v_y$. Thus the two equations describing accelerated motion in the vertical direction are:

$$v_{y2} = v_{y1} + a\Delta t, \tag{13.14}$$

and

$$y_2 = y_1 + v_{y1}\Delta t + \frac{1}{2}a\Delta t^2. \tag{13.15}$$

Both equations rely on the time variable, but some algebraic manipulation can create a new equation without the time variable. The process starts by rearranging Equation (13.14) to solve for t,

$$\Delta t = \frac{v_2 - v_1}{a}. \tag{13.16}$$

This is plugged into Equation (13.15) to get,

$$y_2 = y_1 + v_1\frac{v_{y2} - v_{y1}}{a} + \frac{1}{2}a\frac{v_{y2}^2 - 2v_{y1}v_{y2} + v_{y1}^2}{a^2}. \tag{13.17}$$

Algebraic manipulation reduces this equation to,

$$v_{y2}^2 = v_{y1}^2 + 2a(y_2 - y_1). \tag{13.18}$$

Equations (13.14), (13.15), and (13.18) are useful in finding the results for several simple scenarios.

13.4.1 Going Up

Consider a case in which an object is thrown upward with an initial velocity of $1.5\,\text{m/s}$ within a gravitational field of $-9.8\,\text{m/s}^2$. This object will go upward and slow to a stop before coming back to the ground. What is the height of the peak of flight, and how much time does it take to get there?

Gravity is an acceleration, and thus $a = g = -9.8\,\text{m/s}^2$. It has a negative sign because gravity is downward. The object is moving upward, so the velocity is positive, but it is slowing down because the acceleration is downward. The initial velocity is $v_{y1} = 1.5$, but the final velocity at the top of the peak is $v_{y2} = 0$. The object must come to a stop, even if it is for a very short time, before it starts coming back down. The time of flight is computed by Equation (13.16), and the script is shown in Code 13.6. Lines 1 through 3 set the variables, and line 4 performs the computation, which reveals the answer to be a tad more than $0.5\,\text{s}$. The distance traveled uses Equation (13.15), and the computation is performed in line 8.

Code 13.6 Computing the flight time for a upward motion.

```
1  g = -9.8
2  vy1 = 5
3  vy2 = 0
4  t = (vy2-vy1)/g
5  print('time', t)
6  time 0.5102040816326531
7
8  y2 = 0 + vy1* t + 0.5*g*t**2
9  print('distance',y2)
10 distance 1.2755102040816324
```

This situation is one which is a common experience. 1.3 meters is about 4 feet. Motion upward is the same as motion downward, and if a person where to drop an object from a height of four feet, then a half second of flight seems reasonable. Sometimes, verification of motion equations requires only a moment of thought.

13.4.2 Going Down

Motion upward and motion downward are similar. Without friction, a flight up to a peak takes the same amount of time as flight from that peak back to the ground. This point will be reiterated in the section on projectile flight. For now, the point is supported by use of the same equations as before. If an object were to be dropped from a height of 1.28 meters, then we expect the flight to be a tad more than a half second and that the velocity at the bottom will be about 5.

Lines 1 and 2 set the variables. Line 3 executes the equation, but the result is the square of the velocity. At this point, it is necessary to be careful of the sign of the values. To get the velocity, the square is computed, and Python will return a positive value. However, the correct answer could be negative. Furthermore, as this is the case, the computed value of the squared velocity is negative (line 5). Thus, the square root computation needs to use the absolute value of the result (line 7), and then the sign needs to be reinstated (line 14). The results (lines 12 and 17) agree with the upward problem in the previous section.

Code 13.7 Computing the flight for downward motion.

```
1  y1 = 1.28
2  vy1 = 0
3  vy2sq = vy1**2 + 2*(y2)*g
4  print('velocity squared ',vy2sq)
5  velocity squared   -24.999999999999996
6
7  vy2 = math.sqrt( abs(vy2sq ))
8  print('velocity ', vy2)
9  velocity  5.0
10
11 print('downward velocity', -vy2)
12 downward velocity -5.0
13
14 vy2 = -vy2
15 t = (vy2-vy1)/g
16 print('time', t)
17 time 0.5102040816326531
```

13.4.3   Going Up and Down

Consider a case in which an object is thrown upward ($v_{y1} = 5$) from the ground, reaches a peak, and then falls back to the ground. In this case, the initial height is 0 and the final height is 0. This can be obtained by tossing the object, or by just leaving it sit on the ground. Two possible answers should appear in the computation.

This problem is solved by Equation (13.13) and a modification of Code 13.5. The new script is shown in Code 13.8. Line 1 establishes the known values. Line 2 uses the **roots** function to solve for time via the quadratic equation. There are, indeed, two answers that are produced. The second is 0.0 which represents the case in which the object hasn't moved. The beginning and ending heights are 0. This is not the desired solution, but it is computationally a valid solution. The first answer is 1.02, which is the sum of the time of flights going up and coming down computed in the previous sections.

Since the upward and downward motions are similar, the time of flight is double the time of flight for either leg of the trip. This doubling occurs with the following caveats: the launching and landing heights are the same, there is no friction, and there is no other force being applied.

Code 13.8 Full time of flight.

```
1  x1=0;  x2=0;  v1=5;  a=-9.8
2  t1, t2 = np.roots((0.5*a, v1, x1-x2))
3  print(t1,t2)
4  1.0204081632653061 0.0
```

13.5   PROJECTILE MOTION

Projectile motion combines linear horizontal motion with accelerated vertical motion, which is depicted in Figure 13.3. The object is thrown at an angle from the ground, so it initially has both vertical and horizontal velocities. The computations benefit from the fact that the horizontal and vertical motions are independent of each other. The vertical motion does not affect the horizontal mechanics. Thus, predicting the motion of a projectile just uses the equations that were shown in the previous section. The horizontal motion uses the linear equations, and the vertical motions uses the acceleration equations.

Basic projectile motion is depicted in Figure 13.3. A snapshot of the ball at equally spaced time intervals is shown. The horizontal motion follows the description in Equation (13.1). In the horizontal direction the balls are equally spaced in distance, because the velocity is constant. The vertical motion follows Equation (13.9). In the vertical direction the balls are not equally spaced because the vertical velocity changes in time.

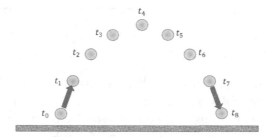

Figure 13.3: Basic projectile motion at evenly spaced intervals.

Consider the flight of Smiley in Figure 13.4. He launches at $y = 0$, with a given velocity v and launch angle θ. The quest is to find the horizontal distance traveled when Smiley lands at $y = 0$. In this example, the initial velocity is $v_1 = 40\,\text{m/s}$ and the launch angle (to the horizontal) is $\theta = 20°$.

Figure 13.4: Distance traveled through projectile motion.

This solution requires three steps:

1. Find the initial horizontal and vertical velocities,

2. Compute the time of flight, and

3. Compute the horizontal distance.

The first step is to find the vertical and horizontal components of the initial velocity vector. Figure 13.5 shows these components which are computed by,

$$v_x = v\cos(\theta)$$
$$v_y = v\sin(\theta)$$ (13.19)

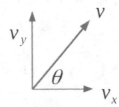

Figure 13.5: Vertical and horizontal components of the initial velocity.

These computations are shown in lines 5 and 6 in Code 13.9. The first three lines establishes the parameters. Python, like most other languages, uses radians for the angles instead of degrees. Line 4 converts the angle of 20° to radians. Lines 5 and 6 compute the initial velocities. In this example, $v_{x1} = 37.6\,\mathrm{m/s}$ and $v_{y1} = 13.7\,\mathrm{m/s}$.

Lines 10 through 12 confirm the velocities. The x and y components of the velocity also obey Pythagorean's theorem, and thus the sum of their squares should be the square to the total velocity. Since computers don't care if they provide the correct answer or not, it is prudent to confirm the computations when possible. Line 12 shows that the computed velocity does match the initial velocity.

The second step is to compute the time of flight. Since the horizontal and vertical velocities are independent, the vertical flight is the same as just throwing the object straight up in the air with an initial velocity of v_{y1}. This calculation was performed in Code 13.8 using different input parameters. Thus, this equation is replicated in line 14. As noted earlier, the computation will produce two answers, one of which is 0. Thus, line 15 selects the larger value, which is the time of flight. In this case, the flight lasts 2.8 seconds.

The third step is to use that time of flight to determine the horizontal distance traveled. Horizontal motion is described by Equation (13.1), which is rearranged to find the distance, given the velocity and the time. This is performed in line 19, and the distance is computed to be 105 m.

13.6 ENERGIES

Much of computations of kinematics is based on the energy of the object rather than computing distances and velocities. If the energies are known, then this other information comes quite easily.

Code 13.9 Determining where the projectile lands.

```
1   v0 = 40
2   angle = 20 # degrees
3   g = -9.8; y1 = y2 = 0
4   theta = np.radians( 20 )
5   vx1 = v0 * np.cos( theta )
6   vy1 = v0 * np.sin( theta )
7   print( 'Initial Velocities', vx1, vy1 )
8   Initial Velocities 37.58770483143634 13.680805733026748
9
10  w = np.sqrt( vx1**2 + vy1**2 )
11  print('w', w)
12  w 40.00000000000001
13
14  t1, t2 = np.roots( (0.5*g, vy1, y1-y2))
15  t = np.max((t1,t2))
16  print(t1,t2, t)
17  2.7920011700054586 0.0 2.7920011700054586
18
19  dx = vx1 * t
20  print('distance', dx)
21  distance 104.94491586719009
```

Energy is expressed in many forms, such as kinetic, potential, electrical, elastic, gravitational, rotational, chemical, and so on. For the case of describing motion in this chapter only two energies will be considered. For this reason, a moving ball will not experience friction, will not be rotating, will not deform, will not make a sound; it will only move in a direction.

The *kinetic energy* is used for an object in motion. It is based solely on the mass of the object and the velocity in which it is traveling. It is described as,

$$K = \frac{1}{2}mv^2, \tag{13.20}$$

where v is the velocity of the object. If the object is not moving, then $K = 0$.

The *potential energy* describes the energy stored up in the object. In electrical systems a battery can store energy, or in a fluid system energy is stored by containing water in a dam. For motion, the potential energy is based on the height of the object, and it is,

$$U = m \left| g \right| h, \tag{13.21}$$

where m is the mass of the object, g is the acceleration due to gravity, and h is the height of the object. Consider a 5 g object (about the weight of nickel) and drop it on Bob's bare toes from a height of 0.1 m. Bob won't mind. Now raise that same nickel to a height of 3 m, and repeat the experiment. Bob will not be happy about this part of the experiment. The same object experienced the same acceleration, but at the end of the experiment, more energy was imparted to Bob's toes when the object came from a greater height. The nickel had more potential energy when at a higher height.

Of course, the experiment could be repeated where the object is again dropped from a very short height, but this time the object as a mass of 2 kg. Again, a lot of energy will be imparted on Bob's toes, but this time the extra energy comes from the additional mass of the object. As a final experiment, Bob can be taken to the moon where a large object drops from a great height and lands on his toes, but since gravity is so small, he's back to being happy again.

The *total energy* is the sum all energies within a system. For the simple system of one object in motion, the total energy is,

$$E = U + K. \tag{13.22}$$

If the system had many objects then the total energy is the sum of the kinetic and potential energies of the individual objects.

$$E = \sum_i U_i + \sum K_i. \tag{13.23}$$

Consider a case of an electric toy car. At the beginning of the experiment, the car is not moving, but there is energy stored in its battery. It has potential energy but no kinetic energy. The switched is turned on and the car zips along its path. The battery is drained so the potential energy goes to 0, but the car is in motion, so there is kinetic energy. The potential energy was converted to kinetic energy. In the real world, the car eventually comes to a halt because there is also friction, which drains away the kinetic energy.

This example can be used to define some terms. If just the kinetic and potential energies are considered, then this would described and *open system*. At the beginning, the car had potential energy, thus the total energy was not 0. At the end, the car has stopped and the battery is drained. The car has 0 total energy. Energy was drained away from the system, thus it is an open system.

A *closed system* would include all parameters. When friction drains away the energy from the car it is converted to some other action, such as heat, sound or vibration. These are also entities which are described by energy. If the total energy also included theses other forms, then no energy actually escapes, it just gets converted to other forms. Hence, the total energy is not changed from its initial value.

The same philosophy is applied to a simple system of a falling object (Figure 13.6). In this case, there is no friction, rotation, vibrations, heat, etc. There is only potential and kinetic energy. The object is manually raised to a height of h (thus putting potential energy into the system). At this point in time, the total energy consists of only potential energy,

The object is released. At any point during the flight, the object has both potential and kinetic energy. The potential is being converted to kinetic, but the total energy remains unchanged. At the end of the flight, the object has no potential energy because $h = 0$, and so the total energy is solely the kinetic energy.

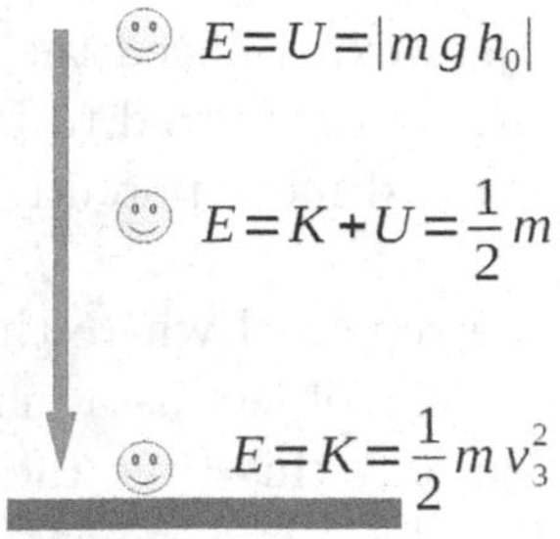

$$\ddot{\smile} \quad E = U = |m g h_0|$$

$$\ddot{\smile} \quad E = K + U = \frac{1}{2} m v_1^2 + |m g h_1|$$

$$\ddot{\smile} \quad E = K = \frac{1}{2} m v_3^2$$

Figure 13.6: The energies of a falling object.

The energy equations provide and easier method of computing some values. Given a mass m and gravity g. The object is raised to a height of h. What is it's velocity at the end of the flight? This could be calculated using the equations from the previous section, but it can also be calculated using the energy equation. At the top the total energy is $E = mgh$, and at the bottom the total energy is $E = \frac{1}{2}mv^2$. Conservation of energy states that these two total energies must be the same, thus,

$$mgh = \frac{1}{2}mv^2. \tag{13.24}$$

The equation is rearranged to solve for v,

$$v = \sqrt{2gh}. \tag{13.25}$$

This is a very easy equation to put into computer code. Furthermore, the mass cancels, so this equation applies to all objects.

Another example is to compute the velocity at the halfway point in the flight. Define that height as $h_1 = h_0/2$. What is the velocity at this point? The solution sets the total energies of the top height equal to the total energy at mid-height,

$$mgh_0 = mgh_1 + \frac{1}{2}mv^2, \tag{13.26}$$

which yields,

$$v = \sqrt{2g(h_0 - h_1)}. \tag{13.27}$$

It is interesting to note that this is a different form of Equation (13.18).

13.6.1 Example 1

As an example, consider an object with a mass $m = 1\,\mathrm{kg}$ starting at a height of $h_0 = 30\,\mathrm{m}$. The potential and total energy are computed in Code 13.10

The total energy is 294.0 at all positions in the flight. To test this, a random height is selected in line 1 of Code 13.11. The time of flight to this point is computed in line 2, and this is used in line 3 to compute the velocity. Example values are shown in line 5. Lines 6 and 7 computed the two energies, and the total is printed in line 9. The total energy is 294.0.

Code 13.10 The total energy at the beginning.

```
1  g = -9.8; m=1; h0 = 30
2  print( abs(m*g*h0) )
3  294.0
```

Code 13.11 The total energy in flight.

```
1  h1 = np.random.rand()*h0
2  t1 = np.sqrt((h1-h0)/(0.5*g))
3  v1 = -g*t1
4  print('hvt',h1,v1,t1)
5  hvt 17.057 15.927 1.625
6  U1 = abs(m*g*h1)
7  K1 = 0.5*m*v1**2
8  print( U1 + K1 )
9  294.0
```

The final computation is shown in Code 13.12. This is the object just before striking the ground. The height is 0, and the kinetic energy is the total energy. Using the same steps as in Code 13.11, the velocity and kinetic energy are computed. The total energy is 294.0.

Code 13.12 The total energy at the end of the flight.

```
1  h2 = 0
2  t2 = np.sqrt((h2-h0)/(0.5*g))
3  v2 = -g*t2
4  print('hvt',h2,v2,t2)
5  hvt 0 24.2487 2.474
6  print( 0.5*m*v2**2 )
7  294.0
```

13.6.2 Example 2

Consider the case shown in Figure 13.7 of a ball bouncing on the ground. Flight between bounces obeys frictionless projectile physics. However, the ball loses 10% of its kinetic energy at each bounce. When the ball bounces it deforms, it makes a sound, and it actually heats up a small amount. All of these losses of energy are bundled into the simple idea that at each bounce, 10% of the kinetic energy is lost.

This problem has several components. It has projectile flights, loss of energy, and some trigonometry. The initial data includes the mass m, the initial velocity v_0, the angle of the initial velocity θ, and the loss of kinetic energy at each bounce (10%).

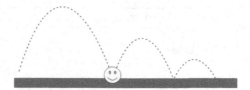

Figure 13.7: A bouncing object.

From that information, it is possible to find the locations of the bounces, the heights of each flight, and the elapsed time between the bounces.

One important change is the description of the angle. This is a reflection problem, and traditionally the angle of incidence and the angle of reflection is measured from a perpendicular to the surface rather than the surface itself, as shown in Figure 13.8. Furthermore, in a reflection problem, the angle of reflection is commonly the same as the angle of incidence. As seen in the figure, the two angles are the same, even though the incident and reflected velocities are not the same.

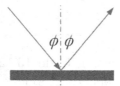

Figure 13.8: Angles of incidence and reflection.

With unequal velocities and equivalent angles, the following relationship is realized,

$$\tan(\phi) = \frac{v_{1x}}{v_{1y}} = \frac{v_{2x}}{v_{2y}}, \qquad (13.28)$$

where the subscript 1 represents the incoming velocities and 2 represents the outgoing.

The problem is established in Figure 13.9. The initial variables are: a mass of $m = 1\,\text{kg}$, the initial velocity of $v_1 = 25\,\text{m/s}$, and an angle of incidence of $\theta = 40°$. This example will compute several items:

- The peak h_1,

- The distance d_1,

- The velocity after the first bounce, and

- The height h_2.

Since the bounce affects the kinetic energy, the problem will be solved through the use of total energy rather than using the kinematics equations. At the beginning, the total energy is the kinetic energy, thus,

$$E = K_1 = \frac{1}{2}mv_1^2. \qquad (13.29)$$

Code 13.13 computes this total energy to be 312.5 J.

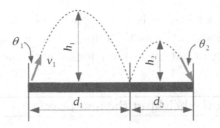

Figure 13.9: Components of the bounce.

Code 13.13 Calculating the time to the peak for the first flight.

```
1  m = 1; g = -9.8
2  v1 = 25
3  theta = np.radians( 40 )
4  K1 = 0.5 * m * v1**2
5  print('K1 = ', K1)
6  K1 =  312.5
```

To compute the time to peak, the vertical and horizontal components of the initial trajectory need to be known. Again, since this problem is abiding by convention, the angle is measured to the perpendicular, thus,

$$v_{y1} = v_1 \cos(\theta)$$
$$v_{x1} = v_1 \sin(\theta). \tag{13.30}$$

Code 13.14 performs the calculations to find the initial velocities. The horizontal velocity, v_x, will remain constant, but the vertical velocity, v_y, will start at v_{y1}, decrease until the object reaches a peak, and then become larger in the negative values as the object falls to the ground.

Code 13.14 Calculating the initial velocities.

```
1  vy1 = v1 * np.cos( theta )
2  vx1 = v1 * np.sin( theta )
3  print( 'vx1 = ', vx1, '.  vy1 = ', vy1)
4  vx1 =  16.06969024216348 .  vy1 =  19.151111077974452
```

The total energy at the peak, h_1, is the same as the total energy at launch, 312.5 J. The total energy at the peak has two components. There is a potential energy component because the object is at a height. There is also kinetic energy. While the object is not moving in the vertical direction, it is moving in the horizontal direction. So, the total energy at the top is,

$$E = \frac{1}{2}mv_{x1}^2 + m|g|h_1. \tag{13.31}$$

The only value which is not known is the height h_1. Code 13.15 shows the process. Line 1 sets the total energy to the value found in Code 13.13. Line 2 computes the kinetic energy by solving Equation (13.31) for h, and line 3 computes the height, which happens to be 18.7 m.

Code 13.15 Calculating the height of the first peak.

```
1  E = 312.5
2  K = 0.5 * m * vx1**2
3  h1 = (E-K)/abs(m * g )
4  print('h1 = ', h1)
5  h1 =   18.712502832699784
```

The distance, d_1, is determined by $d_1 = v_{x1}t_1$ where t_1 is the time of flight. This calculation was done in line 14 of Code 13.9. Code 13.16 computes the time in lines 2 and 3, and it calculates the distance in line 4. Both values are printed. The distance is $d_1 = 62.8$ m.

Code 13.16 Calculating the distance of the first flight.

```
1  g = -9.8; y1 = y2 = 0
2  t1, t2 = np.roots( (0.5*g, vy1, y1-y2))
3  t = np.max((t1,t2))
4  d1 = vx1 * t
5  print('time = ',t,'.  distance = ', d1)
6  time =   3.9083900159131533 .   distance =
       62.80661690128878
```

The flight path going into the bounce is similar to that of the initial launch. The angle of incidence is the same as the angle of launch (to the perpendicular), and the velocity coming into the bounce is the same as the launch velocity. Furthermore, the angle of incidence (going into the bounce) is the same as the angle of reflection (going out of the bounce). The bounce, though, does decrease the kinetic energy by 90%. Thus,

$$0.9\frac{1}{2}mv_2^2 = \frac{1}{2}mv_3^2, \tag{13.32}$$

where $v_2^2 = v_1^2$ is the incoming total velocity, and v_3 is the outgoing velocity. The 1/2 and mass cancel, thus,

$$v_2 = \sqrt{0.9}v_1. \tag{13.33}$$

Code 13.17 shows the computation. Line 1 executes the equation, and the result is the velocity $v_2 = 23.7$ m/s. This is less than the initial velocity of 25 m/s. Lines 5 and 6 find the vertical and horizontal components of the velocity.

With the components of the velocity known, the computation of h_2 replicates that of Code 13.15 with different inputs for the velocity. The result is that $h_2 = 16.8$ m.

Code 13.17 Calculating the velocity after the bounce.

```
1  v3 = np.sqrt( 0.9 ) * v1
2  print('v2 = ',v3)
3  v2 =   23.717082451262844
4
5  vy3 = v3 * np.cos( theta )
6  vx3 = v3 * np.sin( theta )
```

13.7 AIM POINT FOR A FALLING OBJECT

A famous problem in physics is a shot at a falling object, as shown in Figure 13.10. At time t_0, Smiley is attached to a horizontal bar at a distance h above the ground. One the left is a paintball gun which is aimed directly at Smiley. The horizontal distance from the paintball to Smiley is d. The angle from the horizontal of the gun is therefore,

$$\tan \theta = \frac{h}{d}. \tag{13.34}$$

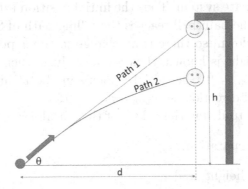

Figure 13.10: The *Shoot the Smiley Face* scheme.

If gravity did not exist, then the paintball would follow Path 1 and hit Smiley. However, gravity does exist and acts on all entities, including a paintball. Thus, the paintball follows projectile path named Path 2. The problem has one more wrinkle. At precisely the same time as the paintball is fired, Smiley drops from the post. Gravity acts on Smiley as well. At some time, t_1, Smiley is in a new position. The question is the following: Does the paintball hit Smiley?

Several steps are required to answer this question. These are:

1. Define the variables.

2. Point the gun at Smiley (compute the angle θ).

3. Decompose the velocity into horizontal and vertical components.

4. Compute the time required for the bullet to travel a horizontal distance of d.

5. Compute the height of the paintball at this time.

6. Compute the height of Smiley at this time.

7. Determine if the paintball hit Smiley.

8. Change the variables and run again.

13.7.1 Define the Variables

The first step is to define the variables, which initially sounds like an easy task. Perhaps the first rule of creating a simulation is that it is never as easy as it first appears. There are two objects (paintball and Smiley) which have an initial position and a final position. Furthermore, these objects are moving in two-dimensions. So, to keep it all straight, more subscripts are required. The paintball will be designated by a p and Smiley will be designated by an s. Thus, the initial position of the paintball is (x_{p0}, y_{p0}), and the final position of the paintball is (x_{p1}, y_{p1}). Likewise, the initial and final positions of Smiley are (x_{s0}, y_{s0}) and $(x_{s1}, ys1)$. Those variables define only the position. Variables are also needed for the velocities and accelerations in the problem.

The design of the problem defines some of these variables. The paintball starts at the origin of the coordinate system. Thus the initial position is $(x_{p0}, y_{p0}) = (0, 0)$. The final location is when the paintball reaches the falling path of Smiley. Thus, $x_{p1} = d$. Smiley drops straight down, so there is no change in the x position, $x_{s0} = x_{s1} = d$. The initial starting height is known, thus $y_{p0} = h$. Just when Smiley starts his fall, his velocity is 0, so $v_{ys0} = 0$ (the initial velocity in the y direction). Smiley never moves in the horizontal direction, so $v_{xs0} = v_{xs1} = 0$.

The user is allowed to define the values of the variables:

- d the horizontal separation,

- h Smiley's initial height, and

- v the initial velocity of the paintball.

The actual numerical values are not critical, as long as they are not ridiculous. For the use of examples, the values are chosen to be $d = 10\,\text{m}$, $h = 7\,\text{m}$, and $v = 80\,\text{m/s}$. This is easily accomplished as shown in Code 13.18.

Code 13.18 Setting the variables for Smiley.

```
1  d = 10.
2  h = 7.
3  v = 80.
```

13.7.2 Point the Gun

Step 2 is to point the gun at Smiley before he drops. Since h and d are known, the angle θ is computed by,

$$\theta = \tan^{-1}\left(\frac{h}{d}\right). \tag{13.35}$$

Code 13.19 performs this calculation, but once again there is a small complication. Python, like almost all other computer languages, use radians instead of degrees for the measurement of angle. The inverse-tangent (or arctangent) function is **atan** which is in the *math* module. Thus, line 1 imports the math module, and line 2 computes the angle **theta**. The result is **theta** in this case is 0.611 radians. The math module contains the **degrees** which converts radians to degrees. The gun angle is nearly at $35°$. The math module also contains the **radians** function which converts degrees to radians.

Code 13.19 Aiming the paintball gun.

```
1  import math
2  theta = math.atan(h/d)
3  print(theta, math.degrees(theta))
4  0.6107259643892086  34.99202019855866
```

13.7.3 Paintball Velocity

The velocity of the projectile was established as $v = 80\,\text{m/s}$. However, that value is at an angle θ as shown in Figure 13.11. Since the horizontal and vertical motions are independent, it is necessary to find the initial velocity in the x direction, x_{xp0} and the initial velocity in the y direction, v_{yp0}. The values of v is the hypotenuse of the triangle which has the symbol θ inside of it. Thus,

$$v_{xp0} = v\cos(\theta), \tag{13.36}$$

and

$$v_{yp0} = v\sin(\theta). \tag{13.37}$$

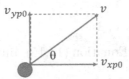

Figure 13.11: Decomposition of the velocity.

Lines 1 and 2 in Code 13.20 compute the two components of the velocity. These are printed in line 4. In this case, confirming the results is easy. The vertical and horizontal velocities form a right triangle and the hypotenuse is the original velocity *v*. The distance formula, using the vertical and horizontal velocities, should produce the initial value of *v*, and this is confirmed in lines 6 and 7. With confidence in the results, the simulation proceeds to the next step.

Code 13.20 Decomposing the initial projectile velocity.

```
1  vxp0 = v * math.cos( theta )
2  vyp0 = v * math.sin( theta )
3  print(vxp0, vyp0)
4  65.53855364152324  45.876987549066264
5
6  print( math.sqrt(vxp0**2 + vyp0**2))
7  80.0
```

13.7.4 Time of Flight

The next step is to compute the time of flight of the project. The flight ends when *x* position of the projectile reaches the *x* position of Smiley. In this case, only the horizontal movement of the projectile is required for the computation. Recall that the velocity in the horizontal direction is constant, so the time of flight of the projectile is simply Equation (13.2) with the names of the variables updated to fit Smiley's scenario,

$$t = \frac{x_{p0} - x_{p1}}{v_{xp0}} = \frac{d}{v_{xp0}}. \tag{13.38}$$

Code 13.21 computes the time of flight as $\Delta t = 0.15\,\text{s}$. This will be applied to both the projectile and Smiley. If the paintball hits Smiley then they both arrive at the same place at the same time. Thus, the flight time must be the same for both.

Code 13.21 Time of flight.

```
1  t = d/vxp0
2  print('Time of flight = ',t)
3  Time of flight =  0.1525819451966713
```

13.7.5 Heights of Objects

The height of the projectile uses Equation (13.15), but the variable names are updated to reflect this problem,

$$y_{p1} = 0 + v_{yp0}\Delta t + \frac{1}{2}g\Delta t^2. \tag{13.39}$$

Implementation is shown in Code 13.22 using Equation (13.15). As seen the computed height is $h = 6.88\,\text{m}$.

Smiley drops from a height of *h* for $\Delta t = 1.53\,\text{s}$. Equation (13.15) computes the

Code 13.22 Height of projectile at Δt.

```
1  g = -9.8
2  hp1 = 0
3  hp2 = hp1 + vyp0 * t + 0.5 * g * t**2
4  print('Projectile height = ',hp)
5  Projectile height =   6.885921875
```

distance traveled by the falling object. Code 13.23 computes Smiley's height at this time in line 2.

Code 13.23 Height of Smiley at Δt.

```
1  vsy1 = 0
2  ys1 = h
3  ys2 = ys1 + vsy1 * t + 0.5 * g * t**2
4  print('Smiley height = ',ys2)
5  Smiley height =   6.885921875
```

At time $\Delta t = 1.53$ s, both the projectile and Smiley are at a height of 6.86 m. They are at the same position at the same time, therefore they collide.

This computation can be run for other values of d, h, and/or v. The result will always be that the two objects collide. Of course, there are parameters which would compute the collision to have a negative height. This means that they collide beneath the horizon.

13.8 ROCKET TEST

The admirable goal of this simulation is to land a rocket on the surface of a planet without crashing. The rocket starts at a given height and succumbs to gravity. Left alone, the rocket would fall to the planet and crash at a great speed. The rocket does have a motor and enough fuel for five burns. If they are all used at the beginning, then the rocket would go up, run out of fuel, and then crash to the ground. In another scenario, the rocket is allowed to fall for a bit of time, then the rocket uses one of the burns to slow the descent. This process continues until the rocket touches the surface of the planet at a sufficiently small speed.

To land the rocket safely, the burns must be scheduled for the correct times during the flight. However, those times are not known. This simulation will thus have two phases. The first is to build the simulation, and the second is to use the simulation to find the correct times for the burns. Just to make the process more complicated, the rocket loses mass from each burn.

13.8.1 Creating the Simulation

The initial parameters are:

- h, the starting height,

- m_0, the initial mass of the rocket,

- k, the rate of mass loss during a burn,

- F, the force produced by one burn, and

- g, gravity.

Several equations are required for this simulation, most of which have been used earlier in this chapter. The position of a falling object is determined by,

$$y_2 = y_1 + v_1 \delta t + \frac{1}{2} g \delta t^2, \tag{13.40}$$

where y_1 and y_2 are the old and new positions, δt is the duration of time, v_1 is the velocity at the beginning of this time, and g is the acceleration due to gravity which must be negative. The equation for updating the velocity is,

$$v_2 = v_1 + g \delta t. \tag{13.41}$$

Acceleration is constant at g, except during the booster burn. Then it is $g + \frac{F}{m_1}$ where F is the force from the burn and m is the mass at the beginning of the burn. During the booster burn, the mass decays by

$$m_2 = m_1 - k \delta t, \tag{13.42}$$

where k is a constant.

Code 13.24 shows the **Init** function which initializes the values. The initial height is 1000, the initial mass is 15,000, and the value of gravity is -2. The value must be negative in order for the rocket to fall. The `time` is the current time of the simulation which starts at 0, and `dt` is the time step used in the simulation. This simulation will compute new values at time steps of 0.1 s. The value of the force is produced for a burn of the rocket motor.

Code 13.25 computes the new values for the acceleration, the velocity, and the position after a single time step. The inputs are the gravity, the current position, the current velocity, the additional acceleration, and the time step duration. The variable `aplus` is the additional acceleration created during a burn. If the rocket is free-falling, then `aplus` = 0, and the only acceleration is due to gravity. The total acceleration is computed in line 3. This is used to compute the new velocity (line 4) and the new position (line 5). These new values are returned in line 6.

Code 13.26 shows the **Burn** function which computes the contribution to the acceleration during a burn and the new mass. The inputs are the current time, the current mass, the force created during a burn, the mass decay constant, and a list of burns. Each burn is signified by two values: the starting time and the duration. Thus, the list of burns is a list of five tuples, each with two values. For example, `burn = [ (10,2), (15,2), (20,3), (30,3), (35,3)]` indicates that the first burn starts at t = 10 and lasts for 2 seconds.

Code 13.24 Initializing the values.

```
1   # lander.py
2   def InitLander():
3       y1 = 1000
4       m1 = 15000
5       g = -2
6       v1 = 0
7       time = 0.0
8       dt = 0.1
9       force = 50000
10      k = 100
11      return y1, v1, m1, g, time, dt, force, k
```

Code 13.25 Computing the new values after a single iteration.

```
1   # lander.py
2   def Iterate(g, y1, v1, aplus, dt):
3       accel = g + aplus
4       v2 = v1 + accel * dt
5       y2 = y1 + v1*dt + 0.5*accel * dt**2
6       return y2, v2, accel
```

Code 13.26 Computing values during a burn.

```
1   # lander.py
2   def Burn( time, m1, force, k, burns ):
3       aplus = 0
4       for t1, d in burns:
5           if t1 < time < t1 + d:
6               aplus = force/m1
7               m1 = m1 - k
8               break
9       return aplus, m1
```

The value of `aplus` is an additional acceleration created by a burn. Its default value is 0, which means that the rocket motor is turned off. In lines 4 and 5, the function determines if the current time is inside of a burn window. In order for this to be `True`, the current time must be more than the start time of a burn and less than that start time plus the duration time. If this is `True`, then the rocket motor is on.

Newton's famous equation relating force, mass, and acceleration is,

$$F = ma. \tag{13.43}$$

In this simulation, the acceleration is computed in line 6, where `force` is the force produced by the motor. This burn is lasting for only a small amount of time (the chosen value is 0.1 seconds). After this portion of the burn, the mass is reduced as in line 7. Line 8 is used to prevent searching for possible burn windows if one has been found. The **Burn** function returns the additional acceleration and the new mass.

Code 13.27 shows the **RunLander** function which runs the simulation. It receives the initial values created by **InitLander** and the list of burns. Line 3 unpacks the initial values, line 4 creates three new lists that will capture the computed values after each iteration, and line 5 sets the ok flag to `True`. When the rocket has reached the ground, this flag will be set to `False` and the iterations will stop.

Code 13.27 Running the lander simulation.

```
# lander.py
def RunLander( initvals, burns ):
    y1, v1, m1, g, time, dt, force, k = initvals
    vs, ys, acs = [],[],[]
    ok = True
    while ok:
        aplus, m1 = Burn(time, m1, force, k, burns)
        y2, v2, accel = Iterate( g, y1, v1, aplus, dt)
        vs.append( v2 ); ys.append(y2)
        acs.append(accel)
        if m1 < 1000 or y2 <= 0:
            ok = False
        y1, v1 = y2, v2
        time += dt
    return ys, vs, acs
```

The iterations begin in line 6. Line 7 determines values if the current iteration is within a burn window. Line 8 computes the new values for position, velocity, and acceleration. Lines 9 and 10 appends these newly computed values to the archival lists. Line 11 considers the stopping conditions. If the mass of the rocket has fallen below a certain value, then it is out of fuel, and there is no reason to proceed because a crash is eminent. If the new position is less than 0, then the rocket as hit the ground. If either of these conditions are met, then ok = False and the simulation will soon come to an end. Lines 13 and 14 prepare values for the next iteration. The list containing computed values is returned to the user.

This function does not determine if the landing was successful. A successful landing is when the rocket reaches the ground with a small velocity, which is a threshold set by the user. For example, if the threshold were 5, then when y2 < 0, the velocity must be less than 5, otherwise the rocket is considered to have crashed.

Finally, the **PlotLander** function in Code 13.28 creates plots of the computed values. These values are scaled so they can be seen on the same graph. The position values are divided by 100, and the velocity values are divided by 5. (Jupyter users will need to use line 3.)

Code 13.28 Plotting the results.

```
1  # lander.py
2  import matplotlib.pyplot as plt
3  %matplotlib inline
4  def PlotLander( ys, vs, acs ):
5      ys1 = np.array( ys )/100.
6      vs1 = np.array( vs )/5.
7      plt.plot(np.zeros(len(ys1)))
8      plt.plot(vs1)
9      plt.plot(ys1)
10     plt.plot(acs)
11     plt.show()
```

Code 13.29 shows a single trial, where the burn values were generated without any forethought. The result is shown in Figure 13.12. The horizontal axis corresponds to time. The smoothly decaying line corresponds to the vertical position, and these values have been divided by 100 so they would fit on this graph. The simulation ended because the rocket did reach the ground, and as seen this curve does end at $y = 0$. The curve with the five vertical thrusts is the acceleration. It is at a value of -2 (the default gravity value for this planet) except during the burn windows. As seen, during the duration of the burn, the acceleration increase.

Code 13.29 A single trial of the rocket lander.

```
1  initvals = lander.InitLander()
2  burns = [ (10,2), (15,2), (20,3), (30,3), (35,3)]
3  ys, vs, acs = lander.RunLander( initvals, burns )
4  lander.PlotLander( ys, vs, acs)
```

The zigzag line corresponds to the velocity of the rocket. It is initially 0, but gravity increases the (negative) velocity. During the burns, the velocity increases. The rocket has successfully landed if this value is below some threshold at the end of the simulation. The plotted values are the original values divided by 5. A believable

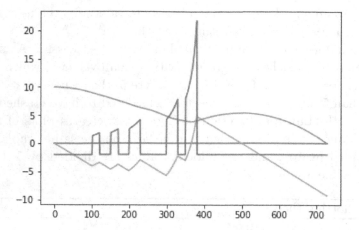

Figure 13.12: The first attempt, showing the position, velocity, and acceleration.

threshold would be that the absolute value of the velocity is less than 5, which means it would have to be between +1 and −1 on this graph. As seen, the final velocity was far away from that threshold, and thus, this rocket crashed. This is not a surprise since the burn values were chosen without any knowledge of how they would affect the outcome.

13.8.2 Finding Correct Parameters

Picking burn values out of thin air is not a good way to find parameters that will land the rocket without crashing. Thus, an automation is needed to find plausible values. A solution is possible. The values `burns = [(4.9761, 0.37088), (19.120, 1.2720), (26.150, 2.4516), (29.103, 4.2291), (34.31, 3.504)]` produce the results shown in Figure 13.13. The final velocity is -3.96 which is below the crash threshold.

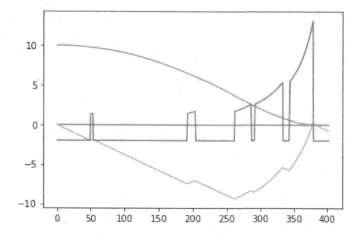

Figure 13.13: A successful attempt.

A simple, but computationally hoggish, method of finding input parameters which will lead to a safe rocket landing is to try random values for the inputs and then run the simulation. This method is easy to write, but is quite unintelligent. Better methods would perhaps select input parameters based on previous results. That is a more involved approach and will not be considered here.

Code 13.30 shows the **ManyTrials** function which considers many trials of random input burns. The inputs are N which is the number of trials, and gamma which is the threshold for a safe landing.

Code 13.30 Running many trials attempting to find valid input parameters.

```python
# lander.py
def ManyTrials(N = 10, gamma = 5):
    goodburns = []
    for n in range( N ):
        burns = []
        for i in range( 5 ):
            a = 35 * np.random.random()
            b = 5 * np.random.random()
            burns.append( (a,b) )
        initvals = InitLander()
        ys, vs, acs = RunLander( initvals, burns )
        if abs(vs[-1]) < gamma:
            goodburns.append( burns )
    return goodburns
```

Line 3 creates the goodburns list which will capture any burn sequence which produced a safe landing. A burn is created in the loop starting on line 6. It creates 5 burn sequences. Each one has a random starting point generated in line 7, and a random duration created in line 8. These burns will not be in sequence, but that doesn't matter as the **Burn** function does not need the burns to be sorted. These burns may also overlap as one burn may still be ongoing when another is scheduled to start. The program will just treat this as one continuous burn.

The default value for the number of trials is N = 10, but this number is far too low. Code 13.31 shows a case in which 100,000 trials were considered. On a laptop, this calculation required 90 seconds. Of the 100,000 trials, 14 led to a successful landing. The first was used to re-run the simulation and create a plot, which is shown in Figure 13.14.

The values for the burns are printed. The first burn starts at 19.0 seconds and lasts for 1.6 seconds. Even though it is the last in the list, it is the first burn in the sequence. The second burn starts at 5.6 s, and the third starts at 27.8 s. Yet the second burn lasts 4.3 s which goes past the beginning of the third burn. In fact, the third burn finishes before the second one does. These two burns are combined to form one which starts at 25.5 s and lasts until 29.9 s

---

Code 13.31 Finding and running a good trial.

```
1  goodburns = lander.ManyTrials(100000,5)
2  print(len(goodburns))
3  14
4
5  initvals = lander.InitLander()
6  ys, vs, acs = lander.RunLander( initvals, goodburns[0] )
7  lander.PlotLander( ys, vs, acs)
8
9  print(goodburns[0])
10   [(31.599719013412123, 1.9699025411046263),
        (25.642625682268516, 4.329796028688244),
        (27.831731814389407, 1.6558932545859055),
        (33.10511518886529, 4.253408813000507),
11  (19.014909104265197, 1.6118603761152923)]
```

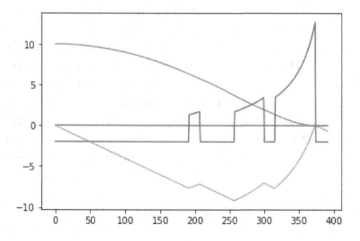

Figure 13.14: A successfully identified safe burn.

The next question, which will remain unanswered here, is if the safe landing values create a predictable pattern. Analysis of the burns exceeds the scope of this chapter, but does pose some interesting questions.

13.9 SUMMARY

This chapter began with implementation of linear motion equations. After these, the chapter reviewed accelerated motion, and applied that to a few simple cases. These naturally evolved into projectile motion, and again Python scripts were used to calculate the outcomes. The measure of motion, both potential and kinetic, provide insights and avenues for easier computations. This chapter reviewed the pertinent energy equations and demonstrated that total energy is conserved.

Two examples were then explored. The first was an aim-point problem, in which a projectile is shot directly at an object hanging in the air. Both objects are subject to gravity, and the Python scripts showed that the projectile strikes the object independent of the initial values. The second example attempted to land a rocket subject to gravity by using a series of motor engagements to provide acceleration which opposed gravity. Several trials were run to find the correct combination of rocket motor burns that landed the rocket safely.

PROBLEMS

1. Derive Equation (13.18) from Equation (13.14) and Equation (13.15). Show your steps.

2. Given and object that moved a distance of $d = 2.4$ m for $t = 9.2$ seconds at a constant velocity. Write a Python script that computes this velocity and prints the result to the console.

3. Given an object that moved at a constant velocity $v = 8.2$ m/s for $t = 23.2$ seconds. How far did it travel?

4. An object initially at rest moving accelerates ($a = 3.5 \, \text{m/s}^2$) for 4 seconds. How far did it go?

5. An object starts with a velocity of 1.5 m/s, accelerates for 4 seconds with a rate of $1.9 \, \text{m/s}^2$. What is the final velocity?

6. An object drops in a gravitational for a distance of 10 m. How much time did it take to make this flight?

7. An object is thrown downward with an initial velocity of $v = 3$ m/s in a gravitational field. After 3 seconds, how far has it traveled?

8. An object is launched from a platform that is 1.5 m high at an angle of $35°$ with a velocity of 4.5 m/s. What is the horizontal distance traveled when it reaches the ground (height is 0)?

9. A 2 kg object is launched from a platform that is 1.5 m high at an angle of 35° with a velocity of 4.5 m/s. Write a Python script that computes the total energy at launch and the total energy at the peak of flight.

10. A 2 kg object is thrown downward at an initial velocity of 1.2 m/s from a height of 11 m. Write a Python script to compute the total energy at the beginning of the flight and at the end of the flight.

11. Repeat the paintball/Smiley test using $v = 100$, height $= 25$, distance $= 35$, and gravity $= -5$. What is the height where the paintball hits Smiley?

12. Repeat the paintball/Smiley test using the original parameters in the text. Except in this experiment, aim the paintball gun at a height halfway between Smiley and the ground. When the paintball reaches Smiley's vertical path, is it still halfway between Smiley and the ground?

13. Repeat the rocket lander simulation using $g = -9.8$. The gravity is too much for the current rocket motor. Double the rocket motor. Find at least one solution that lands the rocket safely. Run the simulation and create the charts of position, velocity, and acceleration.

14. Repeat the rocket lander simulation with four of the burns being (4,2), (12,2), (20,2), (30,2). Find a fifth, non-overlapping burn that lands the rocket safely. Run the simulation and create the charts of position, velocity, and acceleration. Print the final values for y and v.

## CHAPTER 14

Oscillations

A N OSCILLATING object moves back and forth. Without friction, this motion would never cease. There are many examples of oscillating objects of which two are highlighted in this chapter. The first is a spring which compresses and stretches. The second is a pendulum which swings back and forth.

14.1   SPRING THEORY

Figure 14.1 shows a simple spring attached to a wall on the left and attached to a mass on the right. To simplify computations, the spring has no mass and no friction. The block mass also does not have any friction when moving and is not subject to gravity. Basically, once released the mass will move back and forth forever.

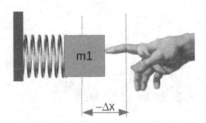

Figure 14.1: A compressed spring.

Each spring has a stiffness which is characterized by a spring constant k. In reality, the spring constant isn't constant. It changes with the stretch of the spring, but such realization complicates computations, so reality will be ignored here. A stiff spring has a large k, and a weak spring has a small k. When the spring is in its *rest state* (not compressed and not stretched) the mass is as a position x. For the computations, the displacement is measured from this position. The displacement, Δx, is not measured from the wall.

In this figure, Michelangelo pushes on the spring, thus compressing it. This action requires force, and thus potential energy is stored in the compressed spring. If he was to remove his finger, then the mass would move to the right, converting potential energy into kinetic energy. The force of compressing (or stretching) a spring is,

$$F = -k\Delta x, \tag{14.1}$$

DOI: 10.1201/9781003226581-14

where Δx is the deviation from the rest position $x = 0$. In this case, when the spring is compressed then $\Delta x < 0$. This equation has a negative sign, indicating that the force opposes the displacement. Thus, the force is always acting on the mass to move it back to the rest state. The potential energy is,

$$U = \frac{1}{2}k\Delta x^2. \tag{14.2}$$

Figure 14.2 shows three stages of motion. The spring is compressed in Figure 14.2a which stores potential energy. When the mass if freed to move, the potential energy creates a force which accelerates the mass. Now, the mass is in motion and thus has kinetic energy. In Figure 14.2b the mass has reached the rest position. The phrase "rest position" only refers to the position. The spring is not stretched or compressed, but it is moving. Thus, the kinetic energy is the total energy. Figure 14.2c shows the spring extended, and at this point, the mass stops moving. Once again the total energy is the potential energy. At any point, the total energy is conserved,

$$E = U + K = \frac{1}{2}k\Delta x^2 + \frac{1}{2}mv^2. \tag{14.3}$$

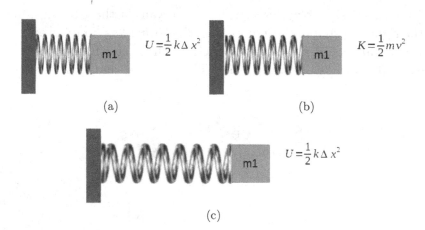

Figure 14.2: (a) The spring is compressed which stores potential energy. (b) The spring is not compressed, but it is moving and therefore has kinetic energy. (c) The spring is extended and again has potential energy.

Newton's Law and Equation (14.1) define the acceleration as,

$$a = \frac{-k\Delta x}{m}. \tag{14.4}$$

14.2 SPRING SIMULATION

In a simulation, the position of the mass will be calculated at equally spaced time intervals Δt. The state of the system (location and velocity) at time t are used to calculate the state of the system at time $t + \Delta t$. The motion of a mass under the influence of acceleration (see Equation (13.9)) is described slightly differently here,

$$x[t + \Delta t] = x[t] + v[t]\Delta t + \frac{1}{2}a[t]\Delta t^2. \tag{14.5}$$

Here the $x[t]$ is the position at time t, the $v[t]$ is the velocity at time t, and the $a[t]$, is the acceleration at time t. The $x[t + \Delta t]$ is the position at a later time.

The velocity is calculated by,

$$v[t + \Delta t] = v[t] + a[t]. \tag{14.6}$$

The Python scripts for these equations are straightforward. The user has the values of $x[t]$, $v[t]$, and k. Code 14.1 shows the script to calculate the next value of $v[t + \Delta t]$ and $x[t + \Delta t]$. The variables with the number 1 are for the previous values, and the variables with the number 2 are for the new state values.

Code 14.1 Computing the state of the spring for one iteration.

```
1  a = -k * x1 / m
2  v2 = v1 + a * dt
3  x2 = x1 + v1 * dt + 0.5 * a * dt**2
```

Code 14.2 shows the implementation of the spring equations. Lines 3 through 8 are the constants defined by the user. These can be changed to simulate different systems. The iterations begin in line 9, and this simulation will be run for 200 time steps. Lines 10 through 12 perform the computations from Code 14.1. Lines 13 and 14 prepare for the next iteration as the newly computed values are converted to the old values.

Code 14.2 The **Spring** function.

```
1   # spring.py
2   def Spring():
3       k = 0.5 # spring constant
4       x = 0.5 # initial stretch
5       m = 1 # mass
6       v1 = 0 # initial velocity
7       dt = 0.1 # time step
8       x1 = x
9       for i in range( 200 ):
10          a = -k * x1 / m
11          v2 = v1 + a * dt
12          x2 = x1 + v1 * dt + 0.5 * a * dt * dt
13          v1 = v2
14          x1 = x2
15          print( i, x2 )
```

Code 14.3 shows the x position for different times steps. The initial stretch of the spring was established in line 4 of Code 14.2 as 0.5. The expected results is that the force will drive the mass back towards $x = 0$. The lowering values in Code 14.3 shows that this is the case.

Code 14.3 The values from the first few iterations.

```
Spring()
0  0.49875
1  0.49500312500000004
2  0.48877186718750004
3  0.4800811718945313
4  0.4689683440038575
5  0.4554828923234377
6  0.43968631255219964
7  0.4216518097687725
8  0.40146396167954296
9  0.3792183241616926
10  0.3550209809292391
```

The results are plotted in the Figure 14.3. The horizontal axis is associated with time and the vertical axis is associated with the x position of the mass. At the beginning the mass is at $x = 0.5$, and as time progresses the mass moves towards $x = 0$. It passes through that point and the spring compresses until the mass reaches $x = -0.5$.

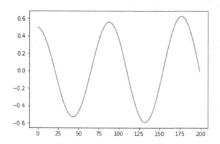

Figure 14.3: Oscillations of the mass on a spring.

However, something has gone wrong. In this system, there is no friction and no external forces acting on the mass during the oscillations. Thus, the mass should oscillate between $\Delta x = -0.5$ and $\Delta x = +0.5$ forever. The chart tells a different story as the peaks of the oscillations are increasing. The peaks go beyond $x = \pm 0.5$.

The equations are valid. The Python script is not in error. What has gone wrong with the simulation?

14.3 CORRECTED SIMULATION

The cause of the problem stems from the conversion of the simulation to a *digital* computer. The equations used are not designed for discrete time steps, but instead are valid for an object smoothly changing in time.

Consider one single time step as shown in Figure 14.4. There are two times, t_1 and t_2, separated by the time step Δt. The thick line is the force from $F = -k\Delta x$. During this time, the mass is moving, thus Δx is changing, thus the force is changing. The acceleration is directly related to the force, $F = ma$, so as the force increases so does the acceleration. However, the Python script over the same time period uses line 10 in Code 14.3. This computes the value of the acceleration and uses this value for the entire time step. In the code, the acceleration and the force do not change over the time step. So, instead of being a slanted line as shown in Figure 14.4, the force in the simulation is a straight line (as shown by the dashed line).

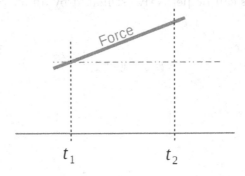

Figure 14.4: Calculation of the force.

The force in the simulation is not the same as the force in the physics equation solely because the simulation is digitized. The physics equations describe a system which is continuous in time, but the Python script describes a system which has discrete time steps. Figure 14.5 shows the actual force as a curved line and the calculated force as a stepped line. Near $y = 0$, the simulation does not produce much error as the curved line tends to bisect the stepped line. The error is the area between the two plots, and the amount above and below the curve is about equal. At both the top and bottom peaks, the calculated force does not emulate the actual force. Thus, there are losses in accuracy that accumulate.

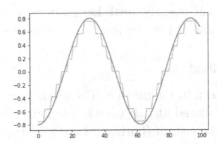

Figure 14.5: The error in the force over a cycle.

This type of problem is not unique to this spring simulation. This is a common problem in creating a simulation of a continuous system. Investment in improving this type of calculation can be important to a variety of applications. The most accurate approach would be to use non-discrete mathematics – calculus, which will be discussed in Chapter 15. So, two other discrete methods are reviewed here, which are more accurate than the original calculations, but still have a small amount of error.

14.3.1 Average Acceleration

Define F_1 as the force at time t_1 and the F_2 as the force at time t_2. If the slanted force line is exactly linear then the force can be replaced by an average force as shown in Figure 14.6. The amount of area under each line (between t_1 and t_2) is the same, and thus, this is a good replacement. However, as seen in Figure 14.5, not all segments between two time steps can be perfectly estimated by an average line, so some error is still expected.

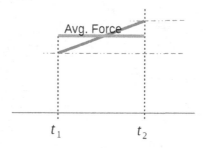

Figure 14.6: Calculation of the average force.

The modified function is **Spring2** shown in Code 14.4, which adds a few lines inside of the for loop. Lines 11 and 13 calculate the acceleration, velocity, and position for time t_1. These lines are the same as in the previous function. In order to calculate the average acceleration, it is necessary to estimate the acceleration for time t_2. This requires knowledge of new position and acceleration. This is done in line 14. Line 15 computes the average of the two accelerations. From this the new position and location can be more accurately computed, in lines 16 and 17.

The output of this function is shown in Figure 14.7. As seen the peaks are very close to 0.5 and −0.5, which is the desired result. This computation is not perfect, and over a large number of iterations, the peak height decays. After 1,000,000 iterations the peak height is only about 0.1, when it was supposed to remain at 0.5.

14.3.2 The Leapfrog Method

The *leapfrog method* is shown in Figure 14.8. The alteration to the original simulation is that the velocity is calculated at half time steps. During the interval between two time steps, the force is still constant (horizontal line), and for the part of motion away from the extremes, this simulation produces a result similar to Figure 14.6. However, at the extreme positions (positive and negative peaks in Figure 14.5), this leapfrog

Code 14.4 The **Spring2** function.

```
1   # spring.py
2   def Spring2():
3       xx = []
4       k = 0.5 # spring constant
5       x = 0.5 # initial stretch
6       m = 1 # mass
7       v1 = 0 # initial velocity
8       dt = 0.1 # time step
9       x1 = x
10      for i in range( 200 ):
11          a1 = -k * x1 / m
12          v2 = v1 + a1 * dt
13          x2 = x1 + v1 * dt + 0.5 * a1 * dt * dt
14          a2 = -k * x2/m
15          a = (a1+a2)/2
16          v2 = v1 + a *dt
17          x2 = x1 + v1 * dt + 0.5 * a * dt * dt
18          v1 = v2
19          x1 = x2
20          xx.append(x2)
21      return xx
```

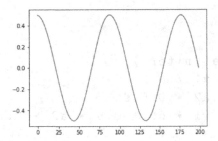

Figure 14.7: Oscillations of the mass on a spring with the correction.

method produces better results. An error is still expected, but it should be less than the averaging method.

The function **Spring** is modified to create **Leapfrog** which is shown in Code 14.5. The changes are inside of the for loop. Line 11 is unchanged from **Spring**. Line 12 changes the time step to 0.5 * dt which is the intermediate time point. Line 13 is unchanged and uses the full time step. After 1,000,000 iterations the peak of the oscillation is still nearly 0.5. For a spring, the leapfrog method provides a good simulation with errors becoming significant after millions of oscillations.

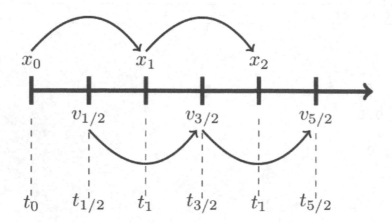

Figure 14.8: The leapfrog method [8].

Code 14.5 The **Leapfrog** function.

```
1   # spring.py
2   def Leapfrog(niter=200):
3       xx = []
4       k = 0.5 # spring constant
5       x = 0.5 # initial stretch
6       m = 1 # mass
7       v1 = 0 # initial velocity
8       dt = 0.1 # time step
9       x1 = x
10      for i in range( niter ):
11          a2 = -k * x1 / m
12          v2 = v1 + a2 * 0.5*dt
13          x2 = x1 + v1 * dt + 0.5 * a2 * dt * dt
14          v1 = v2
15          x1 = x2
16          xx.append(x2)
```

14.4 THE PENDULUM

A pendulum (Figure 14.9) consists of a mass on the end of a massless rod which swings back and forth without friction. The rod is of length L and is initially displaced by an angle θ. The derivation of the following equations uses the small angle approximation, $\theta \approx \sin\theta$, which holds true for small angles (measured in radians).

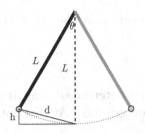

Figure 14.9: The pendulum.

The period of a pendulum is the amount of time required to go from one extreme, to the other, and then back again. For this small angle approximation this is,

$$T = 2\pi\sqrt{\frac{L}{g}}. \tag{14.7}$$

Notably, the mass is absent from this equation. This means that a 1 kg mass will swing with the same period as a 2 kg mass. A grandfather's clock keeps time by swinging a pendulum. Adjustment of the accuracy of the pendulum is achieved my moving the heavy mass up or down, but it is not adjusted by changing the amount of mass. A large mass is used to lessen the effects of friction and to lessen the effect of the mass of the rod of the pendulum.

Another variable not present in the equation is the initial starting angle. Thus, if Carol's pendulum had an initial angle of $\theta = 1°$ and an identical Bob's pendulum had a starting angle of $\theta = 2°$, they would have the same period. Bob's pendulum has a bigger swing, but uses the same amount of time to complete a full swing.

Usually, the position of a mass is measured by (x, y) coordinates. An alternative is to use the polar coordinate system which represents a point in space as (r, θ) where r is the radius and θ is the angle, and the top of the rod is at position (0,0). In this case, the radius is the length L, and it is constant. So, the position can be identified by the single variable θ. At any time t, the angle is,

$$\theta_t = \theta_0 \cos(\omega t), \tag{14.8}$$

where θ_0 is the initial angle and $\omega = \sqrt{L/g}$.

When the pendulum is at its extreme angle, the mass has a height of h, which also means that is has potential energy. When the pendulum is at its nadir, $h = 0$, and thus the only energy it has is kinetic. Through this point the velocity is at a maximum, and it can be determined by using the conservation of energy.

The potential energy is

$$E = U = mgh, \tag{14.9}$$

but h is not yet known.

Consider the triangle $L - L - d$ (from Figure 14.9). The length L and angle θ are known. Using the law of cosines, the length d is calculated as,

$$d = \sqrt{2L^2 - 2L^2\cos(\theta)} = L\sqrt{2 - 2\cos(\theta)}. \tag{14.10}$$

The value of h is determined from the right triangle it makes with d. Using Pythagorean's theorem,

$$h = \frac{d}{\sqrt{2}}. \tag{14.11}$$

Now, the value of U can be determined, and from that the speed of the mass through the nadir can also be determined. At this point the total energy is $E = K = \frac{1}{2}mv^2$, and thus,

$$v = \sqrt{\frac{2K}{m}}. \tag{14.12}$$

An example is shown in Code 14.6. Given a rather large pendulum with a mass of 50 kg, a rod length of 4 m, and a starting angle of 10°, what is the velocity through the nadir? Lines 4 through 6 compute the potential energy at the extreme, and line 8 uses that to compute the velocity, which is $v = 3.1$ m/s.

Code 14.6 Computing the velocity through the nadir.

```
1   m = 50
2   L = 4
3   g = -9.8
4   theta = np.radians(10)
5   d = np.sqrt(2*L**2 - 2*L*L*np.cos(theta))
6   h = d/np.sqrt(2)
7   U = m* abs(g)*h
8   K = U
9   v = np.sqrt(2*K/m)
10  print('v = ',v)
11  v =   3.108590635819263
```

The rather large pendulum is a useful example. Before the days of computer simulations, engineers had to determine the strength of posts that held roadway rail guards. The test is shown in Figure 14.10 in which the post is embedded in the ground. A tall pendulum with a heavy mass was hoisted to a starting angle θ. In doing this, the mass now has potential energy.

With gleeful expectations, the researchers released the mass, allowing it to swing toward the unsuspecting post. At the nadir, all potential energy was converted to kinetic energy. Then the mass smashed through the post, but this collision absorbed some of the energy from the pendulum. The destruction of the post required a certain amount of energy, and that energy was subtracted from the pendulum's energy. However, the pendulum's energy far exceed the post's subtraction, thus, the mass continued on its journey rising to a height, h_2. At this point, the total energy is once again only potential energy. The difference in the starting height, h_1, and the ending height, h_2, is directly related to the loss of energy,

$$E_{loss} = \Delta U = U_1 - U_1 = mg(h_1 - h_2). \tag{14.13}$$

While modern computer simulations do offer the ability to perform thousands upon thousands of inexpensive tests, they do lack a certain entertainment value available to the previous generation of researchers.

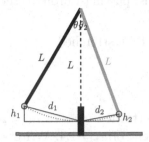

Figure 14.10: A long, heavy pendulum breaks through the post embedded in the ground. The loss of energy in the pendulum is the amount of energy required to break the post.

14.5 SUMMARY

Oscillatory motion moves a mass back and forth in a repeated pattern. Without friction or external forces, the oscillations would continue on forever, without change. The equations governing for a spring and a pendulum have been reviewed here.

From these equations, it is possible to predict the position and period of the oscillating mass. However, the first simulation did not perform as predicted. The oscillations increased in size. This was caused by the conversion of a continuous time event into a digital simulation. Thus, the model had to be modified to correct for this disparity.

Two options were proposed which can provide fairly accurate simulations over thousands of cycles. While these adjustments did not provide the perfect simulation, the results would be close enough to the correct values such that the simulation would be useful.

EXERCISES

1. Given a spring that is attached to a wall on the left, and it is attached to a free moving mass on the right. The spring constant is $k = 4$, and the spring is compressed $x = 2$. What is the force due to this compression, and which direction is the force pointing?

2. Select the choice that best answers: Where is the velocity the greatest?

    (a) When the spring is fully compressed.
    (b) When the spring is passing through the middle (not compressed or stretched)
    (c) When the spring is fully stretched
    (d) Both 1 and 3
    (e) None of the above

3. Select the choice that best answers: Where is the acceleration the greatest?

    (a) When the spring is fully compressed.

    (b) When the spring is passing through the middle (not compressed or stretched)

    (c) When the spring is fully stretched

    (d) Both 1 and 3

    (e) None of the above

4. Given a spring with an attached mass of $m = 2$, a spring constant of $k = 10$, and an initial displacement of $x = 1.4$. Write a Python script that computes the potential energy before the mass is allowed to oscillate.

5. Given $k = 10$, $x = 1$, $m = 1$. Use the leapfrog method to created plots for x and v for 200 iterations. Double the value of k and run again and create a new graph. Write a few sentences on how this affected the system.

6. Use $m = 2$, a spring constant of $k = 10$, and an initial displacement of $x = 1.4$. Write a Python script that uses the conservation of energy to compute the velocity of the mass as it passes through the location were the spring is not stretched or compressed.

7. The presence of friction decays the velocity of the mass. Use the leapfrog method and $m = 2$, a spring constant of $k = 10$, and an initial displacement of $x = 1.4$. Modify this method to reduce the velocity by 1% in each iteration. Run the simulation for 200 iterations. Show the plot of the position and velocity.

8. In this simulation, the spring weakens over time. Modify the Leapfrog method so that k loses 1% of its value in each iteration. Run for 400 iterations with $m = 2$, a spring constant of $k = 10$, and an initial displacement of $x = 1.4$. Plot x and v. In a few sentences, interpret the information provided by the chart.

9. Modify the leapfrog method so that the spring is vertical in a gravitational field. The gravitational field will decrease the acceleration by a value of 1.0 for each iteration. Use $k = 10$, $x = 1$, $m = 2$. Run the simulation for 200 iterations. Write a few sentences that interprets the results.

## CHAPTER 15

Coupled Differential Equations

EQUATION (13.1) relates a change in position, the change in time, and the velocity. It can be rewritten as,

$$v = \frac{\Delta x}{\Delta t}.$$ (15.1)

This is a quantized approach in which both Δx and Δt have small but finite values. Arising from this was errors in the simulation, as seen in the spring example. Two solutions were considered: the averaging method and the leapfrog method. While these did provide better results, they did not provide perfect results. The problem remains with attempting to simulate a smoothly changing action with discrete time steps.

The mathematical solution is to employ calculus, which can calculate actions of smoothly changing entities. In this approach, time steps are reduced to an infinitesimal amount. The notation changes slightly to,

$$v = \frac{\mathrm{d}x}{\mathrm{d}t},$$ (15.2)

where the Δ is replaced by an upright d. The right side of the equation still represents the change in position with respect to the change in time. However, the changes are now infinitesimally small.

This chapter will demonstrate methods by which these types of equations are realized in Python. While this chapter uses calculus equations, the manipulation and derivations of those equations are beyond the scope of this text. The purpose of this chapter is to correctly implement the given calculus equations into Python script.

15.1 SIMPLE EXAMPLE

Consider the equation

$$\frac{\mathrm{d}y}{\mathrm{d}t} = -ky(t).$$ (15.3)

DOI: 10.1201/9781003226581-15

The k is a constant, and the term $y(t)$ means that the variable y is a function of time. At this point, this seems obvious, but later equations with multiple independent variables will be considered, so this notation is adopted here.

The left side of the equation is the change in position y with respect to the change in t. The right side of the equation has the position variable y, and thus, the change in position is related to the current position. The right side of the equation has a negative sign, thus, the change in position pulls the object toward the origin (where $y = 0$). If the position were positive (to the right of $y = 0$) then the change in position is negative (to the left). Likewise, if the position were negative (to the left of $y = 0$) then the change in position is positive (to the right).

In order to solve this problem, an initial condition needs to be defined. In this case, the position y needs to be known at a specific time. So, for the sake of an example, the position is 5 at time $t = 0$. This is written as,

$$y(0) = 5. \tag{15.4}$$

The goal is to calculate the position y for several instances of t. The first step in the computation is to define the time points in which the program will return the position. Equally spaced time points can be created using the **linspace** function, shown in Code 15.1. This function receives three arguments which are the first value, the last value, and the number of values. This latter argument is optional. The result is a list of values, equally spaced, where the first value is 0 and the last value is 10. However, values do not have to be equally spaced. Any set of sorted time values can be used in this calculation.

Code 15.1 Creating equally spaced values.

```
1  tsteps = np.linspace(0,10,20)
2  print(len(tsteps),tsteps)
3  20 [ 0.           0.52631579   1.05263158   1.57894737
       2.10526316   2.63157895
4    3.15789474   3.68421053   4.21052632   4.73684211
       5.26315789   5.78947368
5    6.31578947   6.84210526   7.36842105   7.89473684
       8.42105263   8.94736842
6    9.47368421  10.                       ]
```

The next step is to create a function that models Equation (15.3). Code 15.2 shows this script. The function **model1** receives two arguments. The first is the initial conditions, of which there is only one for this problem. The second is the time locations where the values of y will be calculated. Line 2 sets the constant, and line 3 is the equation. The output of the equation is the left side of Equation (15.3).

Code 15.3 runs the model. Line 2 initializes the starting position to 5. In more complicated systems, there will be more than one initial condition, thus, the initial conditions are stored in a list or tuple, even if there is just one initial condition. Line 3 defines the time points where the computation will be made. Line 4 calls the

Code 15.2 Defining the **model** function.

```
1  def model1(y,t):
2      k = 0.1
3      dydt = -k*y
4      return dydt
```

odeint which stands for ordinary differential equation integrator. It receives three arguments. The first is the **model** function, the second is the initial values, and the third is the time steps. These latter two arguments are used as arguments to the **model** function.

Code 15.3 Calculating the values at given time locations.

```
1  import scipy.integrate as si
2  inits = [5]
3  ts = np.linspace(0, 20)
4  ys = si.odeint(model1, inits, ts)
```

The results for two experiments using two different values of k are shown in Figure 15.1. The upper curve uses $k = 0.1$ and the lower curve uses $k = 0.5$. As k increases, the curve obtains a larger elbow. However, as time increases (moving to the right), both functions approach a value of 0. The object starts at $y = 5$ and moves toward $y = 0$. The strength of the movement is governed by k and the position. Thus, as the object gets closer to $y = 0$ the change in the position becomes smaller.

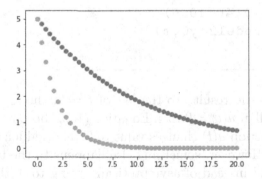

Figure 15.1: The solutions for two values of k.

It is important to note the differences in output of the two functions used here. The function **model** returns the derivative of the variable, dy/dt, whereas the function **odeint** returns values of the variable y at specific time locations.

15.2 TWO VARIABLES DEPENDENT ON TIME

The equation,

$$\frac{dy}{dt} = -y(t) + u(t), \tag{15.5}$$

has two variables dependent on time, $y(t)$ and $u(t)$. However, it computes the change in time for only one of them, dy/dt. The second function is a step function defined as,

$$u(t) = \begin{cases} 0 & t < 10 \\ 2 & t \geq 10 \end{cases}. \tag{15.6}$$

The initial condition is set to $y(0) = 5$. Code 15.4 shows the process. The function **model2** has the same type of inputs as **model1**. Lines 2 through 5 implement the function $u(t)$, and line 6 computes the value for the derivative. The initial condition is set in line 9. Line 10 creates the time points for the desired values of $y(t)$, and line 11 calls the **odeint** function.

Code 15.4 Calculating values for Equation (15.5).

```
1  def model2(y, t ):
2      if t<10:
3          u = 0
4      else:
5          u = 2
6      dydt = (-y+u)/5
7      return dydt
8
9  y0 = [5]
10 t = np.linspace(0,40,1000)
11 ys = si.odeint(model2,y0,t)
12 plt.plot(t,ys)
```

Figure 15.2 shows the result. To the left of $t = 2$, the function behaves as the previous case. After all, if $u(t) = 0$ then Equation (15.5) becomes Equation (15.3). At $t = 2$, though, the function $u(t)$ changes value to 2. The sudden change is responsible for the discontinuity. However, something else happens to the process. The shape of the curve changes, and instead of asymptotically going to 0, the function now goes to 2 as $t \to \infty$. In this part of the process, the $y(t) \to 0$ just as it did in the previous example. However, the value of 2 is added to it, so the system must go to 2 instead of 0 as time progresses.

15.3 DEPENDENT EQUATIONS

Consider the equation,

$$\frac{dy}{dx} + y = x. \tag{15.7}$$

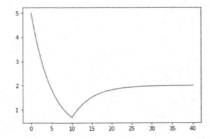

Figure 15.2: The solution for the two variable case.

In this case, y is not a function of time, but it is a function of another variable used in the equation, x. The change in y relies on the value of y and x. The change in y goes up as the value of x increases, and it goes down as the value of y increases. Commonly, a variable x is a spatial coordinate, thus y is dependent on a location, whereas in the previous example it was dependent on time. This is an important distinction, as the later graph shows the behavior of y related to its location in x. In this graph, the horizontal axis is not time.

Code 15.5 shows the process. The function **model3** replicates Equation (15.7). The inputs to the function are still the initial conditions and the values of the dependent variable for which the computations are returned. In this case, the initial condition is $y[0] = 1$, and the points in the list **xs** are the x points at equally spaced points.

Code 15.5 Calculating values for Equation (15.7).

```
def model3(y,x):
    dydx = x-y
    return dydx

xs = np.linspace(0,5,20)
y0 = 1
ys = si.odeint(model3,y0,xs)
plt.plot(xs,ys)
```

The result is shown in Figure 15.3. For the most part, as x increases (horizontal axis), so does the value of y (vertical axis). However, for values of $x < 1$, the behavior is different. The behavior in this area is dominated by the value if y as x is small.

This equation is simple enough to confirm through mathematical analysis. It has a *closed form* solution which means that it is possible to find a function $y(x)$ that satisfies this equation. A calculus-based analysis would derive this solution, but for this chapter, the solution is just provided. It is,

$$y(x) = x - 1 + 2e^{-x}. \tag{15.8}$$

To confirm the Python solution, this equation is plugged back into Equation (15.7).

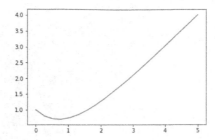

Figure 15.3: The solution for the dependent variable case.

The value of $y(x)$ can be plugged directly into the right side of the equation. For the left side, the derivative of $y(x)$ is needed. Again, the answer is provided without derivation,

$$\frac{dy}{dx} = 1 - 2e^{-x}. \tag{15.9}$$

This equation is plugged into the left side of Equation (15.7), and an intermediate result is,

$$1 - 2e^{-x} + x - 1 + 2e^{-x} = x. \tag{15.10}$$

Algebraic manipulation will eliminate all terms. Everything cancels, which means that the right side was equal to the left side. This also means that Equation (15.8) is a solution to Equation (15.7). Thus, a plot of Equation (15.8) should be exactly the same as the plot created by the Python script. This is the case, so the Python computation is confirmed to be true.

15.4 COUPLED EQUATIONS

So far, the systems described have relied on a single equation, and the analysis tracked the behavior of one variable. This section adds a complexity in that two variables are dependent on each other and are allowed to change their values. This type of simulation is not limited to just two variables, but can extend into a large number, thus approaching realistic systems.

The *predator-prey* model describes the population of two types of animals, where one is the prey and the other is the predator. The system is described by,

$$\frac{dx}{dt} = x(a - by) \tag{15.11}$$

and

$$\frac{dy}{dt} = -y(c - dx). \tag{15.12}$$

The variable x is the population of the prey, for example, H. G. Well's Eloi, and the variable y is the population of the predator Morlocks. These two equations adjust the populations as time progresses based on the current populations. Four coefficients control the behavior.

- The coefficient a is multiplied by x and affects the change in x. If a is large, then the current population of Eloi strongly affects the change in the population of the Eloi. Thus, a is associated with Eloi breeding – more Eloi beget more Eloi.

- The coefficient b is multiplied by both x and y. The term xy is large if both populations are large. However, it affects the change in a negative manner (minus sign). Thus, if there are plenty of Morlock and plenty of Eloi, then the Morlocks eat more Eloi. Thus, b controls the feeding.

- The coefficient c affects the change in the predator population. It is multiplied by the current population of predators, but negatively so. More predators leads to a decrease in the predator population. If there are many Morlocks and few Eloi, then the Morlocks starve.

- The coefficient d is multiplied by xy and positively affects the predator population. If there are large populations of both, then the Morlocks have plenty to eat, and their population will grow.

In the first example, all coefficients are set to 1 (line 1 Code 15.6). The function **predpreymodel** computes both equations (lines 3 and 4). Line 5 puts the results for both equations in a tuple to be returned by the function. Line 8 sets the each coefficient to 1. Since there are two equations, there are two initial conditions (line 9). These are the initial populations for the prey and the predator. While this simulation uses small numbers, they could be interpreted as hundreds of each entity. For example, the initial population is 1.5×100. The input to **predpreymodel** is still the initial conditions and the locations of the computations. However, the initial conditions are now two values in a tuple. These are unpacked in line 2.

Code 15.6 The predator-prey model.

```
1  def predpreymodel(xy,t):
2      x, y = xy # separate the x and y
3      dxdt = x*(a-b*y)
4      dydt = -y*(c-d*x)
5      answ = (dxdt, dydt)
6      return answ
7
8  a,b,c,d = 1,1,1,1
9  x0y0 = (1.5, 1.0)
10 t = np.linspace(0, 12, 100)
11 dx_dy = si.odeint(predpreymodel, x0y0, t)
12 prey = dx_dy[:,0]
13 predator = dx_dy[:,1]
14 plt.plot(t,prey)
15 plt.plot(t,predator, marker='+')
```

The results are unpacked in lines 12 through 15, and the plot is shown in Figure 15.4a. The prey population starts with a value of 1.5 and as time progresses this value falls. At the beginning, there is a large population of prey, so there is plenty to eat, which will inevitably lead to a decrease in the prey population. The predator population starts with a value of 1.0, and as there is plenty to eat, their numbers increase.

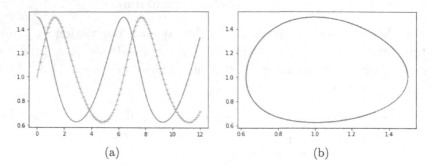

(a)   (b)

Figure 15.4: (a) The curve starting with the largest value is the population of the prey, and the other curve represents the predator. (b) The limit cycle for the predator-prey.

However, the prey population continues to decrease until feeding becomes difficult. Thus, predator population falls, but in doing so, eventually there are so few predators that the prey population can increase again. With the current coefficient values and initial conditions, a stable situation is created. The populations oscillate.

The longer term oscillations are studied through a *limit cycle*, as show in Figure 15.4b. Code 15.7 shows the single command which plots the predator population versus the prey population. The vertical axis is the predator population, and the horizontal axis is the prey population. The simulation starts at point (1.5, 1.0) from the initial conditions, which is the right-most point on the curve.

Code 15.7 The limit cycle for the predator-prey model.

```
1  plt.plot(prey,predator)
```

At the beginning of the simulation, the population of the prey decreases (moves to the left) and the predator population increases (moves up). Thus, the movement along the curve is counter-clockwise. At the top of the curve, the predator population is at its maximum. At the left-most point, the prey population is at its minimum and the predator population is decreasing. The processing continues in a counter-clockwise motion.

This graph shows several cycles of the predator-prey population, and notably the curve is exactly the same through each rotation. Thus, the one predator-prey cycle is precisely the same as its predecessors. This is called a limit cycle, because the cycle has limits. The process stays with the confines of this thin oval shape.

In other simulations, the cycles might be somewhat similar to their predecessors. In these cases, the movement around the cycle will not be exactly the same for each cycle. Thus, the curve will gain some width instead of being a thin line. However, the max and min values will still exist, and thus there is still limits to the cycle. If the coefficients in the simulation where such that the prey population goes to 0 and then the predator population also becomes extinct due to starvation, then the movement of the curve would spiral into the point (0,0). If the size of the populations were to explode, the curve would spiral outward without bounds.

Changing the values of the coefficients changes the behavior of the system. For example, if $a = 2$, then the population of the prey would breed at a faster rate. The result is shown in Figure 15.5a. Again the population of the prey starts at 1.5, but as the process starts, it increases. The population of the predator starts at 1.0 and it also increases to a larger peak value. If the Eloi breed faster, then the Morlocks will have more to eat, and thus their population increases. While the change in the coefficient does affect the values of the curves, it did not destroy the cyclical nature of the system.

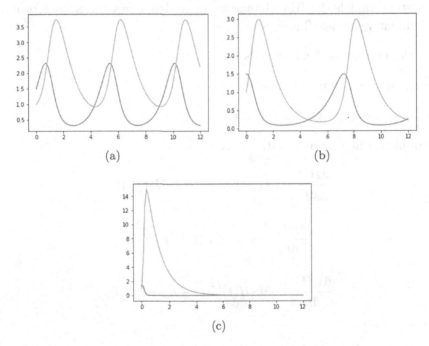

Figure 15.5: (a) The populations in the predator-prey model with $a = 2$. (b) The populations in the predator-prey model with $d = 2$. (c) The populations in the predator-prey model with $d = 10$.

Consider another case, in which $d = 2$. This means that the Morlock population increases faster if both populations are large. The result is shown in Figure 15.5b. Again, the peak values have changed, but the distance between the peaks has also increased. The cyclical nature exists, but more time is needed to complete a cycle. The reason is that Morlocks are breeding faster, and thus decimating the Eloi population. It takes longer for the prey to recover.

Increasing this value too much, $d = 10$, will destroy the system as shown in Figure 15.5c. The Morlock population rises too much, and they eat all of the Eloi. The prey population goes to 0 and remains since there are no Eloi to breed. Without the prey, the predator population decays to 0 as well. At the end, both populations are gone, and only the birds and trees remain.

15.5   HIV SIMULATION

A coupled system can have a large number of variables which are related to each other. For those cases, an equation is needed for each changing variable. Biological systems are notorious for having a large number of variables. However, in this chapter, fascination with large systems is replace by simpler systems which are easier to describe. The example chosen is from

> http://apmonitor.com/pdc/index.php/Main/SimulateHIV .

This system models the HIV (human immunodeficiency virus) as a problem with three dependent variables. These are:

- H – the number of healthy cells.

- I – the number of infected cells.

- V – the number of virus cells.

The coupled, differential equations are:

$$\frac{\mathrm{d}H(t)}{\mathrm{d}t} = k_1 - k_2 H(t) - k_3 H(t) V(t), \tag{15.13}$$

$$\frac{\mathrm{d}I(t)}{\mathrm{d}t} = k_3 H(t) V(t) - k_4 I(t), \tag{15.14}$$

and

$$\frac{\mathrm{d}V(t)}{\mathrm{d}t} = -k_3 H(t) V(t) - k_5 + k_6 I(t). \tag{15.15}$$

The coefficients are:

- k1 : The number new healthy cells which are created each year,

- k2 : The rate of death of the healthy cells,

- k3 : The rate in which healthy cells are converted to infected cells,

- k4 : The death rate of infected cells,

- k5 : The death rate of the virus, and

- k6 : The production rate of the virus from infected cell.

The implementation follows the same process. A model function is created which receives two inputs: a tuple of initial conditions and the time steps where the values are calculated. Code 15.8 shows the **HIVmodel** which performs these calculations. Line 2 establishes the values of all the six coefficients. Line 3 unpacks the initial condition values. The term k3*H*V appears three times in the equations. To be efficient in computing, it is calculated only once and the value is stored as the variable p, as seen in line 4. Lines 5 through 7 compute the right hand side of the equations, and the results are packed into a tuple for a return.

Code 15.8 The **HIVmodel** function.

```
1  def HIVmodel( hiv0, t ):
2      k1,k2,k3,k4,k5,k6 = 1e5, 0.1, 2e-7, 0.5, 5, 100
3      H,I,V = hiv0
4      p = k3*H*V
5      dhdt = k1 - k2*H - p
6      didt = p - k4*I
7      dvdt = -p - k5*V + k6*I
8      answ = (dhdt, didt, dvdt )
9      return answ
```

The program is run by Code 15.9. Line 1 establishes the initial population as 1,000,000 healthy cells, 0 infected cells, and only 100 virus cells. The population of healthy cells is negatively affected by the presence of infected or virus cells as seen in Equation (15.13). However, if both populations are small, then the large value of k_1 will increase this population.

The initial infected population is 0, but the presence of both healthy and virus cells will increase the population of the infected cells as per Equation (15.14). Finally, Equation (15.15) governs the virus population. Initially, there are 100 virus cells, but they increase if there are many infected cells, but decrease if there are many healthy and virus cells.

Code 15.9 Running the **HIVmodel** function.

```
1  hiv0 = [1000000,0,100]
2  t = np.linspace(0,15,100)
3  vals = si.odeint(HIVmodel,hiv0,t)
4  hvals = vals[:,0]
5  ivals = vals[:,1]
6  vvals = vals[:,2]
```

Line 2 in Code 15.9 establishes the time points for the calculations, and line 3 performs the computations. The last three lines unpack the data for plotting, as shown in Figure 15.6a. Time moves from left to right, and the vertical axis is on a scale of 1×10^7. At $t = 0$ the health cells have a count of 1,000,000, and the other two variables are close to 0. The details of the action, though, are difficult to see on this scale. An alternative is to use a log-scale for the vertical axis (Figure 15.6b). The plotting commands are shown in Code 15.10.

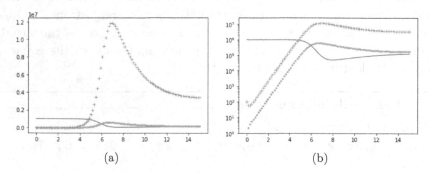

(a)   (b)

Figure 15.6: (a) The results of the HIV model. (b) The results of the HIV model on a log scale.

Code 15.10 Commands to make the semi-log plots.

```
1  plt.semilogy(t,hvals)
2  plt.semilogy(t,ivals,'.')
3  plt.semilogy(t,vvals,'+')
```

The results are shown in Figure 15.6b. This is the same data as the previous plot except that the vertical axis is on a log scale. The healthy cells (line) start at 1,000,000 (or 10^6) cells. This population holds steady until about $t = 4$, then it drops, however, it does slowly rise again.

The curve with the dots represents the infected cells. The population begins at 0 and steadily rises. Once the population of healthy cells falls, the number of infected cells declines, but does not approach 0. Finally, with the + markers represents the virus cells. This population starts at 100, but rises to 10,000,000 before slightly decaying. Even though the healthy cells did make a recovery, the virus and infected cells did not go away.

15.6 THE SPRING MODEL

In the previous chapter, two force equations were used in describing the motion of a spring. The first was Newton's equation $F = ma$ and the second was a restoring force for a spring $F = -k\Delta x$. In actuality, the force equation contains terms for multiple scenarios, some of which are set to 0 in trivial cases. The complete force equation is,

$$F_e = ma - bv - kx, \tag{15.16}$$

where F_e is the applied force, ma is the Newtonian force from acceleration, bv is the friction force, and kx is the restoring force. This equation allows for situations beyond the simple spring model. Consideration will start with modeling a spring more accurately than before. Then the model with mature by adding friction and external forces.

15.6.1 The Spring Model without Friction

Consider a system in which an object is allowed to oscillate but there is no external friction ($b = 0$) and no external force ($F_e = 0$). Equation (15.16) reduces to

$$ma = kx, \qquad (15.17)$$

which is Equation (14.4).

Recall that the acceleration is the change in velocity over the change in time. In derivative notation, this is,

$$a = \frac{\mathrm{d}v}{\mathrm{d}t}, \qquad (15.18)$$

Plugging this equation into Equation (15.17) yields,

$$\frac{\mathrm{d}v}{\mathrm{d}t} = -k\frac{x}{m}. \qquad (15.19)$$

This is a differential equation, but there is a catch. The velocity is the change in position over the change in time,

$$v = \frac{\mathrm{d}x}{\mathrm{d}t}. \qquad (15.20)$$

So, the two sides of Equation (15.19) are connected in a manner not seen in the previous examples, relating the second derivative to its variable, as in

$$\frac{\mathrm{d}v}{\mathrm{d}t} = \frac{\mathrm{d}}{\mathrm{d}t}v = \frac{\mathrm{d}}{\mathrm{d}t}\left(\frac{\mathrm{d}x}{\mathrm{d}t}\right) = \frac{\mathrm{d}^2x}{\mathrm{d}t^2} = -k\frac{x}{m}. \qquad (15.21)$$

To handle this situation, the inputs and outputs of the model equation are modified, and Code 15.11 shows the **SpringModel** function. Like the other models, it receives two inputs. The second is the time steps for which the calculations will be made. The first, a tuple named **xv**, contains the input parameters. Since the velocity relies on the position, the first item in the tuple is the position. Since the acceleration relies on the velocity, the second item in the tuple is the velocity.

The model returns the derivatives of the input variables according to given equations. Thus, the output is a tuple which contains the derivative of the position (the velocity) and the derivative of the velocity (the acceleration). This function is different in that one of the outputs (velocity) is used as an input to the next iteration.

Line 3 computes the derivative as per Equation (15.19). The derivative of the position, though, does not need to be calculated since it is also an input parameter. Line 2 separates the inputs into the variables x and v, and the v is then sent as an output since it is the derivative of the position.

The results are shown in Figure 15.7 which plots the position and the velocity at the chosen time points. The plot with the points represents the position, and the other plot is the velocity. Both oscillate, but they are out of phase. The velocity

Code 15.11 The spring model function.

```
1  def SpringModel(xv,t):
2      x,v = xv
3      dvdt = -k/m*x
4      answ = (v,dvdt)
5      return answ
6
7  k = 5; m=1
8  ts = np.linspace(0,20,100)
9  xv = (1,0)
10 xs = si.odeint(SpringModel,xv,ts)
```

is 0 when the displacement is greatest. In a spring, the displacement is greatest when the spring is stretched or compressed, and these are the locations when the motion changes direction. The velocity must be zero for an instance during this change. A digital spring model was considered in a previous chapter, and the errors in the calculation were noted. In this section, the same spring system is considered by differential equations. This approach best models the frictionless spring system.

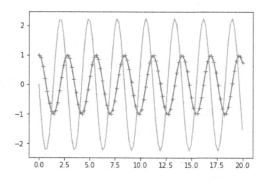

Figure 15.7: A frictionless spring.

15.6.2 The Spring Model with Friction

In the previous system, the oscillations will go on forever because there is no friction. Reality is different, and there is always some sort of friction. Thus, $bv \neq 0$ and the oscillations will become smaller over time. The force equation becomes,

$$0 = m\frac{dv}{dt} - bv - kx. \tag{15.22}$$

The alterations to the code are shown in Code 15.12. Line 3 includes the friction term in the equation, and the variable b is set to 0.3. The result is shown in Figure 15.8a. The amplitude for both the displacement and velocity decay, but the frequency of oscillation remains unchanged. This object goes through several oscillations as the amplitude goes to zero.

Code 15.12 The spring model function with friction.

```
1  def SpringModel(xv,t):
2      x,v = xv
3      dvdt = -b*v/m - k/m*x
4      answ = (v,dvdt)
5      return answ
6
7  k = 5; m=1; b=0.3
8  ts = np.linspace(0,20,100)
9  xv = (1,0)
10 xs = si.odeint(SpringModel,xv,ts)
```

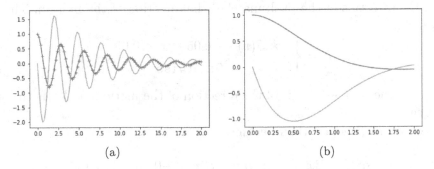

(a)   (b)

Figure 15.8: (a) Amplitudes decay for a system with friction. (b) The motion of a critically damped oscillator.

A system that loses its magnitude over several oscillations is an *underdamped* system. A *critically damped* system is one in which the amplitude of the displacement goes to zero in one cycle. An *overdamped* system is one in which the friction is too great to allow the displacement to return to zero. These are governed by the coefficient b. For example, if $b = 3$ then the system become critically damped as shown in Figure 15.8b. The displacement decays to a value close to 0. The velocity becomes negatively large and then decays to 0 as well.

15.6.3 A Forced System

The final consideration is to add an external force to the system. Figure 15.9 shows a simple case in which a mass is attached to a spring. A magnet is placed at the location where the displacement is 0. It pushes the mass in the direction of its motion. Basically, the mass gets a little push every time is moves through the center position.

The equation of motion is,

$$F = m\frac{\mathrm{d}^2x}{\mathrm{d}t^2} - b\frac{\mathrm{d}x}{\mathrm{d}t} - kx, \tag{15.23}$$

which now adds the external force, F, on the left. The conditions for this example

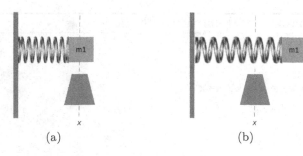

Figure 15.9: (a) When the mass is over the magnet it experiences a force in the direction of its motion. (b) When the mass is away from the magnet, no external force is applied.

are that when the displacement is $-0.05 < x < 0.05$ then the mass gets a push. However, the direction of the push matches the direction of the motion. The force is thus defined as,

$$F = \begin{cases} \gamma \times S(v) & -0.05 < x < 0.05 \\ 0 & \texttt{Otherwise} \end{cases}, \qquad (15.24)$$

where $S(v)$ is the sign, $+1$ or -1, of the direction of the motion, and γ is the strength of the force.

The equation of motion then becomes,

$$m\frac{\mathrm{d}^2 x}{\mathrm{d}t^2} - b\frac{\mathrm{d}x}{\mathrm{d}t} - kx = \begin{cases} \gamma \times S(v) & -0.05 < x < 0.05 \\ 0 & \texttt{Otherwise} \end{cases}. \qquad (15.25)$$

While the equation does have a complicated look, it's implementation is not significantly more difficult than the other models. The **DampledForcedOsc** function realizes the damped, forced harmonic oscillator model (Code 15.13). The major changes are in lines 3 through 6 which uses an `if` statement to select between the two states of the applied force. In this case, lines 3 and 4, the force is applied if the displacement is within a range.

Figure 15.10a shows the response. This system was balanced such that the addition force counters the friction. Had the force been smaller, then the amplitudes of oscillation would decrease. Had the force been larger than the oscillations would continue to increase. Also noticeable is that the oscillations are no longer a perfect sine wave. The force suddenly turns on and off. Such a discontinuity of the force is reflected by the sudden inflections in the save to the oscillations.

Line 14 of Code 15.13 plots the limit cycle of the system (Figure 15.10b). The limit cycle does now have two kinks in the curve as the force turns on in either direction of the oscillation. The curve also indicates that the oscillations do not repeat exactly the same pattern. Each travel around the loop is slightly different. However, the size of the loop is neither expanding or shrinking, so the system is stable.

Stability, though, relies on the values of the coefficients. If γ were increased to 100, then the applied force becomes larger. The oscillations are shown in Figure 15.11a. The size of the oscillations is increased because there is more of a push to the mass

Code 15.13 The damped forced oscillator model function.

```
1  def DampedForcedOsc(xv,t):
2      x,v = xv
3      if -0.05<x<0.05:
4          f = gamma * np.sign(v)
5      else:
6          f = 0
7      dvdt = -b*v/m - k/m*x + f
8      answ = (v,dvdt)
9      return answ
10
11  k = 5; m=1; b=0.3; gamma = 10
12  ts = np.linspace(0,20,100); xv = (1,0)
13  xs = si.odeint(DampedForcedOsc,xv,ts)
14  plt.plot(xs[:,0],xs[:,1]) # limit cycle
```

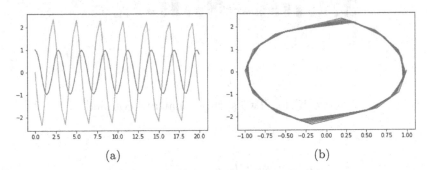

(a)   (b)

Figure 15.10: (a) The damped, forced harmonic oscillator. (b) The limit cycle of the stable, damped, forced, harmonic oscillator.

in the oscillation. However, the frequency still remains unchanged. The limit cycle is shown in Figure 15.11b. By comparing the values of the axes to the previous limit cycle, it is seen that this set of curves has a larger radius. As the size of the oscillations increase, so does the radius of the cycle. Kinks in the system are still seen where the force turns on.

15.7 COUPLED SPRINGS

The final example is shown in Figure 15.12. A mass, m_1 is attached to a springs of length L_1 with a spring constant of k_1. Attached to this mass is a second spring (with L_2 and k_2) which is attached to a mass m_2. Both masses can be initially displaced from their rest states, and both springs can have friction with coefficients b_1 and b_2.

Without bothering with the inconvenient derivations, the equations of forces are,

$$m_1 a_1 + b_1 v_1 + k_1(x_1 - L_1) - (x_2 - x_1 - L_2) = 0, \qquad (15.26)$$

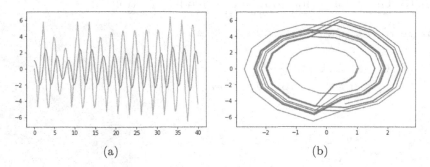

(a)   (b)

Figure 15.11: (a) The oscillator with $\gamma = 100$. (b) The limit cycle of the system with $\gamma = 100$.

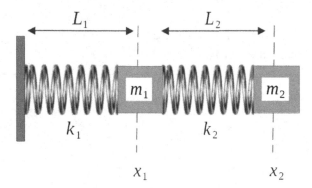

Figure 15.12: Two springs that are coupled.

and

$$m_2 a_2 + b_2 v_2 + k_2(x_2 - x_1 - L_2) = 0. \qquad (15.27)$$

While this system has new complexities, its computation follows the protocol of the previous examples. Code 15.14 shows the **DoubleSpringModel** function. It receives the input parameters and time steps as do the other model functions. In this case, the input parameters are x_1, v_1, x_2, and v_2. These are unpacked in line 6. Lines 2 through 5 set the constants, and in this case, the springs have equal strength and lengths. The masses are equal as well. Lines 7 and 8 compute the two differential equations, and line 9 returns the derivatives of the inputs.

The first trial is run in Code 15.15. Line 1 sets the initial parameters in this order: x_1, v_1, x_2, and v_2. The value $x_1 = 0.5$ and the length of the first spring is $L_1 = 1$ as established in Code 15.14. This means that the spring is compressed. The second spring also has a length of 1, which means that the length of the two springs is 2. The initial position for x_2 is 2.5, which means that this spring is stretched. Neither spring has an initial velocity. 200 time points between $t = 0$ and $t = 20$ are created in line 2.

Figure 15.13a shows the positions of both masses over time. The horizontal axis is time and the vertical axis is the position x. The top plot corresponds to m_2 and it starts at position 2.5. The bottom plot corresponds to m_1. As seen, they oscillate in

Code 15.14 The **DoubleSpringModel** function.

```
1  def DoubleSpringModel( xvs, ts ):
2      m1, m2 = 2, 2
3      k1, k2 = 20, 20
4      L1, L2 = 1, 1
5      b1, b2 = 0.8, 0.8
6      x1, v1, x2, v2 = xvs
7      a1 = (-b1*v1 -k1*(x1-L1)+k2*(x2-x1-L2))/m1
8      a2 = (-b2*v2 -k2*(x2-x1-L2))/m2
9      return (v1,a1, v2, a2)
```

Code 15.15 The first example of coupled springs.

```
1  xvs = (0.5,0,2.5,0)  # compress first, stretch second.
2  ts = np.linspace(0,20,200)
3  vals = si.odeint(DoubleSpringModel, xvs, ts )
4  plt.plot(ts,vals[:,0])
5  plt.plot(ts,vals[:,2])
6  plt.show()
```

time, but eventually friction dampens their activity. The oscillations are not perfect sine waves as the two masses interact.

Code 15.16 show a second case. Both springs start in a stretched position, but the amount of stretch is not the same. The result is shown in Figure 15.13b. In the previous case, the two spring systems were equal in strength, stretch, and mass. Furthermore, the initial case has one spring compressed and the other stretched. This was a symmetrical system, and the resultant plots were smooth. In this second case, the starting positions are no longer opposing and equal. The result shows a cruder oscillation systems. A person riding on one of these masses would feel like their motion was chaotic.

Code 15.16 The second example of coupled springs.

```
1  xvs = (1.5,0,2.25,0)  # stretch the first spring.
2  ts = np.linspace(0,20,200)
3  vals = si.odeint(DoubleSpringModel, xvs, ts )
4  plt.plot(ts,vals[:,0])
5  plt.plot(ts,vals[:,2])
6  plt.show()
```

A third case makes a single alteration in the time points. It uses `ts = np.linspace(0,20,200)` which still has a time span of $t_1 = 0$ to $t_2 = 20$, but

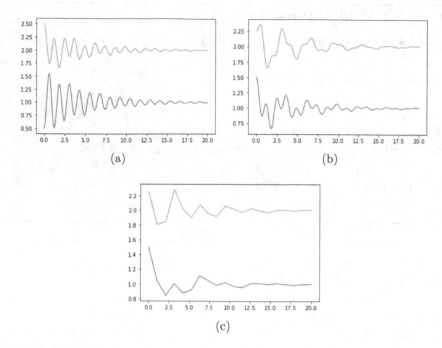

(a)

(b)

(c)

Figure 15.13: (a) Position of two masses over time when starting with opposing stretches. (b) Position of two masses over time when both starting in a stretched position. (c) Position of two masses over time when it is sampled too sparsely.

the number of points is only 20 instead of 200. The plot is shown in Figure 15.13c. Many of the features are lost because the time resolution is too coarse.

The time resolution needs to have at least two points between each peak. This is called the *Nyquist* frequency. If the sampling is too coarse, then the computations will not be accurate. Thus, a proper simulation would consider different time scales to make sure that the features are captured. A possible sign of coarse sampling is the jagged edges in the plot. Decreasing the time steps (Code 15.16) produces a plot with smoothly changing outputs. For this system, which does not have sudden changes in the model, this is a more believable result.

15.8 SUMMARY

An oscillating spring was modeled in Chapter 14, but the simulation had imperfect results because it was a discrete time simulation of a continuous time event. This chapter reviewed tools used to compute results using differential equations, thus allowing for obtaining better answers for continuous time events.

Many real-world systems have more than one variable changing in time, and thus, such systems are described by multiple differential equations which are connected. The state of one variable affects the changes in another. These are coupled differential equations.

The *scipy* module offers tools to easily handle such cases. The programmer must write a model function which contains the equations of the system, and then they feed this into a *scipy* function to obtain the answer at specified time points.

This chapter offered several examples which modeled systems such as predator-prey, HIV, or springs. Altering the input parameters is easy to accomplish, thus allowing the programmer to run multiple trials in a short amount of time.

PROBLEMS

1. Why doesn't Equation (15.3) represent an oscillating spring?

2. Create a model for

$$\frac{dy}{dt} = -k\sqrt{|y|}$$

   with $k = 0.1$, $y[0] = 1$, and the time points equally spaced between $t = 0$ and $t = 40$. Plot the results.

3. Create a model for

$$\frac{dy}{dt} = \frac{y}{(4y^2 - 15y + 18)^2}$$

   with $k = 0.1$, $y[0] = 1$, and equally spaced between $t = 0$ and $t = 40$. Plot the results.

4. Replicate the predator-prey model from the chapter, but alter it such that the Morlocks feed at half of the initial rate. Plot the populations of Morlocks and Eloi versus time.

5. Plot the limit cycle for

$$\frac{dx}{dt} = 5x - 3y$$

$$\frac{dy}{dt} = 9x - 2y$$

   Initial values are $x[0] = 0.5$ and $y[0] = 0.2$. Use 100 time steps between 0 and 5. Plot y vs x.

6. Use the spring model to answer the following questions:

   (a) If k is increased by a factor of 4, what happens to the frequency of the oscillations?

   (b) If k is increased by a factor of 4, what happens to the amplitude?

   (c) If m is doubled, what happens to the oscillations?

   (d) If k is doubled and m is doubled, do the oscillations change?

   (e) If the initial velocity is set to 1, what happens to the oscillations?

   (f) What change is required to any of the variables which will produce oscillations at half of the original amplitude?

7. Alter the two spring model where the first mass is 1 and the second mass is 1.5. The spring constants are 10 and 40 respectively. The lengths of the springs are 0.5 and 1.0 respectively, and the coefficients of friction are 0.1 and 1.5. The initial displacements of the springs are 0.75 and 2.25. Use 200 times points from 0 to 20. Plot the results.

8. Write a Python script that will attempt to find the parameters in which the second mass doesn't move much in the two spring model. The values for the first and second masses should be between 0.5 and 1.0. The values of the spring constants should be between 0.5 and 40.5. The values of the friction should be between 0.5 and 1.0. The value for the first displacement should be between 0.75 and 1.25, and the value for the second displacement should be between 1.75 and 2.25. The length of both springs is 1 and do not change. The time points should be between 0 and 20 with 200 time steps. Run 500 cases with randomly selected values, and report the values of the one in which the second mass moves the least. Plot the positions of each mass in time.

9. Create a model with

$$\frac{\mathrm{d}x}{\mathrm{d}t} = y$$

and

$$\frac{\mathrm{d}y}{\mathrm{d}t} = -x + \mu(1 - x^2)y$$

Run four cases in which $\mu = 0.1$, $\mu = 1$, $\mu = 2$, and $\mu = 5$. Use 500 time points between 0 and 50, and start $x[0] = 0.1$ and $y[0] = 0.1$. Plot the values for both x and y on the same graph.

10. Modify the original spring problem such that the first mass cannot exceed a velocity of 0.7. If the velocity is calculated to exceed 0.7 then it is set to be 0.7. Plot the positions of both masses.

## CHAPTER 16

Extraordinary Number of Solutions

CONSIDER a simple system that generates three outputs, each being one letter from the alphabet, and the goal of this system is to find the sequence of the start of the alphabet: ABC. The first output can be any letter from A to Z, and so can the second and third outputs. The number of possible outcomes of the system is the number of states to the power of the number of nodes, thus, the number of possible outcomes is

$$N = 26^3 = 17,576. \tag{16.1}$$

While the system can generate these outcomes, there is only one outcome that is the correct solution. A computer program can be written to go through all possible outcomes and determine which one is correct. The process would have a three-nested loop, as in Code 16.1. The **GenerateOut** function converts the input integer to an output letter.

Code 16.1 The outline of the ABC program.

```
1  for i in range(26):
2      output1 = GenerateOut( i )
3      for j in range(26):
4          output2 = GenerateOut( j )
5          for k in range( 26 ):
6              output3 = GenerateOut(k)
7              if output1=='A' and output2 == 'B' and output3
                    == 'C':
8                  print('Correct Solution is ', output1,
                        output2, output3 )
```

If the programmer is lucky, then the solution is found in one of the early iterations. Though, there is a possibility that the program would need to go through most of the iterations in seeking a solution.

DOI: 10.1201/9781003226581-16

In any case, 17,576 iterations is not a large number for this type of situation. A modern computer can generate all possible outcomes in seconds. If the problem is increased to finding a string ABCDEFGHIJ, then the number of possible strings is $26^{10} = 1.4 \times 19^{14}$. This simple concept becomes untenable for a standard computer.

Consider a case in which the system has 81 output nodes and each one can have one of 9 different values. The number of possible outcomes is,

$$9^{81} = 2.0 \times 10^{77}. \tag{16.2}$$

If the computer program analyzed 1,000,000 possible solutions each second, it would still take 10^{63} years to finish the computation. Of course a computer which is ten times faster could be purchased, and then the number of years is reduced to 10^{62} years. Obviously, searching all possible outcomes is not feasible. In fact, it is not even close to being feasible. This program would have 81 nested loops. A better way is needed.

This chapter considers a system which generates a huge number of possible outcomes. Instead of generating all outcomes, the system uses a set of rules to eliminate vast number of unwanted. outcomes. The problem with this approach is that all needed rules may not be known beforehand. The process is then iterative. A rule is generated and applied to the system. If the output of the program is insufficient, then the process is examined to find a second rule. This idea repeats until there are enough rules to create a proper output of the system. Some of the rules may not be known until the reaction of the system to the previous rules has been investigated.

To demonstrate this process, the Sudoku game will be used. The number of outcomes for this puzzle far exceeds the brute-force search capability of a standard computer.

16.1 THE GAME

The standard Sudoku game has 81 cells each with 9 possible values. However, at the beginning of the game, some of the cells have known values. A typical game is shown in Figure 16.1a, and its solution is shown in Figure 16.1b. Each cell can contain a digit between 1 and 9, and each row, column, or block must have each digit once.

- Each row has each digit just once,

- Each column has each digit just once, and

- Each 3×3 block marked by thick lines has each digit just once.

A brute-force method of finding a solution would be to try every possible combination of numerical values in the empty cells until one is found that does not violate the rules. In this example, there are 51 empty cells, and thus such a program would have 51 nested loops, each with 9 iterations. The number of possibilities is enormous. Given an empty puzzle, there are 81 squares, and each square can have 1 of 9 different values.

$$9^{81-30} = 4.6 \times 10^{48}, \tag{16.3}$$

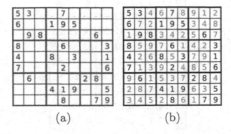

Figure 16.1: (a) A typical Sudoku game. (b) The solution.

which reduces the task to 10^{41} years of computation.

Sudoku puzzlers have developed a set of terms to describe the different aspects of the game. These are:

- *Band* : A single row

- *Stack*: A single column

- *Cell*: One small square

- *Block*: A 3 × 3 area (or equivalent)

- *Candidate*: A possible answer for a cell

- *Tile*: A solved cell

- *Zone, Regions, subgrid* or *nonets*: Cells in a block

- *Givens*: Pre-solved cells

16.2 BUILDING A SOLUTION

The goal is to develop rules which are then used to solve Sudoku puzzles. Before this can be entertained, the data structures need to be created.

16.2.1 Cell Identities

Each cell in the puzzle needs an identifying integer. These are simply numbered in sequential order as shown in Figure 16.2.

16.2.2 Cell Representation

Each cell contains either a solution or a list of candidate solutions. In the beginning of the game, some cells have given values, and these are the solutions for those cells. The other cells have 9 candidate values. This concept is shown in Figure 16.3. Each cell has either a solution or candidates. A set of rules to be created will eliminate candidates from each cell, until only one candidate remains, and this then becomes the solution.

0	1	2	3	4	5	6	7	8
9	10	11	12	13	14	15	16	17
18	19	20	21	22	23	24	25	26
27	28	29	30	31	32	33	34	35
36	37	38	39	40	41	42	43	44
45	46	47	48	49	50	51	52	53
54	55	56	57	58	59	60	61	62
63	64	65	66	67	68	69	70	71
72	73	74	75	76	77	78	79	80

Figure 16.2: The identification of each cell.

Figure 16.3: The layout at the beginning of the solution.

The data structure chosen to represent a cell is a list which contains two items. The first is the solution, and the second is a list of candidates. Thus, the first cell in this puzzle would be represented by [-1, [1,2,3,4,5,6,7,8,9]], where the −1 is used when the solution is not known. The third cell in this puzzle would be represented by [7, []]. At first this may seem to be redundant. Only one of the items in the list is being used at any time. Why not just represent a solved cell by a list with only one entry?

Consider a case in which the number of candidates for a cell have been reduced to just one, [-1, [4]]. The solution to this cell is 4 and will be represented by [4, []]. The difference is the first case has reached a solution, but it hasn't been registered by the puzzle. Basically, it is a pending solution, whereas the second example represents a solved cell.

16.2.3 Puzzle Architecture

Each puzzle has an architecture. The example puzzle uses 81 cells, arranged with a 9×9 cells with 3×3 blocks. There are 9 rows, 9 columns, and 9 blocks. The block, row, or column are the same entity. Each contains 9 cells, and each must eventually have one instance of each numeral. A *group* is defined as either a row, column, or block, and this puzzle has 27 groups. Each group is represented by a list of cell identifiers contained in that group. For example, the first group is the first row, and it contains cells 0, 1, 2, 3, 4, 5, 6, 7, and 8. The first nine groups are the rows. The next nine groups are the columns, thus, group 9 contains cells, 0, 9, 18, 27, 36, 45, 54, 63, and

72. The last nine groups are the blocks. The first of these contains cells 0, 1, 2, 9, 10, 11, 18, 19, and 20.

The Function 16.2 (Code 16.2) creates 27 lists, one for each group, and it returns a list named **groups** which contains the 27 lists. Lines 5 and 6 create the 9 rows, and lines 7 and 8 create the 9 columns. The nested **for** loops create the 9 blocks. The output is the list **groups** which contains 27 vectors, each with the cell identifiers. Code 16.3 calls the function and shows some of the results. Line 3 shows that there are 27 groups. The examples given in the previous paragraph are printed to the console.

Code 16.2 The **Architecture1** function creates a standard puzzle architecture.

```
1  #sudoku.py
2  def Architecture1():
3      groups = []
4      x = np.array((0,1,2,3,4,5,6,7,8))
5      for i in range( 9 ):
6          groups.append( list(x + i*9)) # rows
7      for i in range(9):
8          groups.append( list(x*9 + i) ) # columns
9      x = np.array( (0,1,2,9,10,11,18,19,20))
10     for i in (0,27,54):
11         for j in (0,3,6):
12             groups.append(list(x+i+j)) # blocks
13     return groups
```

Other architectures are possible, and for these puzzles this function will need to be modified. Many of these are called jigsaw Sudoku puzzles which are discussed in Section 16.3.2.

Code 16.3 Example entries in the **groups** list.

```
1  grid = sudoku.Architecture1()
2  print(len(grid))
3  27
4  print(grid[0])
5  [0, 1, 2, 3, 4, 5, 6, 7, 8]
6  print(grid[9])
7  [0, 9, 18, 27, 36, 45, 54, 63, 72]
8  print(grid[18])
9  [0, 1, 2, 9, 10, 11, 18, 19, 20]
```

16.2.4 Creating a Puzzle

The puzzle information, the groups, and the states of the cells are contained within a single dictionary. Creating this is a two-step process. The first step establishes the given values, and the second uses these to create the groups. Each puzzle will need the user to load the given values in the correct cells.

The givens for the example puzzle are established in **Puzzle1** shown in Code 16.4. At first, these are created as a matrix since it is convenient for the user.

Code 16.4 The**Puzzle1** function.

```
1  #sudoku.py
2  def Puzzle1():
3      mat = np.array( (
4          (-1,-1, 7, 9, 6, 2, 4,-1,-1),
5          ( 9,-1,-1,-1, 1,-1,-1,-1, 2),
6          (-1, 1,-1, 8, 5, 3,-1, 6,-1),
7          ( 5,-1,-1, 4, 7, 9,-1,-1, 1),
8          (-1,-1,-1,-1, 8,-1,-1,-1,-1),
9          ( 4,-1,-1, 3, 2, 1,-1,-1, 7),
10         (-1, 9,-1, 2, 4, 8,-1, 5,-1),
11         ( 6,-1,-1,-1, 3,-1,-1,-1, 8),
12         (-1,-1, 8, 6, 9, 5, 1,-1,-1) ) )
13     dct = ConvertMat(mat)
14     return dct
```

In the second step, the function **ConvertMat** (Code 16.5) converts the matrix into the dictionary. The input is the matrix from **Puzzle1**. Line 3 creates an empty dictionary which will hold the puzzle values. The two `for` loops in lines 6 and 7 cycle through the 9×9 puzzle. A list named `box` is created for each cell, and this list has the known value and the list of candidates. Line 9 is used for a cell that does not have a known value, and line 11 is used for the given cells. The output is the dictionary containing the whole puzzle.

Line 1 of Code 16.6 calls the **Puzzle1** function, and two of the 81 cells are shown. The first cell is `dct[0]`, and this dictionary entry has two items. The first is a -1 indicating that this cell does not have a known solution, and the second is a list of the candidate values. Some of these will soon be eliminated. Lines 4 and 5 show the third cell which has a given value of 7 and no candidates because the value of the cell is known.

16.2.5 Presenting a Puzzle

Two functions are used to return information about the current state of the puzzle. The first function returns the number of unsolved cells. If this number is 0, then the puzzle is solved, and it is useful for tracking the progress of the puzzle. Code 16.7 shows the **UnsolvedCount** function, which receives the dictionary representing the puzzle. The `for` loop considers each of the puzzle's cells and counts the number of cells (line 6) which are not solved (line 5). This value is returned.

Code 16.5 The **ConvertMat** function.

```
1   #sudoku.py
2   def ConvertMat( mat ):
3       dct = {}
4       k = 0
5       V,H = mat.shape
6       for i in range(V):
7           for j in range(H):
8               if mat[i,j] == -1:
9                   box = [-1,[1,2,3,4,5,6,7,8,9]]
10              else:
11                  box = [mat[i,j],[]]
12              dct[k] = box
13              k += 1
14      return dct
```

Code 16.6 Output from the **ConvertMat** function.

```
1   dct = sudoku.Puzzle1()
2   print(dct[0])
3   [-1, [1, 2, 3, 4, 5, 6, 7, 8, 9]]
4   print(dct[2])
5   [7, []]
```

Code 16.7 The **UnsolvedCount** function.

```
1   #sudoku.py
2   def UnsolvedCount(dct):
3       answ = 0
4       for k in dct.keys():
5           if dct[k][0] == -1:
6               answ +=1
7       return answ
```

The second function is **PrintSolution** (Code 16.8) which prints the current state of the puzzle to the console. The input is the dictionary and a value L which is the number of columns in the puzzle. Traditionally, this value is 9, but puzzles of other sizes do exist, and this value needs to be adjusted accordingly. Line 5 uses Python formatting which makes sure that each printed value uses three character spaces and that the value is flush to the right. Line 8 creates the newline at the end of each row.

Code 16.8 Output from the **PrintSolution** function.

```
#sudoku.py
def PrintSolution(dct,L=9):
    k = 0
    for i in range(L):
        for j in range(L):
            print("{0:>3}".format(dct[k][0]),end='')
            k = k+ 1
        print('')
```

16.2.6   Rule 1

The puzzle is established and is ready to be solved. As stated earlier, there are too many combinations to try all possible solutions. Thus, rules are needed to eliminate most of the possible solutions. However, all rules may not be known at the beginning of the program build. The strategy is then to create on rule, apply it, and then analyze the results for the of another rule.

Sudoku allows only one instance of each numeral in each group. Thus, Rule 1 is to eliminate candidates of numerals which are solutions in that group. In the example puzzle, the first row (**group[0]**) has several solved cells with the values of 7, 9, 6, 2, and 4. No other cell in this row can have these values, so these values are removed from the candidate lists in all cells in that row (group). The result of the cells in just the top row is shown in Figure 16.4. The candidates have been reduced, which is equivalent to reducing the number of possible outcomes of the system.

Figure 16.4: Applying Rule 1 to the top row.

This rule is applied to all 27 groups (rows, columns, and blocks), and with any luck this will be sufficient to reduce the length of a candidate list to 1 for at least one cell. This would mean that Rule 1 has found a solution to a cell. This rule would be repeatedly applied until the puzzle is solved or the program gets stuck, meaning that another rule is needed.

The results for the example puzzle after the application of Rule 1 are shown in Figure 16.5. Of particular interest are the cells surrounded by thick boxes. In these cells, Rule 1 has eliminated all candidates except for one. Thus, the solution values for these cells are now known.

Rule 1 has three steps.

1. For each group, gather the known solutions.

2. Remove these values from the candidate lists of the unsolved cells in this group.

3. For any cell which has one candidate, convert that to a solved cell.

Figure 16.5: The result of applying rule 1 to all rows, columns, and blocks.

The **Rule1** function (Code 16.9) performs these steps in functions which will soon be defined. Line 3 loops over each group. Line 4 gathers the known values for all cells in this one group. Line 5 removes these values from the candidate lists in all cells in this group. After all groups have been considered, line 6 searches the puzzle for cells with a single candidate, and converts the state of those cells to being a solved cell.

Code 16.9 The **Rule1** function.

```
1  # sudoku.py
2  def Rule1( dct, groups ):
3      for g in groups:
4          aig = AnswersInGroup( dct, g )
5          RemovalInGroup( aig, dct, g )
6      ct = FindSolos( dct )
7      return ct
```

The **Rule1** function calls three other functions which do the brunt of the work. The first of these is **AnswersInGroup** function shown in Code 16.10. The input is the puzzle dictionary and just one of the groups. Thus, this function is called 27 times. The `cellid` the identifier of one cell in this group. Line 5 is `True` if the cell does not have a solution. Line 6 appends this solution to a list named `knowns`, and this list is returned. For the first group in this puzzle, the output of **AnswersInGroup** would be [7, 9, 6, 2, 4].

The second function is **RemovalInGroup** shown in Code 16.11. It receives `aig` which is the list generated by **AnswersInGroup**, the puzzle dictionary, and just one of the groups. It loops through each cell in a group (line 3), and inside this it loops through every entry in `aig`. If the value from `aig` is in the candidate list of this cell, then it is removed (line 6).

The final function is **FindSolos** (Code 16.12). This function loops over all groups (line 4). Line 5 is `True` if the cell is unsolved, and the candidate list has only one value

Code 16.10 The **AnswersInGroup** function.

```
1  # sudoku.py
2  def AnswersInGroup( dct, groupsi ):
3      knowns = []
4      for cellid in groupsi:
5          if dct[cellid][0] != -1:
6              knowns.append( dct[cellid][0] )
7      return knowns
```

Code 16.11 The **RemovalInGroup** function.

```
1  # sudoku.py
2  def RemovalInGroup( aig, dct, groupsi ):
3      for cellid in groupsi:
4          for j in aig:
5              if j in dct[cellid][1]:
6                  dct[cellid][1].remove(j)
```

in it. In this case, the solution for the cell has been found, and the cell is modified to reflect this (line 7). Line 8 prints the change to the console, and the `ct` variable counts the number of cells Rule 1 has solved in this iteration.

Code 16.12 The **FindSolos** function.

```
1  # sudoku.py
2  def FindSolos(dct):
3      ct = 0
4      for cellid in dct.keys():
5          if dct[cellid][0]==-1 and len(dct[cellid][1])==1:
6              ct += 1
7              dct[cellid][0] = dct[cellid][1].pop(0)
8              print('rule 1', cellid,dct[cellid][0] )
9      return ct
```

With the rule in place, the solution to the puzzle can be attempted. Code 16.13 creates the puzzle, applies the given values, and repeatedly calls Rule 1 until it no longer isolates one candidate in any cell. The puzzle is not completely solved, and its current state is shown in Figure 16.6. Not surprisingly, Rule 1 did not solve the puzzle, and a second rule is needed.

16.2.7 Rule 2

Rule 1 did provide solutions for 10 cells in the puzzle, but it is now stuck. A second rule is needed. The revelation of Rule 2 begins with an examination of the current

Code 16.13 Repeatedly applying Rule 1 to a puzzle.

```
groups = Architecture1()
dct = Puzzle1()
for i in range(81):
    ct = Rule1( dct, groups)
    if ct==0:
        break
```

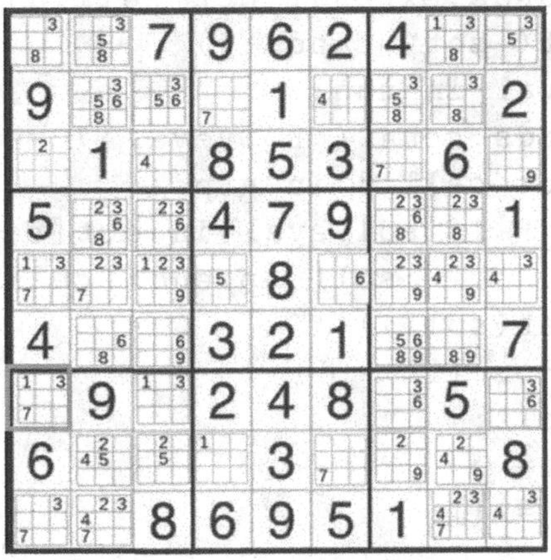

Figure 16.6: The state of the puzzle after repeated applications of the first rule.

state of the puzzle. One cell on the seventh row of Figure 16.6 has a solid box around it. It currently has three potential candidates. Four other unsolved cells in this row also have multiple candidates, but none of these have the value of 7 in their candidate list. Thus, the only cell in this row which can have a value of 7 is the one outlined by the box.

Rule 2 is born. If within a group, a candidate value exists in only cell, then that cell is considered as solved with that value. The **Rule2** function is shown in Code 16.14. The search begins in line 4. The variable grp is one of the 27 groups. The cands list (line 5) gathers all candidates from that group. In line 6, cellid is the identifier for a single cell, and if the cell is not solved (line 7), then all candidates are added to cands (line 8). Line 9 creates a new list, unq which has only one instance of each value from the candidate list. These are the unique values of candidates in this group.

The next step is to determine how many times each candidate exists in the group. Line 10 considers each of the candidates, and line 11 determines if this candidate is seen only once in the group. If line 11 is True, then the program determines which cell has that candidate (line 13). Line 14 gathers the information in a tuple with two items: the identifier of the cell with the candidate, and the value for that cell. These are put into the list soli, of which the duplicates are removed in line 15.

Code 16.14 The **Rule2** function.

```
1  # sudoku.py
2  def Rule2( dct, groups ):
3      soli = []
4      for grp in groups:
5          cands = []
6          for cellid in grp:
7              if dct[cellid][0] == -1:
8                  cands.extend( dct[cellid][1] )
9          unq = list( set( cands ))
10         for solveval in unq:
11             if cands.count( solveval ) == 1:
12                 for cellid in grp:
13                     if solveval in dct[cellid][1]:
14                         soli.append((cellid,solveval))
15     soli = list(set(soli))
16     print('Rule 2',soli)
17     for i,q in soli:
18         dct[i][0] = q
19         dct[i][1] = []
```

Lines 17 through 19 solve for the cell. The value is placed in the first position of the dct tuple and the candidate list is emptied. The cell is now solved. Line 15 prints information for all cells being solved by Rule 2 in this iteration.

Rule 2 is ready for use, but the question remains of how it will be used in conjunction with Rule 1. The combination selected here is to use Rule 1 until it gets stuck, then use Rule 2 once. The process gives priority to the simpler Rule 1, and the is encapsulated in the **SudokuR1R2** function shown in Code 16.15. The ok flag is True when computations need to continue. It is converted to False when either the game is won or it can't be solved by Rule 1 and Rule 2.

Line 5 finds the current number of unsolved cells, line 6 applies Rule 1, and line 7 counts the unsolved cells. If Rule 1 was effective then end2 < end1. If end2 == 0 then the game is won (lines 8 and 9). However, if end1 == end2 and they are not 0, then Rule 1 failed. Thus, rule 2 is employed once (Line 11). The unsolved cells are counted again, and if end1 == end3 then neither Rule 1 or Rule 2 can help solve the puzzle. Line 14 is used when the puzzle can't be solved. Line 15 prints out the final state of the puzzle under any circumstance.

Code 16.16 shows the process. Lines 1 and 2 create the puzzle, and line 3 calls the **goSudokuR1R2** function. It prints the final product to the console, and in this case, the puzzle is solved. Unsolved cells would have a −1 in them, but as seen, all cells have positive values. This function can solve many puzzles, but if there is one puzzle that is not solved, then another rule will be needed.

Code 16.15 The **SudokuR1R2** function.

```python
# sudoku.py
def SudokuR1R2(dct,groups):
    ok = True
    while ok:
        end1 = UnsolvedCount(dct)
        Rule1( dct, groups )
        end2 = UnsolvedCount(dct)
        if end2 == 0:
            ok = False
        if end1==end2:
            hits=Rule2(dct,groups)
            end3 = UnsolvedCount(dct)
            if end1==end3:
                ok = False
    PrintSolution(dct)
```

Code 16.16 Running the **SudokuR1R2** function.

```python
groups = Architecture1()
dct = Puzzle1()
SudokuR1R2(dct, groups)

8 3 7 9 6 2 4 1 5
9 5 6 7 1 4 8 3 2
2 1 4 8 5 3 7 6 9
5 8 3 4 7 9 6 2 1
1 7 2 5 8 6 9 4 3
4 6 9 3 2 1 5 8 7
7 9 1 2 4 8 3 5 6
6 4 5 1 3 7 2 9 8
3 2 8 6 9 5 1 7 4
```

16.3 ALTERNATE PUZZLE ARCHITECTURES

The architecture shown in Figure 16.1a is a standard puzzle with a 9×9 frame and 3×3 blocks. Alternate architectures include 3D puzzles, larger frame size, overlapping puzzles (Samurai Sudoku), and different block configurations. This section will look at just two of these alterations: larger sizes and alternate block configurations.

16.3.1 Larger Puzzles

A larger puzzle is shown in Figure 16.7. This is a 16×16 puzzle with 16 unique values. The same rules apply, each row, column, and block must have each digit only once. Now the blocks are 4×4, and the letters A, B, C, D, E, and F are used to represent the values greater than 9.

		E						4		8	C	5			
	1	8			G	D	4	9	E	3		6	F		
2	9	C				5		A		D					G
		6	3	B				5					9		
1	E			C	4	A		G	9				6	8	F
		E						6	1	8		5			9
	D	B	F	G			6	3				2			
C				8	5	2			A		D		E		
				F				C			3	A		D	
7		8	A				1	E	2		B		3	G	4
3	G		1	5				B	F	7			8		C
	C			2	A	8		D			7				6
		5	3	A		E		D	6		9	G			7
		2	D					5		C			4	A	
		4	C	9			3	G	D	8				B	
		F	E	7			8		5			A			

Figure 16.7: A 16×16 puzzle.

Modifying the functions in *sudoku.py* are tedious but do not require any new logic. The **Architecture** function would need to expand list and range of looping variables. The **ConverMat** function would need to accommodate the larger range of values. Since these modifications do not expand the logic of solving the puzzle, they are not presented here.

16.3.2 Jigsaw Sudoku Puzzles

The second alternate puzzle alters the block configurations, and such puzzles are called *jigsaw Sudoku* puzzles. One example is shown in Figure 16.8. The boundaries for the blocks are no longer 3×3. The rules still apply, each row, column, and block must have each numeral only once.

The only modification is the definition of the blocks as shown in Code 16.17. The **ArchitectureJigsaw1** function still defines the row and column groups in the same manner as before, but the last nine groups are defined in nine lines of code.

Another jigsaw configuration is shown in Figure 16.9, and the code to create it is shown in Code 16.18.

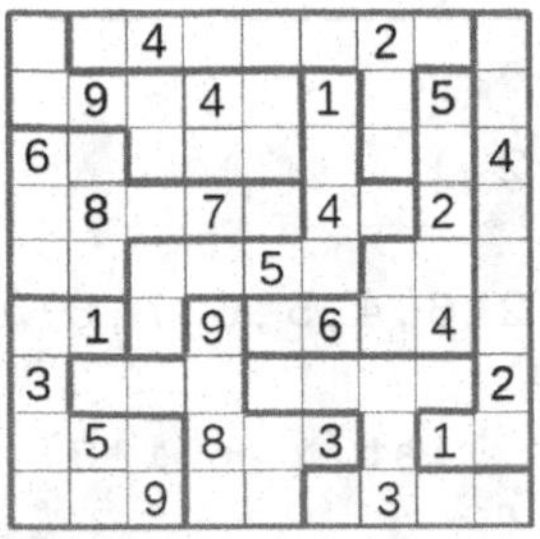

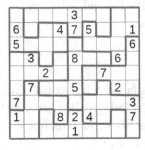

Figure 16.8: A jigsaw Sudoku puzzle.

Code 16.17 The **ArchitectureJigsaw1** function.

```python
# sudoku.py
def ArchitectureJigsaw1():
    groups = []
    x = np.array((0,1,2,3,4,5,6,7,8))
    for i in range( 9 ):
        groups.append( list(x + i*9))
    for i in range(9):
        groups.append( list(x*9 + i) )
    groups.append(( 0, 9,10,11,12,13,20,21,22))
    groups.append(( 1, 2, 3, 4, 5, 6, 7,15,24))
    groups.append(( 8,17,26,35,44,53,62,70,71))
    groups.append((14,23,32,33,38,39,40,41,47))
    groups.append((16,25,34,42,43,49,50,51,52))
    groups.append((18,19,27,28,29,30,31,36,37))
    groups.append((45,46,54,63,64,65,72,73,74))
    groups.append((48,55,56,57,66,67,68,75,76))
    groups.append((58,59,60,61,69,77,78,79,80))
    return groups
```

Figure 16.9: Another jigsaw Sudoku puzzle.

Code 16.18 The **ArchitectureJigsaw2** function.

```
1   # sudoku.py
2   def ArchitectureJigsaw2():
3       groups = []
4       x = np.array((0,1,2,3,4,5,6,7,8))
5       for i in range( 9 ):
6           groups.append( list(x + i*9))
7       for i in range(9):
8           groups.append( list(x*9 + i) )
9       groups.append(( 0, 9,11,12,18,19,20,21,29))
10      groups.append(( 1, 2, 3, 4, 5, 6,10,13,15))
11      groups.append(( 7, 8,14,16,17,23,24,25,34))
12      groups.append((22,31,32,33,40,47,48,49,58))
13      groups.append((26,35,41,42,43,44,50,52,53))
14      groups.append((27,28,30,36,37,38,39,45,54))
15      groups.append((46,55,56,57,63,64,66,72,73))
16      groups.append((51,59,60,61,62,68,69,71,80))
17      groups.append((65,67,70,74,75,76,77,78,79))
18      return groups
```

Code similar to that in Code 16.16 can be applied to the puzzle, with, of course, the use of **ArchitectureJigsaw2**. However, the program does not solve the problem. The solution stops at that shown in Figure 16.10. The conclusion is that the combination of Rules 1 and 2 do not solve this puzzle. Another rule is needed.

Figure 16.10: Partial solution to the puzzle.

16.3.3 Rule 3

Once again, the programmer is faced with examining the puzzle in its current state in order to define another rule. Code 16.19 present the candidates lists for selected cells. Of these are all cells in the fifth row which are not solved. Cells 36 and 44 have only two candidates which are 8 and 9. Thus, the solutions for these two cells are going to be 8 and 9, but at this time it is not known which one will be the 8 and which one will be the 9. It is known, that no other cells in this row can have an 8 or

9. The values of 8 and 9 can be removed from the other cells in this row (37 and 39). In doing this, no cell is directly solved. However, the removal of 8 from cells 37 does affect the solution. The only cell in the second column with a possible solution of 8 is now cell 1. Rule 2 can now solve for cell 1.

Thus Rule 3 is defined. If there are two cells in a group with identical candidate lists of two values, then those values can be removed from the other cells in this group.

Code 16.19 Isolating Rule 3

```
for i in (1,36,37,39,44):
    print(i, dct[i], end='\n')

1 [-1, [4, 5, 6, 8, 9]]
36 [-1, [8, 9]]
37 [-1, [5, 6, 8, 9]]
39 [-1, [5, 6, 9]]
44 [-1, [8, 9]]
```

The function **Rule3** is shown in Code 16.20. Line 4 considers each group, and for each a temporary dictionary, `tdct`, is created. The keys for this dictionary are the candidates, and the values of the entries in the dictionary are the number of times that a particular combination is seen. The candidates are currently contained in a list so the items can be modified. A list cannot be a key to a dictionary for the same reason. Thus, each candidate list is converted to a tuple (line 7). If this particular candidate tuple has not been seen before, then an entry is created in the dictionary (line 11). If it has been seen before, then the count is increased (line 9).

By line 12, all cells in this one group have been considered. Rule 3 seeks the case in which the candidate tuple has exactly two values, and that this tuple has been seen only twice. This condition is checked in line 13. If this line is `True`, then Rule 3 is enacted. The two values from this rule are removed from the other cells in this group. However, they are not removed from the two cells which contained the exact combination of the two values.

This rule does not necessarily solve any cells. As seen in the example, the use of Rule 3 in one row helped solve a cell in another row. Thus, Rule 3 will be used, but the solutions to other cells will come with subsequent use of Rules 1 and 2.

Rule 3 can be modified to catch similar situations. It is possible that in a group there would be three cells with the same three candidates. These would be removed from the other cells in the group. The modifications would be to change the values of 2 to 3 in line 13.

With Rule 3 in place, the driver function needs modification. Function **Sudoku** (Code 16.21) is similar to **SudokuR1R2** except that it now has Rule 3. The program will repeatedly use Rule 1. It measures the number of unsolved cells before and after the application of Rule 1. The value `end2` is less than `end1` if Rule 1 solved some cells. If these two values are the same (line 10), the Rule 1 failed. Rule 2 is used and

Code 16.20 The **Rule3** function.

```
# sudoku.py
def Rule3( dct, groups ):
    print('Rule 3')
    for grp in groups:
        tdct = {}
        for gcell in grp:
            v = tuple(dct[gcell][1])
            if v in tdct:
                tdct[v] += 1
            else:
                tdct[v] = 1
        for t in tdct:
            if len(t)==2 and tdct[t] == 2:
                for gcell in grp:
                    if tuple(dct[gcell][1]) != t:
                        for tt in t:
                            if tt in dct[gcell][1]:
                                dct[gcell][1].remove(
                                    tt)
```

its effectiveness is measured as **end3**. If this Rule didn't solve any cell (line 13), then Rule 3 is used. Rule 3 is different than the other two rules in that it does not solve cells. Thus, once Rule 3 is invoked (line 13) then the other rules are called again (lines 14 and 15). The game ends if all cells are solved (**end** = 0) or it needs another Rule (**end** = **last**).

Code 16.22 solves the example puzzle. Both Rule 1 and Rule 2 will print which cells are being solved to the console. As this is a long list, it is omitted from being shown here.

The Sudoku puzzle originally had a very large number of outcomes, but by creating and employing rules, the number of possible outcomes was reduced to 1. Some of the rules were created after a previous rule failed to solve a puzzle.

16.4 CREATING GAMES

The previous section showed the method to solve a puzzle. This section demonstrates a method on how to create a puzzle. The process must create a puzzle that is solvable, but also that there is only a single solution. Normally, Sudoku puzzles have a symmetry in how the given cells are arranged. The following programs do not include that symmetry, but it can be easily added.

There are two steps to this process. The first is to create a solved puzzle, and the second is to determine which cells are to be the givens.

Code 16.21 The **Sudoku** function.

```python
# sudoku.py
def Sudoku(dct,groups):
    last = 0
    ok = True
    while ok:
        end1 = UnsolvedCount(dct)
        Rule1( dct, groups )
        end2 = UnsolvedCount(dct)
        if end1==end2:
            Rule2(dct,groups)
            end3 = UnsolvedCount(dct)
            if end1==end3:
                Rule3(dct,groups)
                Rule2(dct,groups)
                Rule1(dct,groups)
        end = UnsolvedCount(dct)
        if end==last or end==0:
            ok = False
        last = end
    PrintSolution(dct)
```

Code 16.22 Solving a puzzle with Rule 3.

```python
groups = ArchitectureJigsaw2()
dct = PuzzleJigsaw2()
Sudoku(dct, groups)

2 8 4 5 3 6 1 7 9
6 2 3 4 7 5 9 8 1
5 1 8 7 9 2 3 4 6
4 3 9 1 8 7 2 6 5
9 5 2 6 4 3 7 1 8
8 7 1 3 5 9 6 2 4
7 4 5 2 6 1 8 9 3
1 9 6 8 2 4 5 3 7
3 6 7 9 1 8 4 5 2
```

16.4.1 Creating a Solved Puzzle

Once the software for solving a puzzle is in place, then creating a new puzzle is relatively easy. This process will consist of three steps:

1. Create a trivial solution,

2. Modify the trivial solution to become a viable solution, and

3. Sequentially remove values from cells until the puzzle can't be solve. Back up one step.

One of the issues of creating a puzzle will not be addressed here, although it can be easily enforced. Many puzzles are symmetric in the placement of the given values. If the first cell has a value, then the last cell will have a given value. This symmetry is not important to the process of creating a puzzle, and thus is reserved for assignments for the reader.

16.4.2 The Trivial Solution

This method of creating a puzzle starts with a known solution. It is possible to start with any solved puzzle, but this case will start with a trivial solution. This is a solved puzzle which is easy to make, but will never be used because of its regularity (Figure 16.11).

The first row is the values, in order, from 1 to 9. The row is the same pattern, but shifted three cells to the left. It must be shifted by a three cells rather than one or two. It is shifted by only one, then the first block would have two instances of 2 and of 3. The third row is the second row shifted by another three cells. The next three rows are replicates of the first row except all rows are shifted one cell to the left. The last three rows are the previous three rows shifted by one cell to the left. This puzzle satisfies the rules of one of each value being in each row, column, and block.

1	2	3	4	5	6	7	8	9
4	5	6	7	8	9	1	2	3
7	8	9	1	2	3	4	5	6
2	3	4	5	6	7	8	9	1
5	6	7	8	9	1	2	3	4
8	9	1	2	3	4	5	6	7
3	4	5	6	7	8	9	1	2
6	7	8	9	1	2	3	4	5
9	1	2	3	4	5	6	7	8

Figure 16.11: The trivial solution.

Code 16.23 creates this trivial solution by the 16.23 shows the **TrivialSolution** function. Other trivial solutions exist, but only one is needed here. The output is a 9×9 matrix.

Code 16.23 The **TrivialSolution** function.

```
1   # sudoku.py
2   def TrivialSolution():
3       puzzle = np.zeros((9,9),int)
4       puzzle[0] = (1,2,3,4,5,6,7,8,9)
5       puzzle[1] = (4,5,6,7,8,9,1,2,3)
6       puzzle[2] = (7,8,9,1,2,3,4,5,6)
7       puzzle[3] = (2,3,4,5,6,7,8,9,1)
8       puzzle[4] = (5,6,7,8,9,1,2,3,4)
9       puzzle[5] = (8,9,1,2,3,4,5,6,7)
10      puzzle[6] = (3,4,5,6,7,8,9,1,2)
11      puzzle[7] = (6,7,8,9,1,2,3,4,5)
12      puzzle[8] = (9,1,2,3,4,5,6,7,8)
13      return puzzle
14  puzzle = TrivialSolution()
```

16.4.3 Modifications to the Trivial Solution

The second step in creating a Sudoku puzzle is to modify the trivial solution. Consider the simple case of swapping two values. The 4's are converted to 9's, and the original 9's are converted to 4's. This will still create a valid puzzle, but the regularity has been changed. This example is shown in Figure 16.12a.

While this process can be repeated it will not generate vastly different puzzles. Currently, the value of 1 exists in cells 0, 15, 21, 35, 41, 47, 61, and 73. The value of 1 could be swapped with another value, but this value would be in those same 9 cells. Other alteration methods are needed which don't violate the puzzle rules.

Several alterations are shown here with code. These are:

- Value swapping,

- Rotation,

- Row (or column) swapping,

- Block row (or column) swapping, and

- Reflection.

To create a new puzzle, these alterations are applied in any order and any number of times.

Value swapping is performed by the **SwapCells** function (Code 16.24). It receives the puzzle matrix and the two values to be swapped. Line 3 creates a temporary copy of the matrix. Where the `puzzle` has one value, the program changes that value in the `ans` matrix. The first swap occurs in lines 4 and 5, and the second swap takes place in lines 6 and 7.

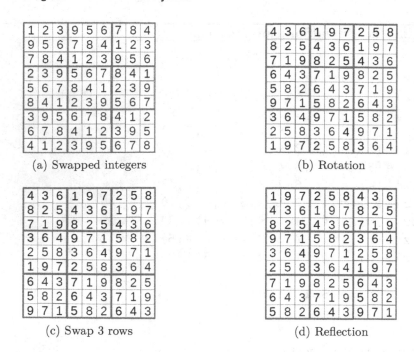

(a) Swapped integers (b) Rotation

(c) Swap 3 rows (d) Reflection

Figure 16.12: Various operations which alter the solution to a Sudoku puzzle.

Code 16.24 The **SwapCells** function.

```
# sudoku.py
def SwapCells( puzzle, val1, val2 ):
    ans = puzzle + 0
    v,h = (puzzle==val1).nonzero()
    ans[v,h] = val2
    v,h = (puzzle==val2).nonzero()
    ans[v,h] = val1
    return ans
```

A puzzle can be rotated in increments of 90 degrees. An example is shown in Figure 16.12b. This is still a valid solution. Since the puzzle is contained in a Python matrix, the *numpy* functions for rotation can be used. Code 16.25 rotates an image 90°. It receives the matrix and the number of times it is to be rotated, thus providing rotations of 180° and 270°.

The third alteration is to swap sets of rows (or columns). Python provides an efficient manner in which this can be done. To explain this, consider a smaller random 3×3 matrix as shown in the first 6 lines of Code 16.26. Line 8 uses a list as an index to a matrix to extract specified rows. In this example, the command retrieves the rows 0 and 2, as shown in lines 10 and 11. Line 13 uses this syntax to swap two rows. Line 14 uses this same technique to swap two columns.

The **SwapBlockRows** function (Code 16.27) swaps two sets of three rows in the Sudoku puzzle matrix. There is a check to make sure that the row values are 0, 3,

Code 16.25 Rotating a matrix.

```
1  puzzle2 = np.rot90(puzzle,1)
```

Code 16.26 Swapping rows of a matrix.

```
1  a = np.random.ranf((3,3))
2  a
3  Out[]:
4  array([[0.5315192 , 0.64188433, 0.42657679],
5         [0.1167365 , 0.54676454, 0.91419294],
6         [0.44495479, 0.11483729, 0.39876951]])
7
8  a[[0,2]]
9  Out[]:
10 array([[0.5315192 , 0.64188433, 0.42657679],
11        [0.44495479, 0.11483729, 0.39876951]])
12
13 a[[2,0]] = a[[0,2]] # rows
14 a[:,[2,0]] = a[:,[0,2]] # columns
```

or 6. Other values are not allowed for this type of swap. Lines 7 and 8 perform the swaps of three consecutive rows. There is a similar function named **SwapBlockCols** but it is not shown here since the only difference is in line 8, where the index accesses columns instead of rows.

The final operation is to reflect the entire puzzle either horizontally or vertically. The *numpy* module offers the functions **fliplr** and **flipud** to perform these functions. The first reflects horizontally, and the second reflects the matrix vertically. Calls to these functions are shown in Code 16.28.

The five alterations have been created. A new puzzle is created by applying these alterations multiple times. Basically, they can be chosen at random. Some of the functions, though, require some additional input. For example, the value swapping requires the two values which are to be swapped. Three possible rotations exist. The reflection can be vertical or horizontal. So, the process randomly picks the modification and then random selects the input values. The number of modifications is up the user.

16.4.4 Paring the Puzzle

In order to create a game, values need to be removed from the solution. However, these need to be removed without destroying the ability to solve the puzzle. The process starts with the full solution, randomly selects a value to remove, and then tests to see if the puzzle can be solved. Eventually, the process will have removed one too many cells, and the puzzle can't be solved. Thus, it puts that value back in as a given, and the new puzzle is ready for publication.

Code 16.27 The **SwapBlockRows** function.

```
# sudoku.py
def SwapBlockRows(puzzle, rndx1, rndx2 ):
    if rndx1 not in (0,3,6) or rndx2 not in (0,3,6):
        print('Index input must be 0,3,or 6')
        return 0
    ans = puzzle + 0
    for i in range(3):
        ans[[rndx1+i,rndx2+i]] = ans[[rndx2+i,rndx1+i]]
    return ans

p2 = SwapBlockRows(puzzle,0,3)
p2 = SwapBlockCols(puzzle,0,3)
```

Code 16.28 Calls to the **fliplr** and **flipud** functions.

```
p2 = np.fliplr(puzzle)
p3 = np.flipud(puzzle)
```

Early, it was mentioned that most puzzles are symmetric in the layout of the givens. In order to achieve this, the selection of which cell values to remove would need to include two cells which are symmetric in position. Symmetry is a minor modification to the process.

Removing the value from a random cell is performed in **RemoveRandomCell**. Line 3 finds the cells that do not have a −1 as the solution. These are the cells in which a value can be removed. Line 5 picks one of these at random, and line 6 sets this cell to −1.

Code 16.29 The **RemoveRandomCell** function.

```
# sudoku.py
def RemoveRandomCell(puzzle):
    v,h = (puzzle!=-1).nonzero()
    ndx = list(range(len(v)))
    r = np.random.choice(ndx)
    puzzle[v[r],h[r]] = -1
```

The **CreatePuzzle** function (Code 16.30) creates a new puzzle. Line 3 retrieves the standard architecture. Line 4 sets the ok flag to True. As long as this is True then the program will remove cells and determine if a solvable puzzle remains. Line 4 also establishes a copy of the puzzle as oldpuz. Known values will be removed until the process has removed one too many cells, then it reverts back to the previous state of the puzzle, which is contained in oldpuz. This matrix is returned in the last line.

Code 16.30 The **CreatePuzzle** function.

```python
# sudoku.py
def CreatePuzzle(puz):
    groups = Architecture1()
    ok = True;       oldpuz = puz + 0
    while ok:
        RemoveRandomCell(puz)
        dct = ConvertMat(puz)
        Sudoku(dct,groups)
        a = UnsolvedCount(dct)
        if a!=0:
            ok=False;
        else:
            oldpuz = puz + 0
    return oldpuz
```

A random cell value is removed by line 6. Lines 7 and 8 attempt to solve this puzzle. If successful then line 9 will return a 0. If it returns any other value, then the puzzle was not solvable, and the previous version of the puzzle is printed to the console. If the puzzle is solvable, then line 13 prepares the puzzle for the next iteration. Line 11 also sets the ok flag to False thus ending the iterations.

Finally, there is the task of classifying a generated puzzle as Easy, Medium, or Hard. The **CreatePuzzle** function merely creates a puzzle without regard to the difficulty. However, it is expected that some of the puzzles it generates are easier than others. Some of the metrics by which a puzzle can be classified are:

1. The number of givens, and/or

2. The number of times Rules 2 and 3 were used to solve the puzzle.

16.5   SUMMARY

Sudoku is an example of a situation in which the number of outcomes is enormous, but only outcome is the correct one. It is impossible to create computer loops to consider all possible outcomes. The solution is to create a set of rules which rapidly eliminate a large number of these outcomes.

The needed rules may not defined before the programming process begins. In this Sudoku example, one rule was created, but it could not solve the Soduku puzzle. The puzzle was examined to define a second rule. Application of the two rules can solve many puzzles, but one was found which did not come to a solution. This puzzle was examined to define a third rule. Rules 2 and 3 were not known at the beginning of the program creation, and they were determined after considering the state of puzzles which could not be solved by the current rules.

A process was presented to create new puzzles. It started with a trivial solution, modified this to a non-trivial solution, and then sequentially removed cells until the puzzle could not be solved. It backed up one step, and thus a solvable puzzle with many cells absent of given values was thus created.

PROBLEMS

1. Write a Python script to solve the puzzle in Figure 16.13a. Print the answer to the console.

2. Write a Python script to solve the puzzle in Figure 16.13b. Print the answer to the console.

3. Using the puzzle in Figure 16.13c, create a function name **Jigsaw3** which creates the architecture for this puzzle. To facilitate grading, print out the group index value and the sum of the values in that group's list, for all groups. Example: if the first group had cells [0,1,2,3] then output would be 0, 6 (the 0th group summed to 6).

4. Write a function named **Jigsaw4** which creates the puzzle shown in Figure 16.13d. Write a function named **PuzzleJigsaw4** which inserts the puzzles given value. Write a Python script that solves this puzzle and prints the answer to the console.

5. The puzzle in Figure 16.13e is an easy puzzle, and the one in Figure 16.13f is a hard puzzle. Measure the difficulty of each puzzle using the ratio of the number of times (Rule 2 or Rule 3 was used) divided by the number of times any rule was used. Count only the times in which the Rule changed the puzzle. In other words, if in an iteration Rule 1 was applied, but it didn't make any changes making the program go to Rule 2, then only Rule 2 is counted. Write a modified version of **Sudoku** to solve this puzzle and print this ratio to the console.

6. Make a new puzzle by applying the following steps to the trivial puzzle:

   (a) Swap cell values 1 and 3.
   (b) Swap cell values 4 and 9.
   (c) Swap cell values 3 and 5.
   (d) Rotation 90 degrees.
   (e) Reflect the puzzle horizontally.
   (f) Swap the first and last block rows.
   (g) Rotate the puzzle 90 degrees.

   Print the new puzzle to the console.

7. Solve the puzzle created in the previous problem, and print the answer to the console.

8. Modify the appropriate functions such that when a puzzle is created, the given values are symmetrically placed in the puzzle. (Example, if a given is in the 6th cell on the 2nd row, then there must be a given in the 4th cell on the 7th row. Create a new puzzle and print it to the console. Create a new puzzle that is symmetric and print it to the console.

9. Write the appropriate functions to solve the puzzle in Figure 16.14. Print the answer to the console.

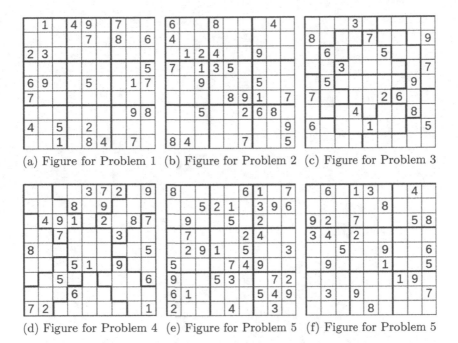

(a) Figure for Problem 1 (b) Figure for Problem 2 (c) Figure for Problem 3

(d) Figure for Problem 4 (e) Figure for Problem 5 (f) Figure for Problem 5

Figure 16.13: Figures for several homework problems.

Figure 16.14: Figure for Problem 9.

## CHAPTER 17

Agent Based Modeling — Virus Spread

IN 2020, the coronavirus spread rapidly across the planet, and scientists produced predictions of the virus behavior through several complicated models. Realistic simulations of a virus spread include several parameters such as population density, social distancing, hospital capacity, etc. Agent based models (ABM) were employed to offer insights as to how best reduce the devastating effects of the virus.

This chapter will present a simplistic model, demonstrating the foundations of an ABM approach. A data structure is created for each person in the population. These people move about and come in contact with each other, thus enabling the spread of the virus. Each agent has variables (such as location, status of infection, etc.) and actions (functions to move, transfer the virus, etc.). The agents move about the environment independently. Unless they come into direct contact, the actions of one agent are independent of the others. Several other important modeling parameters can be place atop of this basic model, but this chapter will leave the realistic parameters for more involved research and dedicated publications.

17.1   THE ABM MODEL

The proposed model consists of a two-dimensional environment, in which exist several people (agents). Each has a position and velocity. Collisions with the walls of the environment or other humans results in a change of direction of the agent. Basically, they bounce off of the walls and each other. Each person has a state of virus infection (healthy, infected, immune). Some people are initially healthier than others, and this is captured in a health factor. Infection will lower the health factor, and if the factor falls below 0, then the person is considered to have been killed by the virus. Human responses (such as social distancing and vaccination) can be modeled by adjusting the parameters.

DOI: 10.1201/9781003226581-17

17.1.1 Movement

For this simulation, the dimensions of the environment is 100×100. The agents therein have a location expressed by a position vector $\vec{x} = (x, y)$ where x and y are the horizontal and vertical position of the agent represented by floats. Each agent also has a velocity $\vec{v} = (v_x, v_y)$.

Movement of an agent follows non-acceleration motion as shown in Figure 17.1a. However, acceleration may be desired for future simulations, thus the two dimensional equation for motion is defined as,

$$\vec{x}_2 = \vec{x}_1 + \vec{v}_1 t + \frac{1}{2}\vec{a}t^2. \tag{17.1}$$

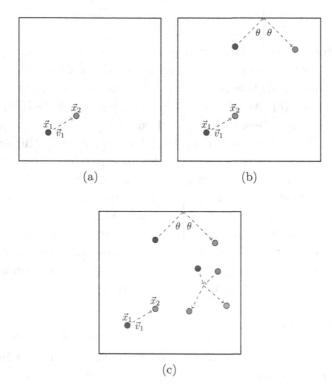

(a)   (b)

(c)

Figure 17.1: (a) The velocity of an agent. (b) Agents bounce off of the walls. (c) Two agents colliding.

This equation can be described by two one-dimensional equations,

$$x_2 = x_1 + v_{1x}t + \frac{1}{2}a_x t^2 \tag{17.2}$$

and

$$y_2 = y_1 + v_{1y}t + \frac{1}{2}a_y t^2. \tag{17.3}$$

For now, acceleration will not be used, so $\vec{a} = (0, 0)$.

A collision of an agent with a wall results in the change of direction of the agent following simple reflection rules. The speed of the agent does not change, but the direction does. The angle of reflection equals the angle of reflection as shown in Figure 17.1b. Since the walls are exactly vertical and horizontal, this computation is simply a change of sign of one of the components of the velocity. In the figure, the agent bounces off of the top wall, which does not change the horizontal velocity. The vertical velocity keeps the same value but changes from a positive value to a negative value. If the walls had any other orientation, then this computation would become slightly more complicated.

17.1.2 Agent Collision

The collision with another agent requires a bit more math. Figure 17.1c adds this case. The same concept is used in that an agent will bounce off of the collision, changing direction but not velocity. However, the change of direction is more than a change in sign of a velocity component.

The agents are not infinitesimally small, but rather they have a radius r. For now, all agents have the same radius. Thus, a collision occurs when the centers of the agents are within a distance of $2r$. If one of the agents is infected, then the collision could pass the virus onto the other agent. The simulation can control the chance of transfer and immunity.

It should be noted that this is not a kinematic collision. Momentum and energy are not conserved. In a kinematic collision, the speed of the agents would change. The agents here represent people, each with their own personality. Some people move quickly about the world and others do not. This personality should not change because of a meeting with another agent. Thus, an agent leaves the collision with the same speed as they had before. Only the direction changes.

The agent collision uses the idea of bouncing off of a theoretical wall, but the orientation of the this wall needs to be determined. Consider the collision shown in Figure 17.2a in which the two spheres represent two agents. The centers of these spheres are connected by the double-headed arrow, $\vec{c}$. The theoretical wall (dashed line) is perpendicular to this arrow, and passes through the point of contact of the two spheres. The angle from the horizontal (shown by the large arc) is described as α. The lower ball collides with the upper ball. The angle of reflection to the wall, θ, is the same as the angle of incidence to the wall.

The approach to calculating the reflection off of a wall at an angle is accomplished by rotating the system to a horizontal plane, compute the reflection, and then rotate the system back to the original orientation. The rotated system is shown in Figure 17.2b. This system is rotated by the angle $-\alpha$, such that the incoming agent is approaching the wall from the top. The computation of the reflection is simply to change the sign of the y component. The system is then rotated by an angle α to return to its original orientation.

The velocity vector is $\vec{v} = (v_x, v_y)$ containing the values for the horizontal and vertical components of the velocity. The standard notation for the rotation of a vector

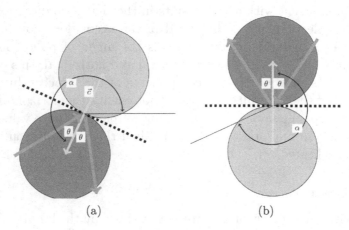

(a)   (b)

Figure 17.2: (a) Rotation for determining a collision, and (b) determining the reflection.

is,

$$\vec{v}' = \mathbf{R}\vec{v}, \tag{17.4}$$

where $\vec{v}'$ is the rotated vector, and $\mathbf{R}$ is the rotation matrix,

$$\mathbf{R} = \begin{pmatrix} \cos(\alpha) & -\sin(\alpha) \\ \sin(\alpha) & \cos(\alpha) \end{pmatrix}. \tag{17.5}$$

The steps for the computation are thus:

1. Rotate the agent's velocity vector by $-\alpha$,

2. Compute the new velocity by changing the sign of the second element in the vector, and

3. Rotate the new velocity by α.

17.1.3 An Example

Consider a case in which the incoming object has a velocity of $\vec{v} = (0.6, 0.8)$, and the collision is such that the vector between the two sphere centers is at an angle of 32° to the horizontal (Figure 17.3a). The dotted line with two arrowheads is the vector to the two sphere centers. The dashed line is the perpendicular, and thus the theoretical wall that the sphere reflects the sphere. The incoming velocity creates an angle of 36.9° to the vertical.

This space is rotated by an angle of 90° + 32° (Equation (17.4)) as depicted in Figure 17.3b. The old dimensions are shown as rotated to assist in keeping where the values were calculated. The new representation of the incoming vector is $(0.36, -0.932)$. This is the direction that the vector points, and it is not the position of the tail of the vector. The outgoing vector is a reflection of the incoming vector. Since it is

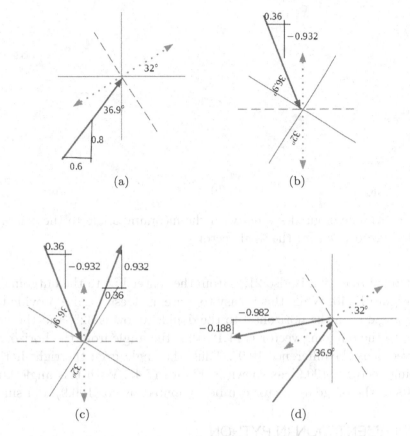

Figure 17.3: (a) Initial parameters in the collision, (b) the rotated space, (c) the reflected vector, and (d) rotation back to the original space.

reflecting off of a horizontal wall, the only change to the vector is the sign of the vertical component, as shown in Figure 17.3c.

The final step is to rotate the system back to the original orientation, by an angle that is in the opposite direction of the original rotation. The result for this example is shown in Figure 17.3d. The outgoing vector is $(-0.982, -0.188)$. The angle between the incoming vector and the dotted arrow line is the same as the angle from that dotted arrow line to the outgoing vector.

17.1.4 Alternate Computation

An alternate method of computation is shown in Figure 17.4a. While this method does not rotate the space, it does require about the same number of computational steps when put into Python script. Both methods provide the same answer.

The angle to the vertical of the incoming vector is already known to be 36.9°. The angle from the horizontal to the double arrow is known to be 32° which is true for the region under the horizontal on the left. The angle between the vertical and horizontal is 90°, and thus the angle between the arrow and the incoming vector is 21.1°.

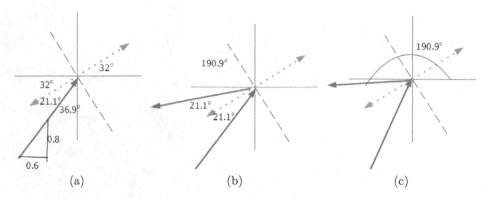

Figure 17.4: (a) The original system with the incoming angle to the center line, (b) the reflected vector, and (c) the final vector.

The angle of reflection is also 21.1° from the center line to the outgoing vector as shown in Figure 17.4b. While this is easy to write, it doesn't quite provide the vector itself. The angle from the horizontal to the double arrow is 32°, and the angle from that arrow to the outgoing vector is 21.1°, thus the angle from the horizontal to the outgoing vector is the difference 10.9°. Thus, the angle from the right horizontal to the outgoing vector is 190.9° as shown in Figure 17.4c. With this angle known, the components of the outgoing vector can be computed by cos(190.9) and sin(190.9).

17.2 IMPLEMENTATION IN PYTHON

Python offers multiple ways in which and agent can be realized in the script, and two such ways will be explored here. The first is to define each agent as a class-object. While this creates code which is easier to read, the program will run slow. The second approach will be to rely on *numpy* tools which will create fast code, but it is harder for the programmer to read.

17.2.1 Agents as Objects

An object can contain associated variables and functions. This suits ABM well. In this example, the class houses information for a single agent. A population is multiple instances of this class.

A single agent has these variables: Each agent in this simulation owns several parameters. These are:

1. x: A two dimensional array for the position, which initially is at a random location.

2. v: A two dimensional array for the velocity, which initially has random values between 5 and 10.

3. a: A two dimensional array for the acceleration, which is initially (0,0).

4. alive: A True/False flag to indicative if the agent is still alive.

5. `infected`: A `True/False` flag to indicate if the agent is currently infected.

6. `immune`: A `True/False` flag to indicated if the agents is currently immune to infection.

7. `health`: A random value between 50 and 100. A healthy agent has a higher value. These values are lowered when the agent becomes infected. If the agent's `health` reaches 0, then the `alive` flag is set to `False`.

8. `bottom`: A random value between −50 and 100. This is an agent's value where they reach the end of the infection. If this number is positive, then when the agent's health declines to this value, the illness ends and the agent becomes immune. If the number is negative, then the agent is doomed to a sad ending.

Each agent also has several functions:

- **Move** Move the agent.

- **Boundaries** Ensure that agents do not move beyond the boundaries.

- **LowerHealth** Lowers the health of an infected person.

- **Cured** Sets the agent's parameters when they are cured of the illness.

- **Death** Sets the agent's parameters when an agent has died.

- **Distance** Returns the distance of two agents.

- **Collide** Manages the collision of two agents.

Other functions are needed to manage the population of agents and iterations of the simulations. All functions will be explained shortly.

Building the class begins starts in Code 17.1. Several of the following codes will be appended to this class as they are introduced. Line 2 in Code 17.1 creates the class. The constructor (`__init__` function) begins in line 3. This function is automatically called when an instance of the class is created (line 13). Lines 4 through 11 establish the randomized variables for a single `Person`. Bob is a `Person` and his values can be accessed by a command such as `Bob.alive`.

Printing all variables could be inconvenient as it requires several commands. Python allows for the definition of the `__str__` function, which creates a string that returns a user-defined string for the class. Code 17.2 is appended to the Person class. Code 17.3 creates a new Bob, and line 10 uses the `__str__` to create a string which is then printed by the `print(Bob)` function as seen in Code 17.3.

Each agent will need to alter their values such as movement or dealing with the virus. Movement is governed by the accelerated motion equation, and the addition to the class is shown in Code 17.4. This function will adjust the position based on the current position, velocity, and acceleration.

The **Move** function could move the agent beyond the boundaries of the environment. In such cases, the agent is to be reflected off of the wall by changing the sign of

---

Code 17.1 Defining a class for a single agent.

```
1  # virus.py
2  class Person:
3      def __init__(self):
4          self.x = np.random.rand(2)*99
5          self.v = np.random.rand(2)*10+5
6          self.a = np.zeros(2)
7          self.alive = True
8          self.infected = False
9          self.immune = False
10         self.health = np.random.randint(50,150)
11         self.bottom = np.random.randint(-50,100)
12
13 Bob = Person()
```

Code 17.2 The function to create a string.

```
1  # virus.py   class Person:
2      def __str__( self ):
3          st = ''
4          temps = vars(self)
5          for item in temps:
6              st += str(item) + ': ' + str(temps[item]) + '\
                   n'
7          return st
```

Code 17.3 Creating an agent.

```
1  Bob = Person()
2  print(Bob)
3  x: [38.72591893 19.9980103 ]
4  v: [ 9.38775062 14.68920354]
5  a: [0. 0.]
6  alive: True
7  infected: False
8  immune: False
9  health: 83
10 bottom: 45
```

Code 17.4 Moving the agent.

```
# virus.py    class Person:
    def Move(self, dt = 0.1):
        self.x = self.x + self.v*dt + 0.5*self.a*dt*dt
```

one of the velocities. Furthermore, the movements are in discrete time steps, so it is possible for the calculation to place agent beyond the perimeter. When an agent goes d distance beyond the boundary, then it is placed a distance d inside of the boundary.

Part of the **Boundaries** is shown in Code 17.5, and this is also appended to the Person class. One corner in the environment is assumed to be (0,0), and the other is defined as (V, H). These two values are the input to the function. Lines 3 through 8 show the reflections for the x[0] variable. Similar code for the x[1] variable is not shown, but would be placed on line 9. Line 3 considers the case in which x[0] has become less than 0. Line 4 positions the agent, and line 5 alters the velocity.

Code 17.5 The **Boundaries** function.

```
# virus.py    class Person:
    def Boundaries(self,V,H):
        if self.x[0]<0:
            self.x[0] *= -1
            self.v[0] *= -1
        if self.x[0] > H:
            self.x[0] = H - (self.x[0]-H)
            self.v[0] *= -1
        . . . # code for x[1] and V
```

If an agent is infected, then their health rating decreases with each iteration. Code 17.6 shows the **LowerHealth** which lowers the health of the agent if the agent is infected and the health is still greater than the bottom.

Code 17.6 The **LowerHealth** function.

```
# virus.py    class Person:
    def LowerHealth(self):
        if self.infected==True and self.health>self.bottom:
            self.health -= 1
```

The lucky agents who have a positive bottom value can be cured of the illness. As seen in the **Cured** function in Code 17.7, when the health falls below the bottom, then the infection flag is turned to False, indicating that the agent is no longer infected. Furthermore, the immunity is set to True preventing this agent from being re-infected.

Code 17.7 The **Cured** function.

```
# virus.py   class Person:
    def Cured(self):
        if self.health <= self.bottom:
            self.infected = False
            self.immune = True
```

Some agents do not become cured. If their **bottom** value is negative, then eventually their **health** value will fall below 0. When this occurs, their **alive** flag is unceremoniously set to **False**. This is handled by the **Death** function shown in Code 17.8.

Code 17.8 The **Death** function.

```
# virus.py   class Person:
    def Death(self):
        if self.health < 0:
            self.alive = False
```

After an agent moves, it needs to determine if it has collided with another agent. This occurs when the distance between the centers of the two agents is less than 1. The **Distance** function (Code 17.9) computes the distance from the considered agent to a second agent defined as the input **you**. This function merely computes the distance, but it doesn't make any decisions.

Code 17.9 The **Distance** function.

```
# virus.py   class Person:
    def Distance(self, you ):
        dist = np.sqrt(((self.x-you.x)**2).sum())
        return dist
```

Most of the tools for the **Person** class are set. The final function is the components of a collision. The mechanics of a collision were discussed in Section 17.1.2. The **Collide** function converts that theory into Python script. This function is called twice to alter the behavior of both participants in the collision.

The input to the **Collide** function is the other agent in the collision. Lines 3 and 4 compute the vertical and horizontal distances between the two agents, and line 5 computes the angle α as defined in the theory of collisions. Line 6 creates the rotation matrix, and line 7 applies it. Line 8 computes the reflection, and lines 10 and 11 rotate the system back to the original space. Lines 15 and 16 transfer the infection if the conditions are suitable. If the programmer wishes to not have a 100% transfer rate, then line 16 would be modified.

Code 17.10 The **Collide** function.

```
1   # virus.py   class Person:
2       def Collide(self,you):
3           ypart = you.x[1] - self.x[1]
4           xpart = you.x[0] - self.x[0]
5           alpha = np.arctan2( ypart, xpart )
6           R=np.array(((np.cos(-alpha),-np.sin(-alpha)),
7                        (np.sin(-alpha),np.cos(-alpha))))
8           vrot = R.dot( self.v)
9           wrot = vrot * np.array((1,-1))
10          R=np.array(((np.cos(alpha),-np.sin(alpha)),
11                       (np.sin(alpha),np.cos(alpha))))
12          w = R.dot(wrot)
13          self.v = w +0
14          # transfer infection
15          if you.infected==True and self.immune==False:
16              self.infected = True
```

17.2.2 Iterations

A single iteration moves each person and computes the events of any collision. The steps are:

1. Move the agent,

2. Reflect the agent off of the walls if needed,

3. Lower the health of infected agents,

4. Determine if any agents have overcome the virus,

5. Determine if any agents have died, and

6. Compute the effects of a collision.

The **Iterate** function (Code 17.11) performs a single iteration in the simulation. The function is external to the **Person** class. The inputs are **people**, **V**, and **H**. The V and H are the spatial limits of the environment. The variable **people** is a list of agents, each created by **Person()**. Each agent is considered in the loop starting in line 2. If this agent is still alive (line 3), then its movement is calculated (line 5). Line 6 checks for movement beyond the boundaries. Lines 7 through 9 check the conditions to alter the health, the immunity, the disease state, or if the agent has died.

The **CreateWorld** function (Code 17.12) creates a population of agents. The inputs are the number of agents and the extent of the environment. This function creates a homogeneous distribution of agents. Alterations to the density of the initial position of the agents would be created here.

Code 17.11 The components of an iteration.

```
1   # virus.py
2   def Iterate( people, V, H ):
3       for me in people:
4           if me.alive:
5               me.Move()
6               me.Boundaries(V,H)
7               me.LowerHealth()
8               me.Cured()
9               me.Death()
10              for you in people:
11                  if you.alive == True and me!=you:
12                      if me.Distance(you) < 1:
13                          me.Collide( you )
14                          you.Collide( me )
```

Code 17.12 The **CreateWorld** function.

```
1   # virus.py
2   def CreateWorld( NPeople=100, V=100, H=100):
3       people = []
4       for i in range( NPeople ):
5           people.append( Person() )
6       return people
```

Line 14 begins the process of manipulating the agents in a collision. The current agent (me) is compared to each of the other agents (line 12). If the other agent is alive and the distance between the two agents is less than 1, then the agents collide. Both agents need to alter their velocities, and this is handled in lines 14 and 15.

The simulation is run in Code 17.13. Line 1 creates 300 agents, and lines 2 and 3 infect the first 10. The two lists **alives** and **infects** will collect the number of living and infected people after each iteration. These collections will be plotted at the end of the simulation.

The iterations begin with the `for` loop starting in line 6. Line 7 calls the `Iterate` function which moves the agents and performs the steps regarding collisions. Lines 8 through 15 collect the number of living and infected people. The last three lines plot the results, of which an example is shown in Figure 17.5. The top line is the number of living agents. It starts at 300 and declines, but as the number of infections goes to 0, the number of living agents stabilize. The bottom curve is the number of current infections. It rises with the pandemic and falls mainly because all agents have become infected. The final value of the number of living agents is about 2/3, which is the same as the number of agents with a positive `bottom` value.

Code 17.13 A trial.

```
1  people = virus.CreateWorld(300)
2  for i in range( 10 ):
3      people[i].infected = True
4  alives = []
5  infects = []
6  for i in range( 200 ):
7      virus.Iterate(people, 100, 100 )
8      ct = 0; cu=0
9      for me in people:
10         if me.alive:
11             ct += 1
12             if me.infected:
13                 cu += 1
14     alives.append( ct )
15     infects.append( cu )
16 plt.plot( alives )
17 plt.plot( infects )
18 plt.show()
```

Simulations wanting to capture a second wave of infections would need to make some alterations. Not all agents would become infected in the first wave, or the immunity does not last forever. The latter would require that another variable be added to the **Person** class which would control how long an immunity lasts.

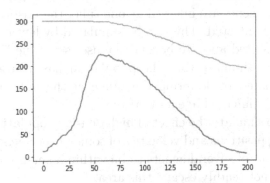

Figure 17.5: Plots of the number of infected and number of living agents for each time step.

17.2.3 Altering the Simulation

This program has several variables which can be altered to produce different simulations.

- `NPeople` is the number of agents at the beginning of the simulation. Increasing the number of agents also increases their density in the environment, which can have a profound effect on the infection rate.

- `NIters` is the number of iterations.

- `X` and `Y` are the limits of the space. By increasing these, the density of agents goes down. It is also possible to create a rectangular space will limits travel in one dimension.

- The velocity of an agent is a random value between 5 and 10. By increasing this range, the agents are likely to have more collisions. To activate *social distancing* the velocity of the agents are lowered.

- The acceleration was not employed in the example. It can be used to slow down agents who are infected or speed up those who disregard social distancing.

- The health factor is a value between 50 and 150. If this range is raised, then it takes more time steps for the infected agent to recover.

- The `bottom` factor is a value between −50 and 100. That means that 1/3 of infected agents will die. By raising this range, the number of agents who can survive the virus increases.

- The distribution of agents is homogeneous, which means that initially everyone has about the same number of neighbors. Highly dense populations can be created in the initialization stage.

Consider a case in which the simulation wishes to use the influence of hospital capacity. If too many agents are infected at one time, the hospitals are over capacity and cannot care for all infected. This can be simulated by lowering the `bottom` factor for agents who are infected and are beyond the user-set value for hospital capacity.

Another case is to simulate that the population has a large number of at-risk agents. This is simulated by lowering the range of the `bottom` value as that will increase the number of infected agents that die.

Another case is to simulate the effect of high density population. This is controlled by the initial starting positions and velocities of some of the agents. For a high density region, set the locations of several agents to be within a small region, and lower their velocities so they do not readily escape this area.

To simulate the presence of a miracle cure, at a certain time, random agents have their `bottom` value increased. As time passes, more agents receive the medicine and their `bottom` values are increased.

Currently, agents who have recovered are considered to be immune. This can be changed as well. One scenario would set the `immune` flag to `False` after a period of time. Another simulation might not set the immunity flag for all agents. Perhaps a recovered agent has only a 75% chance of developing an immunity. This would allow agents to contract the illness repeatedly.

Simulating the opening of public establishments would be to attract some agents to a specific location. This would require an alteration to the acceleration which would alter the direction (but not necessarily the velocity) of the motion toward a bar or a beach.

17.3 SPEED OF COMPUTATION

One of the issues of interpreted languages such as Python is that some coding approaches can create slow computation times. The previous section simulated 300 agents for 200 iterations. The computation required about 90 seconds on a standard computer. While 90 seconds is not too bad, it will grow exponentially with the number of agents, because each agent must interact will the other agents to determine if there is a collision. That is a double nested loop and significantly impacts the computation time as the number of agents increases. This code works well for small populations, but it will perform poorly for large populations.

To increase the speed of computation, a new data structure is used. The cost is that the code will be more difficult to understand and hence maintain. Each agent has three types of data. They have float values for position, velocity, and acceleration. They have binary values for the alive, infected, and immune flags. They have integers for their health and bottom values.

This new data structure will rely on the speed of *numpy* functions which means that the data must be contained in arrays. Three matrices are established. Each row in a matrix is associated with one agent. Thus the 10th agent will be associated with the values in the 10th row of each matrix. The first matrix is **M** which contains the float values. The number of rows is the number of agents, and there are six columns: two each for position, velocity, and acceleration. The **B** matrix contains the binary data which are the alive, infected, and immune flags. The **I** matrix contains the integer values for health and bottom.

These matrices are created by the **InitVirusMats** function shown in Code 17.14. Lines 3 through 5 create the three matrices, but they don't have any data yet. Line 6 sets the first two columns of the **M** matrix to random values between 0 and 100. These are the vertical and horizontal locations of the agents. Line 7 establishes the initial velocity of all agents. Lines 8 and 9 set the random numbers for the agent's health and bottom values. Lines 10 through 12 set the flags such that every agent is alive, healthy, but not immune.

Code 17.15 shows the **CollideM** function which manages the collision of agents. The math within this function is the same as described above.

The **IterateM** function (Code 17.16) computes one iteration and follows the same logic as in Code 17.11. Line 5 computes the new location. Lines 6 through 11 keep the agent within bounds in one direction. The same code for the other directions is not shown (line 12) to save space. The next lines compute the distance from the agent to the other agents and determines if they collide.

Code 17.17 shows one simulation. This time the number of agents is 300, but the number of iterations is 500. Line 2 creates the matrices. The **for** loop runs the

Code 17.14 The **InitVirusMats** function.

```python
# virus.py
def InitVirusMats(NPeople = 100):
    M = np.zeros((NPeople,6)) # a, x, v
    B = np.zeros((NPeople,3), bool) # alive, infected,
        immune
    I = np.zeros((NPeople,2),int) # health bottom
    M[:,:2] = np.random.ranf((NPeople,2))*99
    M[:,2:4] = np.random.ranf((NPeople,2))*10+5
    I[:,0] = np.random.randint(50,150,NPeople)
    I[:,1] = np.random.randint(-50,100,NPeople)
    B[:,0] = True # everyone is alive
    B[:,1] = False # not infected
    B[:,2] = False # not immune
    return M, B, I
```

iterations and saves the number of infected and living agents to their arrays. The simulation results is shown in Figure 17.6.

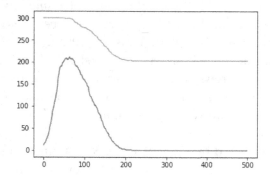

Figure 17.6: Plots of the number of infected and number of living agents for each time step.

The results for the first 200 iterations are similar in both programs. The main difference is that the first simulation required 90 seconds to run 200 iterations, and this second version required 9 seconds to run 500 iterations. The reason is line 16 in Code 17.16. This line computes the distance from one agent to all agents in a single line of Python. This is still a nested loop process, but one of the loops within the *numpy* functions, and thus it is significantly faster.

The cost, though, is that the script is tougher to read. The programmer will need to remember what each of the columns in the matrices represent. Furthermore, the values of the agents are more susceptible to confusion. Line n in each matrix corresponds to agent n. However, there is no mechanism that actually ties them together. It is possible to shift the data in one matrix one row and completely mess up the entire simulation. Thus, the programmer needs to express a bit more care in

Code 17.15 The **CollideM** function.

```
# virus.py
def CollideM(M,B,me, him):
    alpha = np.arctan2(M[him,1]-M[me,1],M[him,0]-M[me,0])
    R = np.array(((np.cos(-alpha),-np.sin(-alpha)),(np.sin
        (-alpha),np.cos(-alpha))))
    vrot = R.dot(M[me,2:4])
    wrot = vrot * np.array((1,-1))
    R = np.array(((np.cos(alpha),-np.sin(alpha)),(np.sin(
        alpha),np.cos(alpha))))
    w = R.dot(wrot)
    M[me,2:4] = w +0
    if B[him,1]==True and B[me,2]==False:
        B[me,1] = True
```

Code 17.16 The **IterateM** function.

```
# virus.py
def IterateM(M,B,I):
    alive = B[:,0].nonzero()[0] # index of the living
    for me in alive:
        M[me,:2] = M[me,:2] + M[me,2:4]*dt + 0.5*M[me
            ,4:6]*dt**2
        if M[me,0]<0:
            M[me,0] *= -1;    M[me,2] *= -1
        if M[me,0]>X:
            M[me,0] = X - (M[me,0] -X);    M[me,2] *= -1
        if M[me,1]<0:
            M[me,1] *= -1;    M[me,3] *= -1
        # similar code for Y direction goes here
        them = list(alive)
        them.remove(me)
        them = np.array(them)
        dist = np.sqrt(((M[me,:2]-M[:,:2])**2).sum(1))
        closendx = (dist<1).nonzero()[0]
        for i in closendx:
            if i in them:
                CollideM(M,B,me,i)
                CollideM(M,B,i,me)
        ndx = (I[:,0]<=0).nonzero()[0]
        B[ndx] = False,False,False
```

Code 17.17 Running the simulation.

```
1  NPeople = 300; NITERS = 500
2  M,B,I = InitM(NPeople)
3  inf = np.zeros(NITERS)
4  aliv = np.zeros(NITERS)
5  for i in range( NITERS ):
6      IterateM(M,B,I)
7      inf[i] = B[:,1].sum()
8      aliv[i] = B[:,0].sum()
```

ensuring that the data for each agent is in its proper location. An increase of speed of almost 20× is worth the effort.

17.4 SUMMARY

This chapter presented a simple model for the transmission in an environment using agent based modeling (ABM). Each agent represents a person, and it has properties for movement, health, and current status. These agents move about a closed environment, and when they collide, it is possible that an infected person can transmit the infection to an uninfected person. Each agent can gain immunity. The illness takes a toll on the agent's health, and if it falls below a threshold, then the agent is considered to be dead.

This rudimentary simulation omits many important features of realistic simulation, such as economic impact, mental health impact, non-homogeneous environment, non-uniform agent behavior and so on. However, it does show the basic mechanics of building a simulation.

Two Python implementations are presented. The first uses a class as the data structure, which provides easily read code, but it is slow. The second implementation uses *numpy* tools which is much faster. However, this second implementation is more difficult to read and maintain.

Finally, a few alterations to the simulation are presented or discussed. Most of the exercises in the next section are based on modifications.

PROBLEMS

Disclaimer: These simulations are merely for educational purposes. They omit significant factors that would need to be considered in order to simulate reality. Please do not use the results computed here as a factor in governing your personal decisions.

1. Run 3 simulations each with 300 agents and 200 iterations. Show the populations plots for all three cases. Comment on the similarities and dissimilarities within these three tests.

2. Run a simulation with 300 agents and 500 iterations. How many people were infected in this simulation?

3. Simulate a stay-at-home order. Run the simulation for 300 agents and 300 iterations. At iteration 50, the stay-at-home order is imposed. Save all current velocities for later use. Set all velocities to 0. Run for 100 iterations, and then lift the stay-at-home order by reinstating the velocities to the values saved. Plot the results.

4. Run 3 simulations, each with 300 agents.

   • The original simulation with 200 iterations
   • The simulation from the previous problem in which a stay-at-home order was put in place at iteration 50 and lifted at iteration 150.
   • The stay-at-home simulation in which the stay-at-home order was put in place at iteration 35 and lifted at 135.

   In this simulation is a stay-at-home order effective? Explain your answer.

5. In the original simulation, the *bottom* variable is designed such that about 1/3 of the agents will die from the virus. Change this value to about 2/3. Run this simulation, and comment on how the results differ from the original simulation.

6. After 30 iterations, a vaccine was created to provide instant immunity to 90% of the population (selected at random). Some people may have already had an immunity, but they got the vaccination anyway. Run this simulation and show the plots. Comment on the effectiveness of the vaccine from the simulation data.

7. Repeat the previous experiment with a 50% effectiveness for the vaccine. Compare these results to the previous problem.

8. Consider the effectiveness of when the vaccine is available. Run a simulation in which the vaccine is 90% effective but not delivered until iteration 100. Compare this to the case in which the vaccine was 90% effective and available at iteration 30.

9. Create a simulation which has 300 agents and 200 iterations. However, all agents start in a confined area of 10×10. Run the simulation and plot the results.

10. Consider the effect of wearing a mask. In this simulation, the masks do not prevent a person from becoming ill because the virus may enter the body through means other than breathing. The masks do prevent the spread of the virus. To be simple, any agent wearing a mask in this simulation cannot transmit the virus. Run a simulation with 300 agents and 500 iterations. In the original simulation, the first 10 agents in the population are the initial infected agents. In this modification, the first 50 people choose not to wear a mask. This group of 50 includes the initially infected individuals. Run the modified simulation and plot the results.

## CHAPTER 18

Chess

C HESS is internationally renowned as a superior logic game. Many computer programs have been written to play this game against humans. This chapter will review a standard approach to creating a chess-playing game. While the program created here will play a chess game, it won't play a strong game. However, a discussion will ensue as to which steps are needed to improve the performance.

18.1 THEORY

The basis of a chess game model is that a configuration of the pieces on the board is converted to a metric for the players' current state. In order for a computer model to determine the next move, the program scores all possible moves, and then it selects a move based on the top scores. Reasons for not selecting the top scoring move are discussed later.

A score for each possible move can be calculated, but the attributes which contribute to that score are open for discussion. In the model developed here, the scores are based on the value of the pieces, their location on the board, and which pieces they can capture.

However, this is insufficient to create a high-quality simulation as it does not consider opponent's possible responses. A chess program has a 'level' for determining the next move. For level 1, the program only considers the next move without repercussions. At this level, many moves can actually lead the computer into perilous positions because it doesn't consider the possible opponent moves. For level 2, the computer considers its possible moves and the opponent's possible moves. While this improves the eventual selection of a move, it requires more computation time. At the beginning of the game, a player has 20 possible moves. Of course, the number of possible moves fluctuates as the game progresses. However if a player has 20 possible moves and their opponent has 20 responses for each one, then the computer needs to evaluate 400 possible moves. The process increases the computations exponentially. In level 3 the computer would consider its responses to the opponent's moves, now increasing to about 8000 possible moves. In this chapter, level 1 will be considered, but the other levels and their efficient computations are reserved for discussion.

DOI: 10.1201/9781003226581-18

18.2 IMPLEMENTATION

This section will provide examples of implementing a chess game to the first level. This program can play a legal game of chess, but it can be easily defeated.

18.2.1 Piece Values

There are variations on the values to attach to chess pieces, but they are in agreement as to which pieces are more valuable. Some scales do not include the king, because once it is captured the game ends. Thus, its value can be considered to be infinite. A lesser value is used here to accommodate the needs of the computation.

For this model, values are assigned in the function **PieceValues**. Each type of piece is assigned a single letter code for ease of programming. These are noted by the comment statements in the code. The output is a dictionary with the values of each piece. Users wishing to use a different scale would alter the values in this function.

Code 18.1 The **PieceValues** function.

```
1   # chess.py
2   def PieceValues():
3       values = {}
4       values['p'] = 1 # pawn
5       values['r'] = 8 # rook
6       values['n'] = 5 # knight
7       values['b'] = 5 # bishop
8       values['q'] = 10 # queen
9       values['k'] = 50 # king
10      return values
```

18.2.2 Creating the Board

The **InitChess** function creates the chessboard and the standard starting positions. The board is an 8×8 grid of alternating white and black squares with a white square in the lower right corner. In Python, the board is represented as an array of lists, one for each square on the board. Each list contains two items, a string, and a value of the piece. The string for an empty square is space-period. There are two reasons for having the space. This will be useful when printing the board to the console, and more importantly it helps establish the board as an array of strings instead of single characters.

Lines 3 through 7 create the empty board. Lines 8 through 15 create the pieces for the black player. Commonly, the chess pieces are black and white, and white move first. Thus, the computer is assigned the black set of pieces. In line 8, one black rook is created. The locations is [0,0] which is the upper left corner. The string 'br1' indicates this is a black ('b'), rook ('r'), and it is the first of two. The second entry in the list is values['r'] which is the value for the rook established by **PieceValues**.

Code 18.2 The InitChess function.

```
1   # chess.py
2   def InitChess(values):
3       blank = [' .',0]
4       board = np.zeros((8,8),type(blank))
5       for i in range(8):
6           for j in range(8):
7               board[i,j] = blank
8       board[0,0] = ['br1',values['r']] # creates a rook.
9       board[0,1] = ['bn1',values['n']] # knight
10      board[0,2] = ['bb1',values['b']] # bishop
11      board[0,3] = ['bq',values['q']] # queen
12      board[0,4] = ['bk',values['k']] # king
13      board[0,5] = ['bb2',values['b']]
14      board[0,6] = ['bn2',values['n']]
15      board[0,7] = ['br2',values['r']]
16      for i in range(8):
17          board[1,i] = ['bp'+str(i+1),1]
18          . . .       # code for the opponent's pieces goes here
19      return board
```

Lines 8 through 15 finish the first row of pieces for the black player. Lines 16 and 17 establish the black pawns. Lines 5 through 17 are repeated with alterations to establish the white pieces, but not shown here (line 18). The changes are the location of the pieces and the letter 'w' instead of 'b'. The output is an 8×8 array of lists.

The **PrintBoard** function prints the status of the board to the console using the string codes from the board list.

Code 18.3 The PrintBoard function.

```
1   # chess.py
2   def PrintBoard(board):
3       for v in range(8):
4           for h in range(8):
5               print('%5s' % board[v,h][0], end='')
6           print('')
```

The three functions are called in Code 18.4. The board is now ready for play.

18.2.3 Moving

Before getting into the functions to decide on moves to make, functions are needed to actually move the pieces and print the status of the game to the console. Chess players refer to positions on the board by rows and columns. The rows are numbered

---

Code 18.4 Initializing the chess game.

```
1  values = PieceValues()
2  board = InitChess(values)
3  PrintBoard( board )
4     br1   bn1   bb1    bq    bk   bb2   bn2   br2
5     bp1   bp2   bp3   bp4   bp5   bp6   bp7   bp8
6      .     .     .     .     .     .     .     .
7      .     .     .     .     .     .     .     .
8      .     .     .     .     .     .     .     .
9      .     .     .     .     .     .     .     .
10    wp1   wp2   wp3   wp4   wp5   wp6   wp7   wp8
11    wr1   wn1   wb1    wq    wk   wb2   wn2   wr2
```

---

1 through 8, and the columns are identified by letters 'a' through 'g'. However, this is less conducive to a Python implementation. Thus, for the program, positions are the board will be indexed by values from 0 to 7 in both dimensions.

The **Move** function moves a piece from one location to another. The inputs to the function are the board, the coordinates of the old location, and the coordinates of the new location. This function does not determine if the move is a legal chess move, which allows the user to set up mid-game positions if desired. If the moving piece lands on a square with an opponent's piece, then the opponent's piece is removed from play. The output of the functions is either the two default values created in line 3 or the name and value of the piece that was removed. The move is performed in three steps. The first is to get the name of the piece that will be removed (line 5), the second is to move the piece to its new location (line 6), and the third is to clear the information from the old square (line 7).

Code 18.5 The **Move** function.

```python
1  # chess.py
2  def Move(board, oldloc, newloc):
3      nam,val = ' .',0
4      if board[oldloc][0] != ' .':
5          nam, val = board[newloc]
6          board[newloc] = board[oldloc]
7          board[oldloc] = [' .',0]
8      return nam,val
```

18.2.4 Individual Pieces

Each piece has a set of rules that govern its movements, requiring multiple functions to properly determine the moves of the pieces. The rook, bishop and queen have the property of being able to move any number of squares in a single direction. For example, the rook can move along columns or rows of the board until it reaches the end of the board or a square with another piece on it. In the latter case, if the piece is of the same color, then the rook cannot advance to that square. If the square is occupied by the opponent's piece, then the rook can occupy that square and capture the opponent's piece. The bishop can act in the same manner but only along diagonals. The queen can act as the rook or bishop.

For now, consider only the case of moving in a specified direction. The program needs to determine which spaces the piece can go to and if the terminal space is occupied by the opponent. Code 18.6 shows the **GoFar** function which receives several inputs. The first is the board. The variables i and j represent the current position of the piece being considered. The list **poss** collects the locations of the squares that this piece can legally go to. The variables kk and ll define the direction that piece is going. For example, if the piece is a rook moving to the right then kk=0 and ll=1. This function considers only one direction of motion, thus it will be called four times for a rook to find the possible moves in all four directions. The first time this function is called, the **poss** list is empty, and the function populates it with possible moves in one direction. The second time the function is called, it considers moves in a different direction and continues to populate that same list.

Code 18.6 The **GoFar** function.

```
1  # chess.py
2  def GoFar(board,i,j,poss,kk,ll):
3      bw = board[i][j][0][0]
4      ok = True
5      k = i;l=j
6      while ok:
7          k += kk; l+= ll
8          if k<0 or l<0 or k>7 or l>7:
9              ok = False
10             break # you have reached the end of the board
11         if board[k][l][0]==' .':
12             poss.append((k,l))  # open space
13         if (board[k][l][0][0]=='w' and bw=='b') or (board[
           k][l][0][0]=='b' and bw=='w'):
14             poss.append((k,l)) # atrack
15             ok = False
16             break
17         if board[k][l][0][0]== bw:
18             ok = False
19             break
```

A while loop is established since the number of squares that are available for the movement of this piece are not yet known. The piece considers consecutive squares in a single direction via line 7. The program will break out of the function when the `ok` flag becomes `False`. This can occur when the considered squares reach the edges of the board (lines 8 and 10). Lines 11 and 12 are used if the next square being considered does not have any piece in it. Lines 13 through 16 are used if the piece moves to the square occupied by an opponent. Lines 17 and 18 are used if the piece attempts to move to a square occupied by one of its own pieces. Lines 12 and 14 append the considered square to the list `poss` as these are legal moves. The function does not produce an output, but it does modify the contents of the `poss` list.

The rook is one of the pieces that uses this function. Since it can move forward, backward, left, or right, the **GoFar** function is called four times. These are managed in the function named **RookMove** shown in Code 18.7. The empty list `poss` is created in line 3. The next four lines consider the directions of motion available for the rook.

Code 18.7 The **RookMove** function.

```
1  # chess.py
2  def RookMove(board,i,j):
3      poss = []
4      GoFar(board,i,j,poss,-1, 0)
5      GoFar(board,i,j,poss, 1, 0)
6      GoFar(board,i,j,poss, 0,-1)
7      GoFar(board,i,j,poss, 0, 1)
8      return poss
```

The function **BishopMove** (not shown) is quite similar except that motions are along the diagonal. Thus line 4 becomes `GoFar(board,i,j,poss,-1,-1)`. The other three lines suitably adjust the direction of motion. The **QueenMove** function (also not shown here) calls the **RookMove** and **BishopMove** functions to determine the possible moves for this piece.

The king and knight have a limited set of motions. The king can move one square in any direction, thus giving it at most 8 possible moves. The knight can move in a combination of 2 squares and 1 square in a perpendicular direction. For example, it can move 2 spaces to the right and 1 space forward. It's motion is not impeded by intermediate pieces. Thus, it also has up to 8 moves available.

The two functions that govern these are **KnightMove** and **KingMove** of which one is shown in Code 18.8. Line 5 defines the possible moves for the piece with respect to its current position. The loop started in line 6 begins the consideration of each move. Lines 8 and 9 consider cases that move the piece off the board. Lines 10 and 11 prevent the piece landing on a square with a piece from the same player. The **KingMove** function is similar except for line 5 which defines its possible moves.

Even though the pawn is the least valued piece, it has the most complicated function for movement. The pawn moves forward, thus white pawns move in one direction, and black pawns move in the other direction. Usually, a pawn can move one space forward, but there are exceptions. The first exception is that a pawn may move two spaces forward on its first move. The second is that when it captures a piece,

Code 18.8 The **KnightMove** function.

```
1   # chess.py
2   def KnightMove(board,i,j):
3       bw = board[i][j][0][0]
4       poss = []
5       allowed = ((1,2),(-1,2),(1,-2),(-1,-2),(2,1),(-2,1)
            ,(-2,-1),(2,-1))
6       for kk,ll in allowed:
7           k = i+kk; l=j+ll
8           if k<0 or k>7 or l<0 or l>7:
9               pass # off the board
10          elif board[k][l][0][0]==bw:
11              pass
12          else:
13              poss.append((k,l))
14      return poss
```

it moves forward and sideways one space. A pawn cannot capture a piece directly in front of it.

Two pawn moves are not included in the code. They are easy to add and somewhat rare to use. The first is a promotion. When a pawn reaches its last row, it can be converted into any other piece. A player could, in fact, have multiple queens due to promotion. This is quite simple to put into code. The second is *en passant*. When one player moves its pawn two spaces forward, becoming parallel to the other player's pawn, then the other player can capture the piece by moving directly behind the recently moved piece. This is a move in which the one piece captures another, but it does not stay on the square in which the capture occurred.

The main three options are to move forward two spaces, move forward one space, and to capture moving forward and diagonal. Part of the **PawnMove** function (Code 18.9) considers these moves. The inputs are like the other moving functions. Since black and white are moving in opposite directions, there are two parts to this program, but only the movement for the black pawn is shown. Lines 6 and 7 consider the move of one space forward, lines 8 and 9 consider a two space move, and the rest of the lines consider a capture. Since the capture and be forward and to the right or forward and to the left, there are two considerations here. Lines 16 and 17 are the placeholders for the movement of the white pawns, which are going in the opposite direction.

Functions now exist to determine all legal moves for any piece on the board excepting two types of special moves:

- Piece promotion

- Castling

- En Passant

Code 18.9 The **PawnMove** function.

```
1   # chess.py
2   def PawnMove(board, i,j ):
3       poss = []
4       bw = board[i][j][0][0] # black or white
5       if bw == 'b':
6           if board[i+1][j][0] == ' .':
7               poss.append((i+1,j))
8           if i==1 and board[i+2][j][0]== ' .' and board[i
                +1][j][0]==' .':
9               poss.append((i+2,j))
10          if j-1>=0:
11              if board[i+1][j-1][0][0]=='w':
12                  poss.append((i+1,j-1))
13          if j+1<8:
14              if board[i+1][j+1][0][0]=='w':
15                  poss.append((i+1,j+1))
16      # repeat for white
17      . . .
18      return poss
```

The final function unites these functions. The **AllPossible** function (Code 18.10) receives the board information and a specific location. It determines which piece is at this location (line 3) and then retrieves all possible moves for that piece. The output is a list of locations where this piece can legally move to. If there are no such spaces or the current location is empty, then the returned list is also empty.

18.2.5 Assigning a Score to the State of the Game

Many options exist on scores based on position can be assigned. One option is to simply add the points for one player and subtract the points from the other. At the beginning of the game, both players have the same pieces, so the total score is 0. As pieces are removed from the board, the score will tilt in favor of one player. However, this function does not take into consideration the locations on the board. Controlling the center of the board is a sound logic to winning the game, thus pieces which influence the center of the board should have more value than similar pieces at the edge of the board. Another consideration is a piece in jeopardy. If the opponent has three pieces that can attack the queen, then the score should be decreased. When the computer considers moves which removes the queen's peril, then the value of the board should go up. Certainly, other methods can be employed to score the state of the game, but those will be left as exercises for the reader.

Three scoring functions will be considered here, and then a final edict will combine these results into a single score.

Code 18.10 The **AllPossible** function.

```python
# chess.py
def AllPossible(board, i,j):
    p = board[i][j][0][1]
    if p=='p':
        poss = PawnMove(board,i,j)
    if p=='r':
        poss = RookMove(board,i,j)
    if p=='n':
        poss = KnightMove(board,i,j)
    if p=='b':
        poss = BishopMove(board,i,j)
    if p=='q':
        poss = QueenMove(board,i,j)
    if p=='k':
        poss = KingMove(board,i,j)
    return poss
```

1. Score the existence of the pieces,

2. Score the positions on the board,

3. Score the peril of pieces, and

4. Combine the scores.

18.2.5.1 Piece Values

The first score is to sum the values of the pieces for the player and subtract the sum of the pieces from the opponent. This applies to only the pieces that are on the board. The process is simple enough as shown in the function named **ScoreActivePieces** (Code 18.11). The two **for** loops are used to consider each square on the playing board. A single square is denoted by board[i][j]. This is a list, and the first element is the string name of the piece. The first character in that string is the color of the piece. Thus board[i][j][0][0] returns either a 'b' or a 'w'. This is returned to the variable bw in line 6. Lines 7 through 10 get the value of the piece, which is the second item in the list. This value is placed in the variables black or white.

18.2.5.2 Board Control

The second score measures the control of the center of the board, which is defined here as the center 2 × 2 area. Of course, it can be expanded to 4 × 4 with a cost in computational load.

Control of the center is based upon two items. The first is the pieces that are in the center, and the second is those pieces which can reach the center in one move.

Code 18.11 The **ScoreActivePieces** function.

```python
# chess.py
def ScoreActivePieces(board):
    white = 0; black = 0
    for i in range(8):
        for j in range(8):
            bw = board[i][j][0][0]
            if bw=='w':
                white += board[i][j][1]
            if bw=='b':
                black += board[i][j][1]
    return black,white
```

This concept creates a computational burden as now the possible moves for all pieces must be considered.

The **ScoreCenterControl** function (Code 18.12) is a bit lengthy. The first section (lines 4 through 10) gather the value of the pieces that currently exist in the center squares. The loop started on line 11 considers all pieces. It gathers their possible moves (line 15), and then scores the values of the pieces for the pieces that can move to the center of the board.

In this case, a piece can be counted more than once. If a piece can move to two squares in the center, then its contribution to this score is doubled.

The output of the function are scores for both players.

18.2.5.3 Pieces in Peril

The third category for scoring is to find the pieces that are in peril of being captured. This process, unfortunately, has nested loops:

- Loop to consider each piece on the board
  - For each piece, find all possible moves
    - For each possible move, count the value of an opposing piece that is captured by this move.

Code 18.13 shows the **ScorePeril** function which performs this process. The loops started in lines 4 and 5 consider each square on the board. If there is a piece on that square (line 6) then its possible moves are calculated (line 7). Each of these moves are considered in the loop starting on line 9. The colors of the piece being moved (line 8) is compared to the color of a piece at the target square (line 10). If the colors are opposing (line 11) then the value of the piece being attacked is placed in the appropriate integer `black` or `white`. The function returns these two integers.

Code 18.12 The **ScoreCenterControl** function.

```python
# chess.py
def ScoreCenterControl(board):
    black, white = 0,0
    for i in range(3,5):
        for j in range(3,5):
            bw = board[i][j][0][0] # b or w
            if bw=='w':
                white += board[i][j][1]
            if bw=='b':
                black += board[i][j][1]
    for i in range(8):
        for j in range(8):
            poss=[]
            if board[i][j][0] != ' .':
                poss = AllPossible(board,i,j)
            for ii,jj in poss:
                if 3<=ii<=4 and 3<=jj<=4:
                    bw = board[i][j][0][0]
                    if bw=='w':
                        white += board[i][j][1]
                    if bw=='b':
                        black += board[i][j][1]
    return black, white
```

Code 18.13 The **ScorePeril** function.

```python
# chess.py
def ScorePeril(board):
    black, white = 0,0
    for i in range(8):
        for j in range(8):
            if board[i][j][0]!=' .':
                poss = AllPossible(board,i,j)
                bw = board[i][j][0][0]
                for px,py in poss:
                    pbw = board[px][py][0][0]
                    if pbw != bw and pbw != ' ':
                        if bw=='b':
                            black += board[px][py][1]
                        if bw=='w':
                            white += board[px][py][1]
    return black, white
```

18.2.5.4 Combining Scores

So far, three possible methods of assigning a score to the positions on a chess board have been discussed. More can be conceived, but are not presented here. The next step is to combine the scores from the different methods into a single value. A simple approach is to create a weighted linear combination of the different metrics, and to compute the ratio of those combinations. Such is the approach in the **Score** in Code 18.14.

Code 18.14 The **Score** function.

```python
# chess.py
def Score(board):
    b1,w1 = ScoreActivePieces(board)
    b2,w2 = ScoreCenterControl(board)
    b3,w3 = ScorePeril(board)
    b = b1+5*b2+5*b3; w =w1+5*w2+5*w3
    r = np.random.rand()*0.01 # to break ties
    pct = b/(b+w+r)
    return pct
```

Lines 3 through 5 gather the scores from the different metrics for both the black and white players. Line 6 creates a weighted linear combination of those scores. In this case, the center control and peril scores are multiplied by five mainly because they are inherently have lower values than the first metric. Basically, this puts them on the same scale. These scores are integers, thus multiple board states can produce the same score. To alleviate this, a small random number is generated in line 7. This is used in the computation of the ratio in line 8. The ratio is the black score divided by the total score. A score of 0.5 would indicate that the positions are equal. A higher score indicates that the black player has an advantage, while a score below 0.5 indicates the white player has the advantage. This process is to be applied to all possible moves, which is presented in the next section.

18.3 PLAYING THE GAME

Code 18.4 shows the commands to set up the game. The **PieceValues** function establishes the values for the pieces, and the **InitChess** function places the pieces on the board. Finally, **PrintBoard** shows the positions of the pieces. The name of the piece starts with an indication of black or white, then the piece designation, and finally a numeral since there some pieces have more than one instance on the board.

18.3.1 Move Selection

The **Move** function will move a piece from one square to another. If this move captures a piece, then the name of the piece and its value is returned by the function. Code 18.15 shows a typical first move in which white moves the king pawn forward two spaces. For this grid, the piece is moved from cell (6,4) to cell (4,4) as prescribed in line 1.

Code 18.15 The first move.

```
1  Move(board,(6,4),(4,4))
2  Out[]: ('.', 0)
3
4  PrintBoard(board)
5    br1   bg1   bb1    bq    bk   bb2   bg2   br2
6    bp1   bp2   bp3   bp4   bp5   bp6   bp7   bp8
7    .     .     .     .     .     .     .     .
8    .     .     .     .     .     .     .     .
9    .     .     .     .   wp5     .     .     .
10   .     .     .     .     .     .     .     .
11   wp1   wp2   wp3   wp4    .    wp6   wp7   wp8
12   wr1   wg1   wb1    wq    wk   wb2   wg2   wr2
```

The next step is for the black player (the computer) to provide the best move. Thus, the program needs to consider all possible moves and score each one. Code 18.16 shows the **ScoreMoves** function which considers all options. The list **moves** collects all possible moves and their scores for further assessment. The default input is for the black player. This argument can be changed to 'w' to score the moves for the white player.

Code 18.16 The **ScoreMoves** function.

```python
1  # chess.py
2  def ScoreMoves(board, player='b'):
3      moves = []
4      for i in range(8):
5          for j in range(8):
6              if board[i][j][0][0] == player:
7                  poss = AllPossible(board,i,j)
8                  for ii,jj in poss:
9                      tempboard = copy.deepcopy(board)
10                     Move(tempboard,(i,j),(ii,jj))
11                     score = Score(tempboard,player)
12                     moves.append((board[i][j][0],(i,j),(ii
                           ,jj),score))
```

Lines 4 and 5 start the loop which considers each square on the board. Line 6 determines if the piece is the considered color. If it matches, then the program proceeds to process the possibilities. Line 7 returns all possible legal moves for this one piece. Line 8 begins the process of considering each move but creating a duplicate board (line 9) and then moving this piece to a new square (line 10). The score of this potential move is calculated in line 11, and the move with its score is appended to the list in line 12. This entry in the list contains the board piece, the old location, the new location, and the score.

The **PickMove** function in Code 18.17 selects the top two moves from this list. Lines 5 through 7 find the move with the highest score, and the second `for` loop finds the second best move. Of course the first move is the obvious choice, but to alter the path of games, the second choice is offered. In any case, one of these choices is selected, and black makes its move.

Code 18.17 The **PickMove** function.

```
1   # chess.py
2   def PickMove(moves):
3       best = []; bestsc = 0
4       for m in moves:
5           if m[3]>bestsc:
6               bestsc = m[3]
7               best = copy.deepcopy(m)
8       best2, best2sc = [],0
9       for m in moves:
10          if m[3]>best2sc and m[3]<bestsc:
11              best2sc = m[3]
12              best2 = copy.deepcopy(m)
13      return best, best2
```

Code 18.18 shows the selection possibilities. Line 1 scores the moves possible for the black player, and lines 2 and 3 show that there are 20 possible moves. The **PickMove** function selects the best two, which are similar in score. Each iteration will be slightly different as there is a small random number used to break tie scores. In this case, the two choices are to move either of the knights.

Code 18.18 Selecting a good move.

```
1   moves = ScoreMoves(board)
2   print(len(moves))
3   20
4   best, best2 = PickMove(moves)
5   print(best)
6   ('bg2', (0, 6), (2, 5), 0.521043368421897)
7   print(best2)
8   ('bg1', (0, 1), (2, 2), 0.51901938183787)
```

For now, the process sticks to the first choice. Black makes a move, and then the human player must counter with a move. Code 18.19 shows white's move in line 1 and black's next move in line 4. Not shown is the possible moves from line 3. The status of the board is shown by line 5. Of course, the process would repeat until one player wins.

Code 18.19 Making more moves.

```
1  Move(board,(0,6),(2,5))
2  moves = ScoreMoves(board)
3  best, best2 = PickMove(moves)
4  Move(board,(6,3),(5,3))
5  PrintBoard(board)
6    br1   bg1   bb1   bq    bk    bb2    .    br2
7    bp1   bp2   bp3   bp4   bp5   bp6   bp7   bp8
8     .     .     .     .     .    bg2    .     .
9     .     .     .     .     .     .     .     .
10    .     .     .    wp5    .     .     .
11    .     .     .    wp4    .     .     .     .
12   wp1   wp2   wp3    .     .    wp6   wp7   wp8
13   wr1   wg1   wb1   wq    wk    wb2   wg2   wr2
```

18.3.2 Improving the Performance

This chess program only considers one level of logic, thus the computer program is easy to beat. It will make bad moves which imperials pieces because of its shallow logic. For example, it can move a queen into a spot that provides an advantage without considering that white could make a devastating move in which one piece can put the king in check and queen in peril at the same time. The computer would have to save the king and lose the queen. The single level of logic does not consider such a possibility.

To increase the performance of the computer, the number of levels need to be increased. The function **ScoreMoves** considers all possible black moves, but it does not consider all possible white moves. This means that for every possible black move, all possible white moves need to be scored. In this case, the best score is no longer the best move. Consider a case in which black has two legal moves. In each move, white has three legal responses. The scores for the first black move are (0.5, 0.6, 0.35) and the scores for the second black move are (0.51, 0.52, 0.53). The first move offers the best choice (a score of 0.6), but it also offers the worst choice (a score of 0.35). The computer does not control white's move, thus, the assumption is that white will make the best possible move for itself, thus, the lowest scores of each set need to be considered. The lowest score for black's first move is 0.35 and for the second move is 0.51. Thus, the second move has a better score.

Of course, a third level of logic could be added to the program, for each black move, consider the white moves, and for those consider the black responses. This is three levels of logic. The issue with this approach is that the number of computations increases exponentially. For a rough estimate, consider that black has 20 legal moves, white has 20 legal responses to each move, and black has 20 responses to those. The total number of moves to be considered is $20^3 = 8000$. This is not too hard for a computer to manipulate. If the choice is to go into five levels of logic, then the number of possible moves becomes $20^5 = 3,200,000$.

A faster calculation would attempt to remove some of these computations before being considered by the program. For example, in the case of the two black moves used in a previous paragraph, a possible decision is that the first black move leads to a very low scoring response by white. Thus, this move should not be considered further. The black responses to the white move do not need to be calculated.

18.4 SUMMARY

This chapter presented a basic chess playing computer program. The computer makes legal moves based on metrics of position and piece value. However, the program uses only first-level logic and is thus easy to beat. Comments on improving the program are provided.

This program does not include some chess maneuvers such as en passant, castling, and promotion. These are also left as exercises for further exploration.

PROBLEMS

1. Write a function for piece promotion. When a pawn reaches the last row, the program will replace it with a queen (even if another piece would be better suited for the situation).

2. Write a function for piece promotion. When a pawn reaches the last row, the program will replace it with either a knight or a queen. This function should consider both possibilities and select the replacement piece based on computed scores.

3. Add a function named **CastleMove** which will reposition the king and rook according to castling rules. This function merely moves the pieces, but does not decide if castling is the best move.

4. The previous problem created a **CastleMove** function. Add a call to this function in the **AllPossible** function. Create a scenario in which a castling move is possible, and demonstrate that this move is included in the output of **AllPossible**.

5. Create a function that sets up the board as shown in Figure 18.1. Use the **PrintBoard** function to show the state of the board in the console.

6. Figure 18.1 shows a situation in which black can checkmate white in two moves. However, the first move seems perilous at first glance. The moves are for black to move the queen one space up and left. This puts white in check, and the only option for white is to capture the queen with the bishop. Black then moves the

rook to the right of the king. Checkmate. Run the **ScoreMoves** function on
this configuration. Sort the moves by score. Write a comment on how well the
initial queen move scored.

Figure 18.1: An game configuration in which black mates in 2 moves.

Bibliography

[1] S. Park and K. Miller, "Random number generators: Good ones are hard to find," *Communications of the ACM*, pp. 1192–1201, Oct. 1988.

[2] J. Farrier, "When the actors in *Planet of the Apes* donned their makeup, they spontaneously segregated themselves." https://www.neatorama.com/2013/12/15/When-the-Actors-in-Planet-of-the-Apes-Donned-Their-Makeup-They-Spontaneously–Segregated-Themselves/, 2013 (accessed April 24, 2020).

[3] M. M. Yin and J. T. L. Wang, "GeneScout: a data mining system for predicting vertebrate genes in genomic DNA sequences," *Information Sciences*, vol. 163, pp. 201–218, 2004.

[4] J. M. Kinser, *Python for Bioinformatics*. Jones and Bartlett, 2009.

[5] J. S. Sokol, "An intuitive Markov chain lesson from baseball," *INFORMS Transactions on Education*, vol. 5, no. 1, pp. 47–55, 2004.

[6] "https://www.baseball-reference.com/boxes/hou/hou201910300.shtml," Accessed May 10, 2020.

[7] Y. H. Yang, M. J. Buckely, and T. P. Speed, "Analysis of cDNA microarray images," *Briefings in Bioinformatics*, vol. 2, pp. 341–349, Dec. 2001.

[8] http://www.physics.drexel.edu/~steve/Courses/Comp_Phys/Integrators/leapfrog/leapfrog.gif

Index

Printed in the United States
by Baker & Taylor Publisher Services